FIGHT BACK AND WIN!

How to Work <u>With</u> Business and Get What You Want

By

Ellen Phillips

ISBN: 1-4033-0443-2 (e-book)
ISBN: 1-4033-0444-0 (Paperback)

Library of Congress Control Number: 2002102138

This book is printed on acid free paper.

Printed in the United States of America
Bloomington, IN

1stBooks - rev. 10/03/02

Contents

"Even if I do not see the fruits, the struggle has been worthwhile.
If my life has taught me anything, it is that one must fight."

- Ella Winter

Thankyouthankypouthankyouthankyou

Books cannot be written without assistance. To this end, I must thank the following "helpers."

First and foremost, my husband, Bruce, continues to be my biggest supporter and strength, as well as my best friend. Plus, he still thinks I'm pretty!

My family unendingly stands by me, even if they do think I'm obsessive with my consumer advocacy: Nan Haygood, who is not only the "bestest" sister, but also my conscience; my brother and sister-in-law, Joe and Jean Haygood, who have lent their support; and my mother-in-law, Flo Phillips.

My daughter Beth Runkles is an extraordinarily talented artist, as evidenced by the enclosed illustrations. Cody and Tallon, her precious younger children, are joys to behold. My eldest grandchildren, Ellie and Tyler Jeffries, love me as only grandchildren can love, and we enjoy an even closer and more special relationship because of our years together.

My comrade-in-arms and dearest friend, Carol Guiles, and her husband, Michael, maintain their encouragment all the way. Even when beset with very serious illness, Carol not only helped with the editing process, but, as always, continued to push me onward and upward. Thanks, *Sister-Friend*.

I must acknowledge Kelly St. Clair for the use of her clothes, heels, and unmentionables seen (or not) on this book's cover. My other dear friends who lend their support are just too numerous to count; you know who you are.

Even though my Webmaster's services don't come cheap, thank you anyway to Jason Thrasher. I can always depend upon him in times of hysteria when things go wrong (which with me is often).

Kudos must go to two other groups of people. A big thank you to the corporate CEOs or their representatives who provided quotes and information that prove their company's interest in superior customer service. And how can I forget the thousands of consumers who have sought my advice, empowered themselves, became "Ellens" all across the country, and vowed never to give up? Blend these two groups together, and we certainly do have a real partnership. So let's strive for the day when hostilities cease, and products and services become the best they can possibly be. That will be the time when we truly can work with business to ensure success for <u>all</u> of us.

For my mama and daddy,
Lucy and Eddie Haygood,
and
my best friend, Carol Burdette Guiles.

When God calls blessed souls home,
He surrounds those left behind
with guardian angels.

Prologue
An Opening Word or Two

While *Shocked, Appalled, and Dismayed! How to Write Letters That Get Results* was meant totally to empower readers in their battle for consumer rights, *Fight Back and Win! How to Work <u>With</u> Business and Get What You Want* takes a somewhat different path. Even though it exposes and resolves a continuation of issues with which we need to be familiar, pre and post- purchase or contract, this book goes a few hundred miles further. Hopefully, everyone will read the entire book. However, many of you will only read the chapter that affects you and helps the most at a given time. Whichever method you choose, though, I'm confident that you'll come away from the situation a better and more informed consumer.

Fight Back and Win! adds a very important (and absolutely incredible) premise: cooperation and even partnership between corporations and consumer, as opposed to the traditional David and Goliath theme. Not only do corporate executives provide insights about their companies and consumerism as a whole, but also highlighted are a number of companies that are tiptop on the list of satisfied employees and with that topic specifically discussed by company officials. In my opinion, when personnel are happy and take pride in their work, they interact more successfully with consumers. Result? A purchasing public of happy campers.

Perhaps you call one day to discuss your dissatisfaction with a product or a service. Rather than speaking with a customer service representative who perhaps is misinformed, doesn't care, or hasn't been allowed the responsibility to rectify the problem, you find yourself in a cordial conversation with an informed, caring, responsible individual. What an amazing and refreshing difference and, you can bet your booty, you'll buy again and again from this outfit – and tell all your friends to do the same.

These customer friendly companies have discovered methods to attract and to maintain the best staff. Whether a business has instant stock options, an onsite gym and daycare, adoption and tuition reimbursement, and so forth, employees are happier and work harder to ensure the continued success of their employer. The corporate "models," if you will, need to send their message to every other company that deals directly with consumers, customers, patients, or any other *a rose is a rose is a rose*.

What makes good employees? How should company officials better serve their clientele? How do we perceive a great tech company as opposed to a mediocre one? What can companies do to survive mergers and flourish even more? All of these topics ultimately benefit the rest of American buyers.

To our utter horror, on September 11, 2001, we watched the world, as we knew it, flame with destruction. Too many people from too many countries (including our own) decry friendship with America and its people. An important lesson is learned from this experience: all of us must work harder to lessen our biases and to learn more about what makes other individuals and cultures tick. As we realize now more than ever, finding common ground is a lesson that <u>must</u> be learned by as many folks as possible. But even a most important consumer lesson can be learned from those tragic circumstances: by humanizing each experience and each person, corporations and consumers alike learn to value each other, and the *Consumer Revolution* can finally lay down its weapons. "Enemies" shall become buddies, or at least friendlier with one another. The economy will boom. And (as stated in one of my *Shocked, Appalled, and Dismayed!* anecdotes), *"Corporation and Consumer lived happily ever after..."* God bless America!

Chapter 1

Don't Tell Me I Can't

***"True eloquence consists of saying all that is necessary,
and nothing but what is necessary."***
- Mark Twain

Fifty-four years ago, as the lighting cracked and the thunder boomed, a baby girl was born in a small Alabama town. Emerging abruptly into the reality of a harsh, cold world, her complaining screams about this rude injustice resounded throughout the corridors of the tiny hospital, a portent of things to come.

Ellen had arrived!

Hopefully, many of you have read and utilized *Shocked, Appalled, and Dismayed! How to Write Letters of Complaint That Get Results*. If so, you know enough about me to realize my sharp tongue is aimed (usually) at the inequities and wrongs others have suffered and that pen (computer) and paper have taken the place of the oral diatribe. What's even more important is that you've <u>used</u> what you've learned, taken the complaint flag into your own hands by joining the Consumer Revolution, and <u>won</u> your battles against companies who either manufacture or sell inferior products or provide shoddy services. You've also realized that it is your *right* to expect what you pay for, and *nothing* should stand in the way of your obtaining satisfactory results. After an exciting review of letter-writing ground rules and a pop quiz (just kidding – a little English teacher humor), *Fight Back and Win!* will guide you on the pathway to writing different types of complaint letters and correspondence, although I expect I can be persuaded to throw in a goodly number of "normal" complaints along the way.

So what different kinds of missives can you expect to find within? It truly runs the gamut from job performance rebuttals to eldercare, from home building to education and just about everything in between. Just as we found in *Shocked, Appalled,*

1

and Dismayed!, many of us still need special hints for success in any given situation.

While I thoroughly enjoy the vicarious satisfaction of turning the complaint screws on behalf of others, all my *Poison Pen* letters for clients still boils down to two primary ingredients in my own philosophy: determination to get results and the patience to see the problem through to resolution. Many readers have asked what events in my life prepared me for a career of complaints and consumerism. I learned the true meaning of determination and patience early on in my own life: read on, but be forewarned that this is serious stuff.

Until I was seven, my childhood was quite uneventful. My father worked in the family department store and my mother was the best of the old-fashioned term, "housewife." At a little over four years apart, my brother, Joe, our little sister, Nan, and I led a simple life in a small, sleepy Southern town. We played the games that our friends played, we participated in church activities, we minded our parents, we dreamed our dreams. But the summer after my first grade year in school, the ordinary lives of my ordinary family were interrupted by an unforeseen event – one so catastrophic that it irrevocably stamped each of us and ultimately helped to mold me into the person I am today.

Just as horrible and terrifying as the HIV stories of this generation or perhaps even more so because it struck so indiscriminately, the great Polio Epidemic of 1954 swept across America, its icy fingers clasping at anyone who came near its clutches. No one was safe. Rich or poor, young and old, everyone feared the sentence of this dreaded disease. It was highly contagious and, therefore, physicians and scientists could only speculate about its source. Many believed it came from breathing unsanitary air, while others remembered the cold swim that our former president, Franklin D. Roosevelt, enjoyed just prior to his being stricken with polio.

Magazine photographs pictured its victims, especially the children, some who had escaped death only to lie in a huge body-encasing black apparatus. In so many instances, breathing functions ceased because of the paralysis that swept through the body and concentrated in the lungs. Enveloped within this machine that breathed for its captive, the Iron Lung remained a portrait in horror in the minds of everyone throughout America.

Other illustrations come to mind. People who were "lucky" enough to be confined to wheelchairs or who barely walked with the assistance of heavy, cold, steel braces. And especially the children ...

My family's favorite summer vacation, one that arrived like clockwork each year, was an adventure to the beach. Living as closely as we did to the Florida shores, it was a relatively short drive and an inexpensive trip. That year, my father decided we would also benefit from a fishing excursion, killing two birds with one stone. Oh, could my daddy fish! We rented a little cabin in Dunellen, Florida and, along with family friends, set out for what we thought then to be just another summer fun. In our innocence, no one ever thought for a moment that a family's greatest nightmare would prove to soon come true.

Faded black and white photos of us holding up long lines of fish with me in the middle grinning a toothless grin and both hands gripping the biggest catch of all survive in photograph albums and in my memories. I remember the excitement of being the chosen child to accompany our grown-up friends to Cyprus Gardens. Seeing the beautiful dances of the water skiers and performers as they entertained us, smiling directly at me; swimming in the cold waters on that fiery hot day; and then tiredly beginning the drive back to Dunellen. Soon, though, I forgot about the day's joy when I became enveloped in trembling chills. The return drive seemed longer and longer until we finally arrived back at our cabin. As I violently shook from the chills that racked my body and with 104 temperature, my parents immediately hustled me to a local doctor, who diagnosed a possible case of the mumps. To my mother's frantic question (as so many other mothers asked that summer), he reassuringly answered, "Oh, no, this definitely isn't polio." Not reassured at all, my folks bundled me into the car and we raced back to Greenville.

Memories rush back as I remember that day. They are so vivid that over forty-five years vanish and Mama is in the yard picking flowers for me while she waits for the return phone call from our pediatrician in Montgomery. Isolated as much as possible from Joe and Nan, I lie in my parents' bed, my entire body hurting so terribly and my fever rising higher and higher. I desperately need to go to the bathroom, but I don't want to bother my mother. I stand, take a few wobbly steps and then, all of a sudden, I can't feel my legs and I collapse to the floor. "Mama! Mama!" I scream as the remainder of my body goes limp. I try to pinch myself but I can barely move my fingers. I'm so scared. "Mama! Mama!"

My parents grab me up and race for St. Margaret's Hospital in Montgomery, fifty miles away. By this time, my body is almost totally numb and I lie listlessly in my mother's lap. Her hands smooth my hair away from my face and she rubs my neck. Between soft kisses, I hear her words, "It's okay, Ellen, you're going to be fine." She feared and I sensed that those words were only a futile attempt to make us both feel better for I wasn't "fine," and perhaps would never be so again.

The car screeches to a halt at the emergency room. Nurses and doctors dash to meet me and I'm even more frightened by their appearance. Their entire faces and bodies are covered, and I hear only muffled sounds from behind their masks. They, too, are afraid but it's *me* they fear. I'm just seven years old; I can't hurt them. Please, let me see your faces. But they don't listen, and then they place me upon a long bed on wheels and take me away from my parents. Daddy holds Mama back as she struggles to be free to follow me down the corridor.

All of a sudden, we arrive at a large room with bright orange signs posted all over the door. I'm a smart girl; I always had the best reading scores in first grade. Even in my panic, I spell out the words in my mind: *Danger Con/ ta/ mi/ na/ tion*. I know what the first one means but I'm not sure of the second. It's something bad, though, I can tell. I hurt. I want my mama. Suddenly, one of the doctors holds up a long needle and the nurses force my body into a ball. Why are they doing this? Then, like a searing bolt of lightening, they push the needle into my spine. **"Mama! Daddy! Help me! Mama! Where are you?"** Until the day he died, my father said he shuddered as he

4

recalled my screams of pain and fear and having to restrain both my mother and himself from bolting past the barrier, stealing me, and returning to the sanctuary of our home.

Polio. Not simply paralytic but also bulbar, the type that either thrusts its poisonous virus into one's brain and kills or remains in the throat and simply paralyzes. Either way, it was a death sentence: Even if I survived, there was no way I could ever move of my own accord, much less walk freely.

It's hard for me to swallow and even harder to breath. The iron monster engulfs me in one devouring bite. I lie flat within its tentacles, only my head exposed as I watch my tears in the tiny mirror above me. Mama tries to feed me soft-scrambled eggs, particle by particle. "You must swallow," she whispers, "to exercise your throat muscles." She or Daddy never leaves my side, each always on the verge of collapse themselves as they divide their time. One with me, one driving an hour each way, attempting to be a consoling and normal parent to my twelve-year-old brother and three-year-old sister. Both parents praying, always praying. Hundreds of other voices in our little town joined with theirs, and soon these particular supplications were answered for I breathed of my own accord. I would not die.

St. Jude's Hospital, also in Montgomery, was the next stop. Especially equipped for the children of Alabama who had contacted polio, this was probably the first time in my memory that I actively complained about a situation and achieved results. (A portent of things to come.) Because I was completely paralyzed from the neck down, the doctor had left stringent orders that I was not to be moved; however, on one occasion the nun on duty decided to give me a tub bath. That evening, my mother had gone out to dinner with Montgomery cousins, never dreaming that I wouldn't be safe and sound. I protested in vain with the nurse. The doctors were always impressed that for so young a child, I always listened attentively to their instructions. She didn't listen to me, however. For some reason, she made up her mind that I was going to get into the tub and that was the end of any argument. "Getting into the tub" is a rather ironic statement as I couldn't move a muscle to walk,

5

to get in, or to bathe. So she did just what she set out to do, through hell or high water! Remember when I came complaining into the world? When my doctor came for rounds later on that night, I didn't even allow Mama to get the words out of her own mouth first; I lit into the nurse about the mandate she *didn't* follow. The very next day, Sister Headstrong was transferred to another floor.

St. Jude's soon ran out of options and recommended I be sent to FDR's own hospital – the Georgia Warm Springs Foundation where the most prominent polio specialists practiced. Back in the 1930's President Roosevelt had found the warm spring water in the area very therapeutic to his own lifeless legs in this don't-blink-you'll-miss-it community and built a hospital for others like himself. The Montgomery doctors released me to go home to await my acceptance into Warm Springs.

Finally, I was back with my family. I laugh as I remember lying in bed and little Nan taking my useless hands and playing with them. Her own chubby little hands would pick up one of mine and flop it around like a dying fish, slapping me on the arm with it (which I couldn't feel) and then on my face (which I could). Little did we realize then that our game was probably one of the earliest rehabilitative measures for exercising my degenerative muscles. And then the word came: it was time to go.

Montgomery, only fifty miles from home, was one thing; Georgia at several hours away was another. But there was no choice. I had to stay there alone, without Mama or Daddy. Nan and Joe needed them almost as badly as I. My siblings had previously developed a light case of the disease from exposure to me, much like a bad case of the flu, and even though they were completely recovered, they, too, stayed confused and upset over the trauma that surrounded us all. Nan, especially, didn't understand what was wrong. All she knew was that I was very sick and couldn't live with her anymore. She needed constant assurance that "the bad bug" wouldn't come and sweep her away as well. Even when I was hospitalized in Montgomery and throughout my stay at Warm Springs, as soon as my parents walked through the door, she ran to meet them with the plea, "Ellie come home?" But "Ellie" never came. It was a lifetime in a three-year-old's eyes.

My brother experienced his own problems. He, too, needed his mother and daddy to help him through his own uncertainties as his body and attitudes underwent their pubescent transformations. His fear was more hidden, for boys at that time were taught that it's unmanly to cry, and he was hesitant to question. Outwardly he changed from an exuberant and daring kid to one noticeably quieter. He kept his thoughts to himself, but our parents later discovered his introspection was that of anger, resentment, and guilt. Because he was the eldest and a boy, they believed that his handling of the situation was relatively satisfactory when, in fact, at this time in a child's life when he really needs his parents' support and understanding, he felt that Mama and Daddy had no time for him. Within their frantic lives, they attended more to little Nan, but most of their thoughts and all of their weekends were spent with me. Even though my brother knew better, I became the closest solution on which to blame his fears and anxieties. And once again children suffered.

Months at Warm Springs did help. Inanimate arms and legs constantly exercised by the dedicated therapists in the soothing spring waters gained new strength, and soon I could sit up in a wheelchair and my arms did just what I asked of them. Living in a ward with many other children afforded me playmates of a sort, and I even had a best friend – Phyllis – who spent hours with me cutting out and dressing up paper dolls. Daily, I received dozens of cards and letters (the magic word!) from the kind people back home, many of whom enclosed money and all mailed with prayers for my recovery. Soon, I discovered a new pastime. Clasping the money in my greedy little hands, I'd ask an orderly to wheel me to the gift shop where I bought candy - lots and lots of candy - for my friends and (mostly) for me. Photograph albums today portray a *really* large little girl sitting in her wheelchair with a face so bloated an apple belongs in her mouth as she awaits being popped into the oven to bake.

7

But oh, how I was homesick. I missed Mama and Daddy desperately. Three or four times a week, a nurse would call home collect for me and as soon as I heard Mama's voice accepting the charges, I'd break into sobs and beg her to come and get me. Between her crying and mine, there wasn't a whole lot of conversation taking place. Every weekend, she brought stamped post cards for me, and each day I'd write almost the identical words to mail back home accompanied by many *XOXOXO* love and kisses marks.

Dear Mama and Daddy. I miss you. I want to come home.
Please bring me some books to read. I miss Nan and Joe.
Love, Ellen

And not a day passed when I failed to receive letters from my parents, from Joe, and little chicken-scratches from Nan. Letters were such an essential part of my life and I've never forgotten their importance. Perhaps this episode led me on my future journey in writing for others.

"You'll never walk again." Finally discharged from Warm Springs, these words rang in our ears. Even with the braces on my legs, confined to a wheelchair, and covered from breast to hip with a steel back brace to strengthen the S shaped curvature of my spine, such a dire prognosis seemed almost dream-like. Maybe because we were so filled with joy that "Ellie" was finally home and our family once more reunited, or that only my legs were paralyzed when it had once been my entire body. Whatever the rationale, we moved on with our lives as normally as possible.

Excitedly, I learned that Mama and Daddy had planned a short vacation to the beach, just as we had always done. Naturally I couldn't scamper into the water and ride the waves; the huge truck tire innertube with my name stamped on it remained empty. Also impossible was strolling my wheelchair across the sugar-spun sands, even though my folks gave it their best shot. Yet, as I lay there on the sand where they carried me and experienced the tickle of the tide or sat on the porch, I felt the sun as it kissed my face and smelled the bracing salty air. With a parent carefully holding me on each withered side, the warm Gulf waters cradled me in its arms. Yes, I was home.

Later on, I'll speak on kindness that we bestow on others and certainly there had been more than my fair share all throughout this terrible trial. Friends, family, and even those whom we didn't know very well continued their prayers and their support. One of the grandest surprises awaited us when we returned home from that special Florida trip. In 1955, and especially in a small middle-class town, almost no one had a new-fangled television. As we rounded the corner to Redbud Lane, Joe yelled, "Look! There's an antenna on our roof!"

Like excited children on Christmas morning, everyone but me leapt from the car and dashed into the house. There, perched on a new shelf high enough for a little girl lying in her bed to easily view, was a brand-new television set. As amazed as we all were, no one was more surprised than my father when he read the attached card. Daddy had been a loyal member of the local Lion's Club for many years, and this gift — this wonderfully entertaining gift — had been very secretively planned for, purchased, delivered, and installed, all without his knowledge. What a source of joy for each of us as we had family time each evening in my bedroom, staring transfixed at the tiny black-and-white images cavorting across the screen. What hours of happiness followed that, for a time, allowed me in my thoughts to escape my bed and to become one with the characters in front of me. Friends, prayers, thank you.

Being home wasn't always completely wonderful, though. Even though I was long past contagion, many still feared my presence or even that of my family. Well-meaning neighbors would call and offer to bring meals for us, but not *bring* in the traditional sense of the term. Stopping their cars at the end of our driveway, they would place the trays by the street, honk their horns, and quickly speed away. By this time thirteen and four, Nan and Joe sat together for hours on the front porch with only themselves for entertainment. Parades of cars drove slowly past our house, the people within craning their necks and pointing. My siblings weren't allowed to go and play with their friends and no one was allowed to visit, either. About the only real entertainment they both had that first summer I was home were The Great Wheelchair Rides. Each day, Mama asked Joe to take me for a ride down the street. She probably thought she was imposing on his good nature, but little did she know that both he and Nan looked forward to this chore with great anticipation.

"Okay, Mama," he'd sigh with a long-suffering look on his face. He and my mother would carry my wheelchair as well as my own tub-of-lard- self down the back steps, get me situated in the chair, and then he and Nan would very sedately begin strolling me down the driveway to the street. Every moment or two, Joe glanced back to make sure that Mama wasn't watching out the kitchen window and when he was certain, all hell broke loose. VA VA VROOM!

With a loud whoop, Joe tilted the back wheels and raced up and down the street, Nan running as hard as she could alongside, and me holding on for dear life. I screamed as he sprinted, some of my cries from fear of tipping over but mostly for the sheer enjoyment of "running," too. These small, happy events strengthened my parents' and my determination that one day I would escape the prison of my chair and the heavy braces on my legs. Yet even with the occasional flight from reality, the fear continued to gnaw at everyone.

Each subsequent check-up at Warm Springs revealed the same message: never walk, never run, never … Undaunted, Mama and Daddy researched and searched until they finally encountered a nurse trained in the Sister Kenny method of therapy. Sister Elizabeth Kenny, an Australian nurse, had long rejected the use of braces for polio victims. She believed that special exercises and massaging of debilitative muscles would regenerate the nerves in those useless parts. My parents learned the therapy, and the backbreaking ordeal began.

Determination. Several times a day, they lifted me to the dining room table and began the endless hours of exhaustive physical therapy. Months passed. The steel chains came off my legs and holding tightly to my parents, I would twist my body and thrust my legs forward. Determination. As the weeks and months sped by, pinpricks of feeling would make themselves known, and the therapy and "walking" hurt more and more. Determination. The specialists continued their incessant chant, "Give up, it's no use, she'll never walk." These powerful men, schooled in their expertise of polio and its captives, didn't realize the extent of my family's talisman: an indomitable spirit and a vast faith in God.

Then it happened. Early on Christmas Day 1957, I needed to go to the bathroom. I hated to disturb my parents' sleep - they got so little - and so I decided to attempt the journey myself. I feel my determination now. I remember.

I carefully reach for my legs and one at a time swing them over the side of the bed. I sit there for a moment on the edge catching my breath, and then I slowly place them on the floor. Holding tightly to the bedpost, I stand very still, suddenly undecided if I'm brave enough to make this long pilgrimage all alone. Holding on to the side of the wall (it doesn't seem strong enough to support me), I hesitantly take one, two, three faltering steps. Tears puddle my eyes, as my once-useless legs seem to take on a life of their own. Another step, then another. "Mama! Daddy! I'm walking by myself!"

My screams of thanksgiving awaken my whole family and the four of them rush to the doorway. Transfixed, they stand there, all thoughts of a traditional Christmas morning forgotten, as they watch me walk towards their opened arms. Tears of joy streaming down their faces, my parents grab me just before I reach them and hold me so very tightly that even today I feel the power of their arms as we cling to one another. On what other day could this miracle possibly have occurred but on Christmas, the greatest miracle day of all.

Mama and Daddy rushed me back to Warm Springs the following morning and after being apprised of what had happened the day before, the most prominent physicians in the world just shook their heads in disbelief as they staunchly informed us that there was no way whatsoever I could walk. Albeit _very_ slowly, I strutted my stuff across the room filled with these gentlemen who could only stare and murmur amongst themselves. Finally, one of them softly spoke, this man of science who adhered only to medical doctrine. "It *is* a miracle. There's just no other explanation."

Courage, faith, prayer, determination and this miracle had saved me from a life experienced by so many thousands not as fortunate. Even then I knew that I had a destiny to fulfill, an obligation to pay back. I just wasn't sure what it was to be.

Incredibly, another test of faith interrupted what finally had become a peaceful life. At twelve, I was again struck down, this time with nephritis, a deadly kidney disease. That Easter, I once more languished in the hospital, while I fought to survive. After a month, I returned home where I was bedridden for another year. But still again God, our determination, patience, and the prayers of all who loved me prevailed. Still on occasion wearing the steel back brace from my battle with polio, exactly twelve months later I entered junior high school. I was indeed an inspiration, a true miracle-child. Even then, I knew that somewhere, somehow, a specific destiny awaited me. Could it possibly be helping many others and inciting a *Consumer Revolution* when I hit middle age? According to a couple of ladies, this is exactly my task in life.

Christine Casson of Montgomery Village, Maryland is one client whose creed is also "It's not over 'til the you know what kind of lady sings," and she saw none of these particular ladies anywhere on the horizon. She, as so many of us does, bought a personal computer. Hers is primarily utilized for maintaining records for her small business, and it's imperative she depend upon it to stay in working order. Crash after crash occurred almost immediately after the purchase, which resulted in all of her records being lost.

We battled with this giant computer manufacturer and the store that sold it for many months, getting a snippet of help here and there but no real assistance and certainly no semblance of a resolution. Her story is unique in that she first <u>hand</u> wrote her initial letter after her brand-new computer ate up all her data. Now, the problem with the first letter (other than being handwritten) is that Chris is dyslexic; therefore, that complaint looked like gobbledy-gook to the reader. Perhaps because she has persevered over the years to succeed in spite of her handicap (just as I did), Chris refused to allow the uncaring corporates to kick her into submission. First writing a letter to both the manufacturer and the store where she purchased the computer, to our *dismay* these letters, one of which follows, were treated with no more respect or understanding than was Chris' original one.

1944 Determined Drive
Montgomery Village, MD 28887
April 29, 1997

Carla Computer, President/CEO
Execrable Computers, Inc.
1337 Worthless Parkway, Suite 56
San Francisco, CA 94103

Dear Ms. Computer:

After enduring a year-and-a-half of appalling problems with my original computer purchased at Computers-R-Pitiful, happily at the end of 1996 my Execrable Model #MG237ED was replaced by an upgraded unit, the N190. A combination of complaints and short-term technical fixes resulted in the issuance of my new system based upon the recommendation of Computers-R-Pitiful's warrantee provider, Protection Provider. Unfortunately, within two weeks by October 12, 1996, my problems began anew with this current model and, thus, I hope that you will investigate immediately to assist in solving this situation.

- **Because the sound did not work I first contacted technical support at the Execrable 800-number; I had experienced episodes when the sound would return, then shut off over the following two weeks. On**

November 10, I was informed that other customers were calling with the same problem. I was then told to move my unit to an area where cold air freely circulated, which I did.

- By December 10, 1996, the sound cut off once more. Telephoning your company only resulted in a recording explaining that the hold time was ninety minutes and I could not wait for that length of time. On December 14, I received a letter from Computers-R-Pitiful mandating that any computer problems were to be reported directly to Protection Provider, and on December 22, I spoke to its evening supervisor who suggested that the defect was within the sound system and advised me to again call Execrable.

- On January 1, 1997, I turned on my computer and <u>nothing</u> worked. I then re-packed it and called Protection Provider in Denver, Colorado. I mailed them the entire system on January 8 and, supposedly, two technicians worked on the computer, installing a new hard drive, with the computer scheduled for return on January 15. When I finally spoke with John, the Execrable representative, he requested my Master CD ROM disk number, and I then discovered the wrong Master had been installed. John then transferred me to the order department, and I was promised that my new order would arrive by January 17.

- By January 26, after receiving the new Master CD ROM disk, that system again was not working. Bruce, the supervisor, requested my SID number and informed me the crash continued to reoccur because I needed a new fax modem sound card. He then called me and advised not to use my PC until it was repaired.

- On February 22, the service technician from Wang installed a new sound card in less than five minutes. He suspected defective drives were the problem but could not reach your representatives on the telephone. March 1997 resulted in ten more days of freezing up and crashing, and I had to restore everything from the

Master CD ROM disk. The machine would not accept my Microsoft certificate, and when I spoke with Execrable about this latest development, Samuel Slime stated that nothing could be done. He told me to contact Microsoft for support; this was my final call to your company.

Seven months have passed since my "new" Execrable computer arrived. Two years have elapsed since my original purchase of the new computer (copy of receipt enclosed). I am not only frustrated but also enraged by my experiences with two of your models. I have even written to Computers-R-Pitiful expressing my displeasure and complaints. This company's lack of responsiveness and courteous disposition of my computer problems only exacerbates an already horrific situation. My complaint with your organization, however, centers on the defects of your product. Not only has this matter cost me time and aggravation attempting to resolve what appears to be problems within the design or manufacture of the computer, I have also lost valuable billing hours in my business because of the lack of ability to utilize the computer in my day-to-day work.

I initially purchased an Execrable computer for one primary reason: your company is one of a very few that would deliver to a private home and set up computers if a customer is disabled. I suffer from severe dyslexia that makes it impossible to read directions. Therefore, your product was my choice because of its standard of accommodation for disabled and handicapped people. I also believed I could depend upon its professionalism and product name. I now realize I was in error.

I expect to be reimbursed for my computer expenses in the amount of $2072.62. I also believe I am due compensation for my lost revenue because of your product continuing to malfunction. Even though these losses are in excess of $3000, I will accept the $2072.62. Certainly, you will wish to send me a letter of explanation and apology for the time and frustration I have endured in my attempts to procure a <u>working</u> computer.

Thank you, and I look forward to hearing from you within the next ten business days.

Sincerely,

Christine Casson

Enclosures

cc: Daniel Defrauder, President/CEO
Computers-R-Pitiful, Inc.
9840 Demon Drive
Minneapolis, MN 55415

Randy Remote, Northern Division President
Execrable Computers, Inc.
877 Unconcerned Avenue
St. Paul, MN 55101

United States Department of Justice
Civil Rights Division
624 Ninth Street, NW
Washington, DC 20425

National Council on Disability
1331 F Street, NW, Suite 1050
Washington, DC 20004-1107

President's Committee on Employment
of People With Disabilities

1331 F Street, NW, Suite 300
Washington, DC 20004-1107

Robert Burns, Assistant State Superintendent
Division of Rehabilitative Services
State Department of Education
2301 Argonne Drive
Baltimore, MD 21218

The Honorable Donna Shalala, Secretary
United States Department of Health and Human
Services
200 Independence Avenue, SW
Washington, DC 20201

Patricia Jarman-Manning
Commissioner of Consumer Affairs
Department of Business and Industry
1850 East Sahara, Suite 101
Las Vegas, NV 89158

Even more epistles sped through the postal service but to no avail. Our final and no-holds-barred recourse was a petition to then-Attorney General Reno with copies to those same authorities interested in discriminatory practices.

> **19897 Determined Avenue**
> **Montgomery Village, MD 28887**
> **August 7, 1997**

The Honorable Janet Reno, Attorney General
United States Justice Department
950 Pennsylvania Avenue, NW
Washington, DC 20530

Dear General Reno:

As a person with an indomitable spirit and a fierce belief in the American justice system, I turn to you as my last hope.

I have enclosed a packet of letters in chronological order, which fully explains the horrendous problem I have experienced for too long, the latest being dated June 3, 1997. Once an investigator was assigned to my case, Execrable Computer's frantic attempt to cover itself was the June 3 letter to Mary Marvelous, the investigator at the office of Maryland's Attorney General. It contained blatant falsehoods. [Here, we iterated what had been said.]

I have been subjected to abuse that no person should ever have to experience: verbally, emotionally, and financially. While only attempting to do what is right as an American consumer, it is apparent that some within these two corporate giants do not feel the same way.

I am only one small consumer trying desperately to battle on my own with little to no help from those from whom I have requested assistance. One case in point is the Attorney General's office in Maryland, which appears to have given up on any satisfactory resolution. While I do understand that this office is totally separate from your own, I wish you to be aware of what has and has not occurred. [Now is the real reason for this letter. Particular instances, persons spoken with and correspondence are specified, a lá my advice, which follows in point # 2 in Chapter 2.]

Because I remain optimistic, even after all of the trauma that has occurred, I believe with all my heart that there <u>must</u> be justice. Please be my justice and use the resources of your office to investigate and to intervene.

Thank you.

Sincerely,

Christine Casson

Enclosures

To be perfectly honest, we don't know if General Reno stepped in or not. What we do know, however, is that the Maryland Office of Attorney General's investigation immediately gained momentum. In the spirit of what *Shocked, Appalled, and Dismayed! How to Write Letters of Complaint That Get Results* (as well as this book) preaches, Chris never gave up and this spirit resulted in an invigorated investigation. After a lot of hemming and hawing from the two baddies, they finally agreed to a $2000 refund, a letter to credit agencies admitting their error in the debacle, and a letter of apology to the client.

Another specific and determined letter-writer is Jennifer Hamilton. You may recall her *Lemon* automobile case in *Shocked, Appalled, and Dismayed!* in which her son almost lost his life because of a defective airbag. I detailed her ongoing battle in my previous book– one that finally reached an exciting climax in December 1998 after publication and almost two years after her problems first began. Mrs. Hamilton now drives a new car and the "Cruel Crooks" dealership lost its corporate license. Undaunted perseverance? You betcha!

So over forty years later, the strongest word in my vocabulary is still *determination*. Whether on the part of self and family or clients who often become friends along the way, from complaint letters to love letters, this word is my guide to doing what is necessary to get the job done. I'm reminded frequently of what opera diva Beverly Sills once said, "You may be disappointed if you fail, but you'll be doomed if you don't try."

Complaint letters that get results are, indeed, easy to write. But what's more important is to become worthy soldiers in,

19

what I've termed, *The Consumer Revolution*. Customer satisfaction, product quality, an improved economy, and the national financial and emotional well-being – all are achieved through writing professional letters of complaint <u>and</u> helping businesses to live up to their responsibilities. Alright, soldiers, are you ready to begin the first surge in our battle plan? Forward, march!

Chapter 2
A Brief Review

"You can't be treated like a doormat if you don't lie down."
- Barbara K. Mehlman

As far as I'm concerned, our national cry should be **CONSUMER REVOLUTION**. I'm tired of big business's attitude that consumers will continue to just sit back and beg to be screwed one more time. I'm also disappointed in the attitude of many consumers who believe that nothing they do can resolve their difficulties with poor quality or service. Sure, some folks have made a couple of attempts but achieved little to nothing, then given up. And I understand that our lives are filled with obligations that consume us and complaints are left dying by the wayside. But it's time to get off your duff! We must take our own financial and emotional destinies in our hands. As consumers, you have been wronged; this is your fight, and you must not give up the battle or the war. Raise the banners! Sound the trumpets! To the ramparts! Not only do you owe yourself, but every complaint letter you write benefits society as a whole, thereby improving product quality, satisfaction and the economy for all of us. And this is my soapbox, dear friends.

According to the Better Business Bureau, companies must spend between two to twenty times as much to win a new customer as to retain an existing one who has a complaint. This sounds to me that money is slipping through those corporate fingers for no good reason. After all, think of the number of fellow consumers that *one* individual tells about a positive experience with resolving a problem. Lots cheaper, huh? How does each of us start that first step to resolution?

When writing letters to any source and about any topic, there are certain guidelines to be followed. Complaint letters *really* need to follow the rules if you intend to win – whether it's because you want to receive some kind of compensation or just a simple apology. Rather than going into all of the detail found within *Shocked, Appalled, and Dismayed! How to Write Letters of Complaint That Get Results* (and ruining your incentive to rush out and buy a copy if you don't have one already), I've chosen to simply reiterate the series of steps necessary to begin the letter-writing process for yourself. While adherence to these steps is mandatory for the complaint letter to achieve the best results, you'll find them useful for many other formats as well. But first, complainers – heads up!

What can you do to achieve the same results as Chris Casson and Jennifer Hamilton? Just follow these simple steps:

1. Calm down. The very first pledge we must make to ourselves is to remain calm, cool, and as detached as possible from the situation. Try to stand back and view the problem as an outsider would. I know you're really ticked and allowing the anger to die down may take a few hours or even a few days. (Got a punching bag to fall back on?) However, once you feel calm enough to begin sorting through your information without steam blowing from your ears, you're ready to begin. Don't wait too long, however. With twenty-five slices of life punching us in the face everyday, you'd be amazed at how quickly we can forget events, and it's most important to relay the facts accurately and completely.

2. Document and organize. There are folks who keep every tiny bit of data and know exactly where it's stored (me), while others must plunder through purchases and drawers to find that one essential receipt (my husband). For either category into which you fall, gather all of the information that is on hand; include every scrap, no matter how insignificant you may think it might be. There are probably people with whom you have spoken personally about the problem, and you have written down each of their names (you have, haven't you?). It may have been a secretary, a supervisor, or the manager. Hopefully, you have maintained some sort of record keeping so that you have the dates and the times of the conversations, as well as the names of the persons with whom you've spoken. Is there any prior correspondence? This, too, must be included. It's one of those slaps-in-the-face to the recipient that you've already previously addressed this problem in writing, and just because it hasn't yet been resolved, you don't intend simply to lie down and die like a dog.

3. Keep receipts. These are your proof of purchase, either for a product or for a service. When you enclose them within the letter, remember to mail only <u>copies</u> and not the originals; otherwise, the only firsthand documentation is gone to that great shredder in the sky. This includes not only receipts for purchased products but also for other types of verification, such as airline boarding passes. Your stack of ammunition should now be growing as fast as Pinocchio's nose (after all, remember *he* turned into a jackass when he didn't do what he was supposed to do). To make your case easier to follow, it's imperative to place any and all data in proper chronological order as it occurs. Once you have compiled everything from your list (or as much of it as you can find), then you are ready for the next better-listen-up step.

4. Discover the name of the person at the highest level. Whether we don't or won't take the time to research and to obtain the name of the person or persons to whom the letter should be addressed, this step is *so* important. It is *critical* to unearth the name of the Head Honcho, the company's CEO and/or president. This is the person at the top, the one with the authority to solve your problem or to pass it to someone with equal authority.. If you should hit a dead end – maybe because of a non-responsive customer service representative - then check the reference section of your local library. Books, such as <u>Standard and Poor's Register of Corporations</u>, <u>Trade Names Dictionary,</u> <u>Forbes</u>, or <u>Dun and Bradstreet Directory</u> are valuable resources to elicit that one certain name and title. Check the appendices of my earlier book for much of this same information, even though you'll have to update most names. Calling the corporate office and asking for this low down may easily and simply access the names of local management. (In fact, go online to www.ConsumerReports.org/Home/Manufac/index.html for toll-free phone listings and Web sites for a huge number of manufacturers.) Your local Chamber of Commerce or city/county offices may also be of help.

Ellen Phillips

There are many times when CEOs are so *shocked, appalled, and dismayed* with the information presented that they themselves set the ball rolling, and you'll hear directly from him or her. These folks realize that if you're satisfied with the manner in which you've been treated, you're going to talk about it and you're going to tell your friends and family, which translates to more sales. Because competition in today's business world is so feverish, few corporations and companies wish to tick off their past, present, and future customers.

5. Use polite language. No one reacts well to being attacked or abused, and a potentially sympathetic ear quickly becomes purely defensive. You're looking for a fair hearing of your problem, and it's not to your advantage to come across as a rude or a hostile person, even if you feel like calling the Boss a #!@%#. It's most important to be as objective and detached as possible, even if you pretend that you're writing the letter for someone else. Recall my advice on Internet "flaming" in Chapter 4. Flame not, lest ye be flamed.

6. Write in standard business letter format. Type or word process all letters; do <u>not</u> hand write, and never, ever think of sending E-mail. Note from the preceding letters that the body is always single-spaced. The only abbreviations allowed are the names of the states in the heading and the inside address, as well as some titles, such as Mr. or Dr. Review the examples found throughout the book, such as where the heading (your address and the date) and the inside address (the same as will appear on the envelope) are situated. Make sure your signature is written <u>above</u> your typed name; it's amazing how many folks make these tiny errors and ruin the whole professional format.

7. Grab the reader's attention as the letter begins. The very first sentence must be an immediate attention getter, in order to grab the recipient's eye. My favorites, of course, are *shocked* and *appalled*, such as "I am shocked and appalled at the unprofessional manner to which I have been subjected by your company's manager, [name of person]" or "I trust that you will be as shocked and appalled as I have been over the recent problem which I have encountered with your company." Really, though, any WAKE-UP term is appropriate to use here. Words like *inexcusable* or *outrageous* will also arouse a note of curiosity on the part of your reader and is a not-so-subtle encouragement to keep on reading. Avoid slang. "Your products suck!" simply won't get the response you want.

8. Be succinct. When presenting your problem, be as to the point as possible. No one, particularly a busy executive, is going to want to wade through ten sheets of paper. If your reader snoozes, you're the loser or, worse, he or she pitches this novel into "File 13." The letter itself should be no more than one to one-and-a-half pages long unless it is an extremely involved case with loads of *pertinent* documentation.

9. Review the history. Introduce your problem and the ways in which you have tried first to solve the difficulty. After all, you want the Big Cheese to understand that you have a legitimate problem, you've tried any means possible to solve it yourself to no avail, and he or she is, indeed, the last possible resource. Be sure your dates, your costs, your prior conversations and correspondence, the persons with whom you have been in contact, and any other relevant information is placed in chronological information. Again, if *BC* has to search throughout the letter for what happened on which date, you'll lose again.

10. Suggest Lost Profits. State that you'll decline to have future dealings with or purchase from the company, if your legitimate problem isn't solved. This particular part of the letter is also an implied "threat" to its loss of income, because guess what? You're gonna tell family, friends, colleagues, and even strangers on the street who are also "appalled" at your problem and the manner in which you have been treated. Your CEO will surely realize that that this wide realm of people will think twice before they, too, may lose money on a product or service offered by his or her company. After all, the Big Boss's stock options won't be as enormous if profits fall, and his pockets will be quite a bit leaner (which might not be so bad, as this would place *BB* on a par with the rest of us lowlies).

11. State your expectations. Do you want repair, replacement, refund, or will just a simple apology make you feel less like a victim? If you don't specify exactly what it is you

25

want, then the recipient can only guess. Always specify that you've been "a loyal customer" or even better, a "faithful credit card holder for years" if such is the case. When expectations are fair, legitimate, and reasonable, it is indeed rare that a *poison pen* customer doesn't get something back.

12. Close firmly and politely. You should thank the reader in the last paragraph, not only for reading your letter but also for the anticipated response. Moreover, stress to the Honcho that you expect a quick answer within a stated time frame. This can be in the form of "immediately" or a fixed deadline such as, "I expect to hear from you within seven business days (or one month) regarding this situation." While it has been my experience that most people rarely hear quite as quickly as "within seven business days," this specificity does place the big wig on alert that you'll be waiting for the reply on that fixed date. You're expecting quick action to be taken with the inference being that if it isn't, you'll really step up the (poisonous) pace.

13. Proofread for errors. Even if you need someone else to check it for you, the letter must be grammatically correct. There are many inexpensive books available to use as a tool for foolproof editing. If you have access to a computer, utilize the spell check function, although the final copy still would need a thorough eyeballing. The more professionally you write your letter, the more likely you are to receive a prompt and positive response. Be <u>really</u> careful with what you think is your final copy; none of us is perfect. Once, to my absolute humiliation, I telephoned a client to check on any responses to our complaint letter. Imagine my horror when she informed me that she never mailed it because of a couple of spelling errors. Groveling at her feet (pretty hard to do when you're on the telephone), I nicely reprimanded her for not immediately calling this to my attention, sent her new <u>corrected</u> copies, and learned a valuable lesson from the experience.

14. Copy Key People. This can be your most potent tool. Trust me, prospective writers, your "carbon copy" list will *definitely* be the signal for your addressee to wake up and smell the coffee. You should send a copy of your letter to any and all agencies that either investigate issues such as your problem or who simply may be interested in what's going on. The bodies fall within state's attorneys generals for possible fraud issues to state consumer protection divisions to national regulatory agencies and consumer organizations. The more, the merrier! To obtain current names and addresses of companies and agencies for yourself, request a free copy of the <u>Consumer Action Handbook</u> from the U.S. Office of Consumer Affairs. This is an excellent reference book, which lists a huge number of agency and corporate contacts and is partial payback for all those taxes you paid. Each year, I simply call (1-800) 688-9889 and look forward to receiving the updated version, or I can speed up the process by turning to the Internet for **http://www.pueblo.gsa.gov**, which offers up-to-date handbook information. The handbook also offers facts and tips to help you gain knowledge about your rights and how to make the right choices — and, yes, how to protect yourself. In addition, I've also tried to incorporate as many ccs as possible within the enclosed sample letters.

15. Shop some place else. This is truly the icing on the cake. Why should you be loyal to a business or a company that doesn't respond with loyalty when a problem arises with its product or service? Sure, it's inconvenient to drive ten miles to another supermarket, cleaners, and so forth. But if enough Consumer Revolution soldiers make known our *written* displeasure and then sashshay elsewhere to spend our money, then many of these companies will realize consumers mean business (and once they change policy to a more customer-friendly one, you can then return to your neighborhood florist).

16. Never give up! I could lie and tell you that each and every letter you write will provide instant relief or even that you'll receive results 100% of the time. Unfortunately, sometimes your "seven business days" becomes three weeks and your "one month" becomes three. I always tell my clients that if a month passes with no satisfactory response – and especially if none at all — to fire off another epistle, along with a copy of the original and a brief cover letter to every single person or agency on your carbon copy list. Personally, I've written several times over a period of months for some resistant authorities, as have a few of my clients. But the secret is that you harangue, you harass, and, quite simply, you <u>never</u> give up. You may get discouraged, but the fight must continue. This is your *cause* and, if you do wish to "Work with Business to Save Time and Money and Get What You Want," then fighting back (and never giving up the fight) is the answer. Ms. Casson and Mrs. Hamilton, among others, certainly didn't give up on their long and hard-fought battles. I had faith in them, and I have faith in you. Don't ever forget that determination and patience are the attributes you'll now lay claim to in order not only to avoid future victimization, but also the means by which you'll shake hands with your (corporate) enemies and discover they really can be your friends.

Helpful Agencies and Services

The **Consumer Action Handbook** lists consumer agencies and corporate contacts and may be obtained by writing the Federal Consumer Information Center, Pueblo, CO 81009. View the Handbook online at www.pueblo.gsa.gov for up-to-the-minute revisions.

The **Major Consumer Action Program (MACAP)** is a third-party dispute resolution program of the major appliance industry. Write them at 20 North Wacker Drive, Suite 1500, Chicago, IL 60606 or telephone (800) 621-0477.

Chapter 3

So What's All the Fuss About Service?

"One man can make a difference. All men should try."
John F. Kennedy

As I often state, one of my biggest *faux pas* comes when I oversimplify customer service – or even service in general – as an oxymoron. This is patently unfair to those in the industry who work long and hard hours in an attempt to satisfy dissatisfied customers and to preserve the integrity of the company for which they work.

On the other hand, however, we know there are many within the ranks who seek to race through their workday with the least amount of hassle possible. These are the folks who seemingly could care less about the state of our health or our wallets. While Chapter 12 discusses what companies and their executives can do to alleviate the worsening employee situation and Chapter 9 deals with certain chronic consumer-service issues, this chapter details how companies themselves *perceive* consumers and, based upon those perceptions, how they then treat us. Tastes of additional information may be found in other applicable chapters, but for now "Caveat emptor." Let the Buyer Beware.

For instance, take the dot-com craze – the stuff of which many millionaires have been almost instantly made – which has provided a speedy and clickable manner to shop. Not only do we avoid long lines and potentially surly salespersons, but also we're promised (or at least these companies imply) that we'll be pleasantly surprised by the sites' service. HOLD UP! It ain't necessarily so.

What about going through the ordering process only to discover upon checking out that the product is out of stock? Or if there's a question about a product or service, having to spend another ten minutes searching for the correct "Contact Us" e-mail address or phone number? The problem isn't always just an out-of-stock or a delayed shipping, or the very gift you want sent to Great Aunt Hortense doesn't arrive gift-wrapped. Much deeper and more aggravating is the issue of pathetic-to-nil service on many sites, even the better known. Don't make us search through pages or give up the valuable time that we're supposedly saving by Net shopping in the first place. E-tailers need to sit up and take note that if service problems aren't resolved, then way too many of their customers will follow my Rule # 15, which is to "Shop some place else."

If I've got a problem or a question, I expect a E-tailer - or, for that matter, a "regular" company - to provide an answer via many mediums: e-mail, telephone, fax, chat, and so forth. The more, the better. And I don't want to wait forty-eight hours or longer to receive an answer in return, either, or I get testy. If they're truly serious about talking and keeping market share, Dot-coms (and traditional bricks and mortar companies) better cough up whatever amount of money it takes to put these better-service devices in place. I read with great interest of 1-800-Flowers that employs several <u>thousand</u> extra customer service representatives to help their customers during peak holiday hours. These folks will chat online for twenty or more minutes (basically, as long as it takes) to assist with the purchase of the perfect bouquet of flowers. Or look at Lands' End. The company has 2,500 sales reps whose jobs are to answer your questions online. More than half of the shoppers who place items in Lands' End shopping carts end up buying, as opposed to only twenty-two percent for the industry average. Thank you to these dear, online, speedy, and knowledgeable representatives.

And what about Nordstrom's as another example? While I tout this company's particularly great service in the retail chapter, it even goes a step further online. Nordstrom, Inc. continues to see the light; it purchased a million dollar plus software program that enables a customer service rep to lead a client literally to the specific item for which she or he is searching. And you'd better believe that the types of unheard of service from all three of the aforementioned companies elicits repeat customers as well as many new ones since the latter tells others about his or her wonderful shopping experience.

(I'm reminded of a radio interview I had with a station in Wisconsin and the host wishing that he had access to a Nordstom's in his area. He remarked how much he missed that special touch the store delivered to its customers.)

Speaking of repeat customers, why not reward them for returning to a Website (or a store)? What better form of advertising and positive press is a measly five or ten percent taken off the price of the purchase. Ten percent off a $50 purchase is only $5.00. Even if we're talking five percent off a luxury item (for example a $50,000 automobile equals $2,500 discount), the laurels thrown by the customer definitely ensures additional business and more company profits. An incentive doesn't even have to be in the form of a discount, but a gift for repeaters. What could it cost the company to provide something for which it pays a few bucks or probably even a few cents as a reward for shoppers coming back to spend some more money. And it doesn't have to be an incentive for the biggest spenders, either. Sure, our profile shows that we only spent $29.95 last month while Frannie Fartenagle spent $299.95, but don't differentiate between Frannie and me because of the *amount* we each spent. Rather, recompense both of us because we returned to this site and bought *more* items.

Restaurant surveys found that gripes about service have tripled over the past five years (and, believe me, this is one of the better industries). Furthermore, according to the Department of Transportation, complaints about air travel more than doubled in 2001. Some research proves that if you're not a big spender (remember Freddy Fartenagle?), then you simply don't always receive decent service. According to the October 23, 2000 issue of *Business Week*, a gentleman who works as a customer service rep at an electric utility company relates an interesting and scary story. Six people service the top 350 business clients. Another six representatives serve the next level of 700 customers. Two customer service personnel handle 30,000 consumers, and those 300,000 at the lowest rung of the ladder (I guess they can't afford to use enough electricity to warm them in winter) get no personal service at all, although I don't how "personal" a two to 30,000 ratio can get. The have-nots must play hit-or-miss with an 800 number.

Enter the world of big spender versus the more economical buyer. We're told that companies increasingly and deliberately decide to give different service to different people. We already know that if one is a Platinum frequent flyer, he or she receives more attention and perks than a member of the lowly, plain ole' frequent flyer program. But did you know that E-tailers as well as regular stores are keeping tabs on your spending profile? The big spender may return an item for a full refund, without a receipt. On the other hand, Ms. Economical often must have the receipt, the store and manufacturer tags, *and* get her item back within a ten-day period – or less. Fair?

Even the Maytag Repairman – that poor, lonely, white-suited gentleman who bemoans that he has no customers to visit – would be aghast to learn what's going on these days. If a consumer buys a more expensive product from the Maytag Corporation, his or her extra spending definitely gets more for the money. How about a special group of customer support personnel, an out of the ordinary toll-free number to call, and *very* rapid repair service? Dale Reeder, Maytag's customer service general manager, stated in that same *Business Week* article that those who spend more "deserve" more service. Well, excuse me! What are the rest of us who pay $500 for a washing machine instead of $1000? Chopped liver? To answer this question, maybe you'd better go back and read George Orwell's *1994*. The author's predictions concerning "Big Brother" don't necessarily mean the government in this day and time.

Horror of horrors, we have allowed the day to arrive where, on many occasions, we must <u>pay</u> for service. Because Business sees us as overly demanding (but really just because we've become more aware, more consumer-savvy as to our rights), some companies have instigated a fee-based service program. Those consumers willing to pay to avoid the seventeen options and the thirty-minute phone wait will receive quick and helpful service, while the rest of us remain in the Never-Never-Land of Sit-Down-Shuttup-and Maybe-We'll-Get-to-You-Sometime-in-the- Future "customer service." As I preach over and over 'til I'm blue in the face, <u>all</u> of us must complain if we're treated unfairly or if we don't receive the service we ought to when we first make the purchase. Be damn to companies who make us pay extra for what we should get in the first place. Consumers, unite!

Yet, as much as we love to tell Big Business its "business," another extremely important fact remains: if we don't follow the Golden Rule, why should they? I wrote of the need for civility, not only in our personal lives but also in the workplace, in *Shocked, Appalled, and Dismayed!* And from that same perspective, a few more pieces of advice for individual or business etiquette (ignore at your own risk - literally).

- **Watch the mouth** (and this tip from yours truly, the *Mouth That Roared*). For instance, if the waiter doesn't take your order quickly enough because he's busy elsewhere, don't snarl at him or leave a five percent tip. (If he's lazy or inattentive, the five percent is okay, but no snarling, please.)

- **Be careful with body language**. Nonverbal communication sometimes can be nastier than verbal. What kind of a message does one demonstrate when he or she ignores an outstretched hand or leaves a meeting without shaking hands, for example? (And for goodness sake, do *not* throw up that middle finger when someone cuts you off on the road. It could mete you nothing shy of a pistol-whipping.)

- **Are we rude with our cell phones**? This action often provokes a whole boatload of *re*action from people around you. Whether playing double jeopardy when talking in traffic to the absolute height of rudeness when talking in a restaurant or a movie or the theatre, this nonsense needs to be immediately stopped. Unless an emergency is present, nothing is so important that it can't wait until we're out of earshot of others.

- **What about when we travel**? Must you take up the whole space in the overhead compartment? Is it necessary to push in front of another person when boarding the train? Manners, manners, manners, please…

- **Or party**? Sure, the buffet table looks great and maybe you haven't eaten since breakfast. Still, that's no excuse for abandoning your partner, client, guest, etc. to make a mad dive for the food. Along this same line, do a people study the next time you're around "eaters." How many talk with their mouths full or eat their peas with a spoon. Not only do behaviors like these show a distinct lack of proper upbringing, but also the former is downright disgusting. Don't forget to consult those *Grande Dames* of whom I wrote in *Shocked, Appalled, and Dismayed!*'s Chapter 10 for an introduction (or a re-introduction) to acceptable table manners.

I could go on and on but I think you get the point. Just as we expect those within Corporate America and elsewhere to treat us with respect, responsibility, and responsiveness, the treatment goes both ways. The way each of us treats one another in any situation – whether with civility or with rudeness – mandates the manner in which society either moves forward or remains the stereotypical "Ugly American." And hey, Consumers, the further we advance, the more Corporate must listen to and remedy our valid tales of woe. To conclude this chapter, take a gander at the following joke that really does exemplify the attitude we *shouldn't* have when dealing with customer service. And by the way, the "joke" is proclaimed to be an absolutely true story.

A crowded United flight was canceled, and a lone agent was rebooking a long line of inconvenienced and frustrated passengers. Suddenly an angry passenger pushed his way past all the others, slammed his hand down on the countertop, and yelled, "I HAVE to be on this flight and it better be FIRST CLASS!"

The agent replied, "I'm sorry, sir. I'll be happy to try to help you, but I must assist these folks first. I'm sure we can work something out, though, when it's your turn in line."

Obviously unimpressed by the agent's gentle reprimand, the man then screamed, "Do you know who I am?"

Without hesitation, the agent smiled and grabbed her public address microphone. "May I have your attention, please?" her voice bellowed throughout the terminal. "We have a passenger here at Gate 26 WHO DOES NOT KNOW WHO HE IS. If anyone can help him to discover his identity, please come to the gate."

Aware of all the other passengers surrounding him and laughing hysterically, the man glared at the agent, gritted his teeth and swore [and I'll use the less crude version of the term], "*Screw* you!"

Without flinching, this very professional gate agent just smiled and replied, "I'm sorry, sir, but you'll have to stand in line for that, too."

Chapter 4

Netiquette and the Internet

"Adhere to the same standards of behavior online that you
follow in real life."
- Virginia Shea

I concluded *Shocked, Appalled, and Dismayed!* with a chapter entitled, "The Art of a Perfect 'Thank You' Note," in which I vented my own feelings regarding proper etiquette and its place within the realm of all letter writing, complaint or otherwise. Therefore, it's only appropriate that I begin *Fight Back and Win!* with a semblance of the same category. "Netiquette" is the term coined for computer etiquette. Involving the courtesy, respect, and ethics essential for corresponding on the Internet, it is a process with which we should all be familiar. Certainly, this doesn't take the place of old-fashioned letter writing around which both books are showcased, but it functions in its own manner. Just be careful in utilizing this process as a means of formal communication. Attorney John Morrison has some thoughts on the subject:

"My preliminary impression of this medium is that users tend to write everything that comes to mind as it comes to mind, and then send it upon completion without going through the difficult and time consuming process of organizing thoughts and editing what has been written. While this method of instant 'electronic conversation' may be useful among 'friends,'
I recommend that when using e-mail for communicating a timely complaint, users be reminded that the substance of the complaint remains more important than the method used to transmit the complaint. ('Haste makes waste' remains a valid warning.)" [**]

[**] John C. Morrison, Esquire, Morrison and Reynolds, Alexandria, Virginia

E-mail can be an extremely useful tool in certain circumstances, but you must be very cautious when utilizing it as a means of complaint correspondence. As a matter of fact, I really don't recommend its use for this purpose. Although it may be forwarded to a company's manager or to a CEO, it truly isn't confidential information. If e-mail is directed to others on down the line, a new problem may arise. Let's say that you've included personal information, such as your store account or your bank card number (as you would in an official complaint letter), but a disgruntled or an unscrupulous individual within the company – plus any hacker who's surfing around - sees this on the e-mail message. What's to stop this person from having a shopping spree at your expense? Your next credit card statement might be a shocker when you see the purchases you didn't make, such as a new wardrobe, a trip to the Caribbean, or an expensive new car! This is as deadly as leaving copies of credit card receipts lying in your front yard for any vagabond to steal to use your card number.

Internet activity also can place you in a most embarrassing situation if you've made comments that you wouldn't wish anyone else to see. Just as in a letter, you're accountable for the language you use in the "public domain" — the area accessible for others to see or to read.

One end result may be that your server annuls your e-mail services altogether, and then you'll really be stuck. It's better to be safe than sorry by remembering the following points:

- A simple click of the mouse can send a message to the wrong person.
- Avoid sending or forwarding defamatory, obscene, or offensive messages. You may end up opening the wrong can of worms (and, believe me, you can kiss any resolution goodbye).
- Forwarding chain letters or the like is against the law, just as it is with traditional letters or "snail mail" as it's called in Cyber jargon.
- E-mailing to large listings within an ISP (Internet Service Provider) is a big, bad no-no.

- And if you use company computers for messages, usually *everything* you send or receive is fair game for company inspection. Don't jeopardize your job because of policies such as this.

I'm reminded of a story I read a few years back in *The New York Times* (June 8, 1997) regarding the use of technology and its grave potential for trouble. Slander and libel laws do certainly apply to the Internet, even if First Amendment rights may be questionable within this gray area. We're on extremely shaky ground if and when we circulate damaging or false information about a company on the Internet. Personal web sites that cast open and available aspersions upon corporations or individuals are now widely in use. Surfers vent their hostilities regarding dissatisfactions in an attempt to bring other and equally vocal proponents to their side. It's risky business, though. Federal courts have thus far banned the use of a company's name to steer folks to another site without the express permission of that company, maintaining that by doing so, we use the company's trademark illegally. Additionally, many lawsuits have arisen with the personal Website owners becoming the loser in most cases.

It's just too easy to send wrong information, especially in the heat of anger. If we receive misinformation about a person or a company from a friend or other source whom we think of as reliable, we might tend to copy the posting to other friends or groups. (Just think of all the virus hoaxes passed on.) This can all too quickly (and to our chagrin) land us in Brer Rabbit's briar patch, because the Web is just too similar to television and newspapers. Even if the New York Times article is not a recent one, it offers a surprising raising of the relevant red flag from no less than Stephen Brobeck, the Executive Director of the Consumer Federation of America. "*The overwhelming majority of information about consumer issues on the Web is either biased, because it is provided by marketers, or unreliable, because it has not been evaluated by any credible source.*"

Virginia Shea's book, Netiquette (speaking of Web sites, take note of her publisher, Albion Books' www.albion.com)

40

offers some great advice on avoiding human error when writing [complaints] on the Internet. Ms. Shea relates some funny and true examples of what can happen if we're not careful.

- By accident, you send your letter to the person about whom you wrote the complaint. (Been there, done that.)
- The person who receives your message forwards it on to the person you wrote about.
- You unintentionally send the missive to an international mailing list, rather than to the individual you intended to receive it.

And she concludes her book with her own special doctrine: "*The rules of Netiquette can only work if they're adopted by a majority of the people in Cyberspace — if they become a community standard.*"

We must remember that e-mail is vastly different from traditional letter-writing. So far as complaints are concerned, it's usually disrespectful, defiant, dictatorial, and filled with grammatical errors. Seldom do we achieve results with this type of "correspondence," which directly contrasts with a professional, detached, coherent, and organized letter that can and usually does get results.

Also so far as e-mail is concerned, we must be vigilant little soldiers in order to protect our files and address books from virus enemies set to destroy our hard drives and so forth. Unfortunately, it seems more and more likely that, at some point or another, many of us will become subject to a wormy virus and its heinous hacker hobgoblin. Even if Cupid's arrow passed through an eyeball (!), it would probably be less painful than what could happen to "Cecelia Citizen's" personal PC all the way up to those big boys at the Pentagon or at Amazon.com.

What can we do? A good anti-virus program is a necessity. However, it's only as good as the frequency with which you update it. A "fire-wall" for net surfers also is absolutely essential as a protection against hackers. It doesn't matter if the program is one belonging to Symantec (Norton Anti-Virus), Cnet

(BlackICE Defender), or others, your primary goal is to get your hands ASAP on a reliable one before the next time you open an E-mail attachment with which you're not familiar. Experts at *Kiplinger Personal Finance* magazine (June 2000) tell us the best method to discover computer vulnerability is to hack yourself. Go to www.grc.com to find "Shields Up." If your computer is unprotected, the program usually finds several openings in less than a minute.

You <u>can</u> avoid costly crashes or even someone peeking into your private information by ensuring that *your* love bug is that fat little fellow with wings and a bow and arrow. Anything else can be successfully avoided by following this advice.

The World Wide Web can still prove a beneficial fount of information and knowledge. How many times have we thought of writing a letter to our Senator or Congressperson, but since we haven't voted in the past decade, we don't know to whom to address our concerns? As names of these personages may change every four or two years, just sit down at your trusty computer and pull up the new names and the e-mail addresses, phone numbers, or even Web sites for your own and other states' current Senate and House members. Don't forget to check out the committees on which they serve, also. These may be the very ones about which you have concerns. Regardless if your search involves a complaint letter or simply for one voicing your opinion about matters close to your heart, here again, just as always, the highest-ranking official in a certain territory is the one to write. Up-to-date heads of regulatory agencies may also be discovered surfing the Web. **http://seamless.com** is the best "address" to obtain information for all your complaining needs. It offers a wealth of tips on consumer help. A brand-new one-stop shopping Web site to access the Federal government is now available. **http://www.consumer.gov** (aka *The Consumer Gateway)* offers information by subject. Cooperating partners may be even more numerous when you try this now, but the original ones include the following: the Consumer Product Safety Commission, the Federal Trade Commissions' Bureau of Consumer Protection (the host agency), the Food and Drug

Administration, the National Highway Traffic Safety Administration, and the Securities and Exchange Commission. Each of these sites has its own subject areas that allow consumers to locate and to link up to immediate and current information. Even better, topics are cross-linked to encourage user access. Once more exercising this miraculous Internet invention, we can always keep abreast of whom to vocalize our complaints, *vis-à-vis* the "pen."

Even with my admonitions, I suspect there may still be some readers who still insist on complaining via e-mail. If you absolutely and unequivocally <u>must</u> use this source in lieu of a real letter and nothing I say will change your mind, then at least remember some important rules.

- **Calm down**. As previously ascertained, it's mighty easy to jump on the Internet and blast off quicker than Tinkerbelle can sprinkle fairy dust. Because this is a median with such an immediate "postage stamp," it's really necessary to keep your head on straight.
- **Document and organize**. Just as in a real letter, *poison* or otherwise, no one will give any credence to information that isn't factual and in order.
- **Discover the name of the Big Boy or Girl**. Here again, the higher you go, the better chance you'll have for resolution.
- **Use polite language**. Those much more familiar with this technique than I call veering from the formula "flaming." These inflammatory remarks or messages can take the form of rudeness, threatening remarks, stupid comments, etc. Whatever the "flame," avoid it like the plague.
- **DON'T TYPE IN ALL CAPS**. This method is equivalent to SCREAMING at the recipient.
- **Avoid instant-message programs**. Nothing is more annoying than a message that repeatedly pops up on the recipient's screen. Don't tick off this person since he or she will respond when he or she chooses and not before .

- **Proofread for errors**. *Ellen English Teacher* can't stress this enough. Someone who might have a better grasp of grammar and mechanics than you is reading your e-mail, particularly if you've dashed off the message. Sloppy spelling, for example, is basically the same as wearing dirty clothes when speaking with the recipient in person.
- **Grab the reader's attention at the beginning**. It's always important to let the recipient know you're shocked, appalled, and dismayed right at the onset.
- **Be concise**. Lots of computer experts decree it to be poor Netiquette to hold up the lines (kinda like an old-fashioned telephone party line) by writing and writing and writing. Don't.
- **Review the history**. Again, the key word is concise.
- **Suggest profit loss**. Don't forget this "implied threat" to loss of the company's capital. (Note the term implied as opposed to that of "flaming.")
- **State your expectations**. This goes without saying.
- **Close firmly and politely**. This is the time to declare when you want a response and also to thank the reader.
- **Copy key people**. I've got my doubts about this regulation with regard to e-mail because of the time and the space you've already taken with the complaint itself. I suggest that you limit the amount of cc's or just list each one without writing the addresses on the screen.

Cybershopping

Those consumers familiar with the Internet find themselves with a dazzling array of helpful people, a multitude of organizations, discussion groups, and everything in between. The most spectacular feature of this device for many of us, however, is the stoke of the keyboard and the click of the mouse that instantly brings relief from crowded parking lots, tired feet, and heavy shopping bags – buying online. With a swish of your credit card, you can enjoy shopping for just about any item your heart desires, right in front of your computer. In fact, the figures in for the year 2000 show that over $114 <u>billion</u> was spent on E-commerce. Even as recently as 2001's holiday shopping season, traditional stores took a loss, while Internet shopping sites made money. The outlook for the next decade is simply astronomical, as well. Should we all then 1, 2, 3, race and shop?

Hold up there before your fingers go flying to find that perfect product! Just as we have to be careful when shopping by mail and by phone, the same holds true for shopping from the Net. The Federal Trade Commission advises consumers to remember the following:

1. **Unsecured information can be intercepted**. Always use a secured browser, which will encrypt or scramble purchase information. The credit and charge card companies are currently working on a better level of security measures for online shopping. If you don't have encryption software, it is probably a good idea to call the company's 800 number or fax your order. Even so, Susan Grant of the National Consumers League tells us, "Paying by credit card is the safest way to shop on the Internet because many scam artists are not set up to take credit cards and because consumers have the right to dispute dubious billings under the **Fair Credit Billing Act**." This Act applies to credit card and charge accounts and helps to protect the consumer on a number of fronts. These include billing errors, unauthorized use of accounts, goods or services charged but not received, and against paying charges until an explanation or proof of purchase is provided.

2. **Shop with companies you know (and trust)**. Always determine their return and refund policies <u>before</u> placing an order. Beware of Web site "clones" that are used by hackers to steal personal information. Always check a domain name at <u>www.nsi.com</u>. Type in the prospective site's Web address to see who's operating it and if

details don't match the legitimate site you wanted, then avoid the suspicious one forever.

3. **Never give out your Internet password**. Create a really original one that is impossible for a scam artist to decipher, and avoid like the plague a combination of letters and/or numbers, such as your house number and your pet's name. Also, do not give out your social security number. With today's horror stories of identity theft, react like a wild bull with a red kerchief waved in front of its eyes if an online company asks for this piece of private information.

4. **Always print out a copy of your order and confirmation number for your records**. This documentation is imperative if you need to later write a complaint letter.

The same laws that protect you when you shop by mail or phone apply when shopping through this medium. (See Chapter 9) The only exception to the **Cooling-off Rule** is when a company doesn't promise a shipping time and you're *applying* for credit to pay for your purchase; that business then has fifty days to ship after receiving your order. A fairly new web site is sponsored by the **American Bar Association**. www.safeshopping.org provides information on wise online shopping and offers much of the same advice that I do with regards to E-commerce complaints.

So let's say you've followed all of this advice, and you've placed a very special online order to arrive just in time for your wife's birthday. Unfortunately, she opens the package and instead of the *Marilyn Monroe Sexy-Sexy Bra*, she sees a model that looks too utilitarian even for your great-grandmother. Determined to satisfy your honey's tastes and, at the same time, to reimburse your pocketbook while avoiding divorce, you could write a letter like the following:

899 Ripped-Off Lane
Tulsa, OK 73956
November 21, 2001

Bob Boob, President
Sexy Online Company
1344 Online Avenue
New York, NY 18754

Dear Mr. Boob:

I am appalled at my recent experience with Sexy Online. On October 29, 2001, I ordered one (1) black lace *Peekaboo* bra, size 34B (copy of order and confirmation number enclosed) for $29.95 plus $8.00 for shipping and handling. Instead, my wife was shocked when the package revealed a white *Granny Grumps* bra, size 42DDD.

Under the Fair Credit Billing Act, I am requesting an immediate credit to my charge card (#1234567890). Please note that I returned the bra well within the required sixty days time limit.

I have been well satisfied in the past with my online shopping, and particularly with the services offered by your company. Assuming that this $37.95 credit is applied before my next billing date, I will certainly remain a loyal customer of Sexy Online. I also expect a letter of explanation from you regarding this mix-up.

Thank you, and I look forward to hearing from you within the next seven business days.

Sincerely,

Samuel Strangled

Enclosure

cc: Howard Beales, Director
   Bureau of Consumer Protection
   Federal Trade Commission
   Pennsylvania Avenue and Sixth Street, NW
   Washington, DC 20580

   Jane Wheeler, Director
   Office of the Attorney General
   Consumer Protection Unit
   440 South Houston, Suite 505
   Tulsa, OK 74127

   B. B. Bucks, CEO
   Big Bucks Credit Card Corporation
   909 Money Terrace, Suite 20
   New York, NY 18798

Some final words of caution need mentioning here. Just as there are scams in the "real" world, there are also fraudulent and deceptive activities on the Internet. Some of the very same people who are out to pick your pocket in newspapers, magazines, and on the telephone are now strutting their stuff in Cyberspace. You'll run across these in e-mail advertising, one of which is called classified (yes, just like the garage sale ad you run in your local newspaper) but with a big difference. These are more like infomercials, promising get-well-get-thin-and-get-rich schemes. Others excite the reader who's planning for his or her retirement with investment opportunities. Be sure to close your eyes and don't dial that 900 phone number they are advertising. You may also contact the **Coalition Against Unsolicited Commercial E-Mail (CAUCE)** at www.cauce.org for pointers to avoid unwanted messages.

The second category is what's called "disguised" advertising and is often harder to recognize. A number of these are found on bulletin boards and in chat forums. These "chat forums" are live discussion groups which many scoundrels tap into without disclosing their real intentions. Because the method isn't as obvious as an ad, it's sometimes more misleading to the viewer; therefore, you might get caught up in the venture without realizing that it is indeed a scam. <u>Never</u> give out your bank account or credit card numbers online (or by phone for that matter unless you've instigated the call yourself). Personal information is just that – personal — so keep it to yourself. Remember there are thousands of people on the Net who may be storing away this information for their own unethical use.

One CEO of a (yes!) web site who is very savvy about purchasing online got caught up into purchasing stock options off the Net. The online broker was advertised through another site and everything seemed legitimate – that is until the day soon thereafter that Seth Scammed realized that the information he was given for his purchase was wrong. We wrote the following letter:

NET ELUCIDATION
Chattanooga, TN 46831
(1-800) 964-0000
www.ne.biz

May 17, 2001

David Dastardly, Chairman and CEO
Cybercrook, Inc.
0033 Corporate Drive
Suite 410
Dallas, TX 89036

Dear Mr. Dastardly:

An egregious situation has occurred with your web-based financial site, Stocks for Sale, which I discovered on the Internet site www.stsale.com, and is a matter

that I am certain you will wish to immediately and thoroughly investigate.

- I first became a member of Stocks for Sale in December 2000. Based on the service's information regarding furnishing "correct" symbols for stock options, I purchased two groups of stocks from Get Rich in January 2001 using the symbols your site provided. The information on your site stated that the stock options I was purchasing expired in <u>February 17, 2001</u>; therefore, I purchased twenty-two contracts of QQQHH. The first two contracts were purchased on January 15, 2001 for $1154; the next twenty were purchased on January 25, 2001 in the amount of $1554. (Total sum $2708.) Please see enclosed E-mail dated February 26 for the purchased Call Series.
- In late February, my purchases disappeared from my Get Rich screen. I promptly E-mailed webmaster@stsale.com on February 26, only to learn that not only had the options expired worthless as of January 29, 2001, but also that your service had incorrectly cited the expiration date. Stocks for Sale's apology was as worthless as the Get Rich stock purchase.
- I subsequently wrote many times to Stocks for Sale (see enclosed copies); however, responses have been limited at best. I finally received a return e-mail from Anthony Accomplice on March 1 (both copies enclosed). Mr. Accomplice admitted to the error but stated that Stocks for Sale is blameless because I accepted the licensing agreement. While I admit to accepting the extremely consumer-unfriendly twenty-page agreement, I did so only because the document was <u>supposed</u> to contain accurate information. It did not.
- I then received an E-mail on March 4 from Roger S. Rogue, Senior Vice-President at Stocks for Sale,

who advised me to contact him (copy enclosed). I wrote on March 5 (copy enclosed), in which I advised Mr. Rogue of my attempts to contact him via telephone. Receiving no response, I called again; he eventually did return my call and left a message. However, when I attempted to reach him on many other subsequent dates, he, I assume, simply refused to respond to any of my messages.

- On April 16, I wrote to the Chattanooga Better Business Bureau (copy enclosed). Jerald Jurisdiction, head of the Chattanooga Better Business Bureau contacted me to see if I wanted to file a formal complaint. Thus far I have not done this.

Even after I reported the site inaccuracies to Stocks for Sale, the false information continued to appear on your site for more than a month. As the president of a company that specializes in websites, I ensure that all information is current and correct on my site, and I expect no less from other reputable ones. While I hesitate to term Stocks for Sale's activity as fraudulent, it certainly appears to be a gross misrepresentation of facts given to prospective clients. It is irrelevant that your company blames its vendor; I still suffered a loss of $2708, again based on tainted information provided by Stocks for Sale. I expect an immediate refund or a credit of this amount to my charge card.

Thank you, and I look forward to hearing from you by June 1, 2001.

Sincerely,

Seth Scammed, President

Enclosures

cc: The Honorable Paul G. Summers
Attorney General of Tennessee
Office of the Attorney General
500 Charlotte Avenue
Nashville, TN 37243

Mark S. Williams, Director
Division of Consumer Affairs
500 James Robertson Parkway, 5th Floor
Nashville, TN 37243-0600

Cynthia Carter, Deputy Attorney General
Division of Consumer Protection
Office of Attorney General
425 Fifth Avenue, North, 2nd Floor
Nashville, TN 37243-0491

The Honorable Donald L. Evans, Secretary
United States Department of Commerce
Fourteenth Street and Constitution Avenue, NW
Washington, DC 20230

Office of Consumer Protection
United States Department of Commerce
Room 5718
Fourteenth Street and Constitution Avenue, NW
Washington, DC 20230

Federal Bureau of Investigation
935 Pennsylvania Avenue, NW
Washington, DC 20535-0001

Michael Powell, Director
Federal Communications Commission
1919 M Street, NW
Washington, DC 20554

National Association of Consumer Agency
Administrators
1010 Vermont Avenue, NW, Suite 514
Washington, DC 20005

National Association of Securities Dealers, Inc.
33 Whitehall Street, 8th Floor
New York, NY 10004

Daphne D. Smith, Assistant Commissioner
Department of Commerce and Insurance
Securities Division
Davy Crockett Tower, Suite 680
500 James Robertson Parkway
Nashville, TN 37243-0485

US Commodities Futures Trading Commission
Lafayette Centre
1155 21st Street, NW
Washington, DC 20581

Jerald Jurisdiction
Better Business Bureau
6525 Business Drive, Suite 410
Chattanooga, TN 47777

Editor
Business Week
1217 Avenue of the Americas
New York, NY 10001

Editor
Forbes Magazine
85 Fifth Avenue
New York, NY 10003

Editor
Fortune Magazine

Ellen Phillips

1271 Avenue of the Americas
New York, NY 10001

Editor
Investors Business Daily
19 West, Forty-fourth Street
New York, NY 10031

Editor
PC Magazine
650 Townsend Street
San Francisco, CA 94103

Editor
Wall Street Journal
200 Liberty Street
New York, NY 10281

Editor
Yahoo! Internet Life Magazine
650 Townsend Street
San Francisco, CA 94103

Editor
Ziff Davis Publications
650 Townsend Street
San Francisco, CA 94103

Even though it took a second and even a third attempt, "Seth" finally got results.

So what can we do to ensure our Internet buying time is spent wisely? The following snippets of advice can help you to make wise decisions before a complaint letter is necessary:

- **Make sure the merchant service has a secure browser**. This padlock symbol assures the consumer that the personal information we type in, such as our names, addresses, credit card information and so forth, doesn't land up in the hands of unscrupulous hackers. If we're not cautious and this *appalling* situation does happen, then we can find ourselves faced with the threat of identity theft (more on this topic in Chapter 6).

- **Never give out your social security number**. Even the IRS has stopped placing taxpayers' numbers on their forms. If this merchant does ask for your social security number, shut down its web page — pronto!
- **Check the return policy**. Just as in "regular" purchases, a legitimate Web merchant should state its policy and include its <u>physical</u> address and (preferably) a toll-free number. If you're not sure about the policy, then call. If the company isn't sure, then rethink purchasing from it. When returning an item, it doesn't hurt also to send it certified mail, return receipt requested (your "proof"). Insure the return if it's a big ticket item.

Many companies have passed a review of the **Better Business Bureau** and have agreed to binding arbitration to settle disputes. The BBB's logo should appear on these sites. Don't forget, however, that binding arbitration means that you as well as the company must agree up-front to any subsequent decision made after filing a complaint. It certainly wouldn't hurt to visit the **www.bizrate.com** site. This Net service reports the service and dependability of more than five hundred Internet merchants. Additionally, to be extra careful, check out **www.scambusters./org/scamcheck.html** for scam alerts.

- **Read warranties**. You wouldn't dream of buying an expensive item in the real world without checking the warranty; do the same when you cybershop. There are three types to consider and the **Magnuson-Moss Warranty Act** requires merchants to make copies available. The first is a <u>full</u> warranty that states that the item will be repaired or replaced within a specified time and covers parts and labor. The full also protects secondary owners if you later sell or give away the product in question. The second type of warranty is the limited one for which parts are covered but no labor; this one does not apply to secondary owners. The final warranty is an implied one. Watch out for this third warranty as it simply means that the item is fit for "normal" use (and what's normal for some buyers may not be the same for others). If, for some reason, the company doesn't follow through on its warranty promise, then immediately write your complaint letter to the **Federal Trade Commission** at Pennsylvania Avenue and Sixth Street, NW, Room 240, Washington, DC 20580 and send a copy to your state attorney general's office, too. Also, contact the **National Fraud Information Center** at www.fraud.org to file a complaint and to read other complaints. A brand-new policing site, the **Internet Fraud Complaint Center**, is one that combines the expertise of the FBI and the National White Collar Crime Center. If you think you've been swindled, hacked, victimized, or otherwise scammed, contact www.ifccfbi.gov. Your complaint will then be forwarded to the appropriate local, state, or federal law-enforcement agency for investigation.

- **Always print out a copy of your order and confirmation number for your own records**. You'll need this information if you later find a complaint letter necessary. Unless otherwise stated, your products must be delivered within thirty days, and if delays are necessary then the company must contact you. This is the law.

But maybe you're not shopping but simply surfing the Web. How can you remain anonymous to avoid unwanted spam, having marketers access your virtual profiles, or even criminals exploiting your data to commit fraud? Actually, there are several easy remedies to these potential problems.

- **Use an alias**. Maybe you've always wanted to be a Marilyn Monroe or a Clint Black; now's your chance. Always register using the fictitious name and, even better

- **Get a free e-mail account** (there are lots of these Web-based services out there). For example, you can become <u>Marilyn@yahoo.com</u> or <u>Clint@hotmail.com</u> and every time you register this alias make sure you decide on a password that you'll use each time. (Maybe sexyblonde or countrysinger.) Then your *real* e-mail address, as well as your user name and password, is protected from the lurkers.

- **Avoid spammers another way.** These folks or marketers employ something called "bots," programs that copy all the e-mail addresses they can discover. You could use your real address but add a word that doesn't belong, such as <u>pznpen@gotcha.com</u>.

- **Thwart the Internet Protocol (IP) number.** Each time you're on the Net, you're given an IP, which is a special number that tells servers how to send messages to you. There are several good software programs on the market to defeat the IP, such as the Anonymizer (<u>www.anonymizer.com</u>).

- **Avoid spam like the plague.** For a long time I would hit the reply key with the message "Unsubscribe" as directed. Messages didn't stop, however. I finally realized that each time I told them to take me off their mailing lists, I was actually notifying these creeps that I was reading their mail. So don't reply, just delete.

While we do have recourse if those "nice" folks on the Internet place us in a stranglehold of sorts, who helps us by *monitoring* the Web? People who know me are aware that I don't have a whole lotta use for the Better Business Bureau as an agency that helps disgruntled consumers. However, as mentioned previously, the **BBB Online** is helpful in other areas. Its Privacy Program stamps a "seal of approval" (yep, just like *Good Housekeeping* magazine) on those sites that promotes and adheres to consumer privacy. And there's even a Kids Privacy Seal to help parents protect their children from less desirable elements.

The other monitor is **Internet Fraud Watch** (www.fraud.org). It bears repeating that this site points out the bad guys and is a spot on the Net we all had better pay attention to on a consistent basis. It's also of interest to go online with this organization and check complaint statistics. (How about the one that states consumer complaints have risen over 600% in three years - pretty discouraging, huh? Obviously, this number doesn't reflect all you Consumer Revolution warriors.)

But let's say that you know all this safety information. In fact, let's go even further and state that you're a good cybershopper. Too bad that things still go wrong; so, in that event, perhaps you should consider a letter like the following:

8901 Cybershoppe Stree
Jacksonville, FL 32203
July 29, 2001

Sharon Sells, President
Internet Books, Inc.
9867 Readable Road
New York, NY 99998

Dear Ms. Sells:

I am shocked and outraged by your failure to ship Oprah's 2000 Book Club Picks to me at the appropriate time. When I placed this order on June 25, 2001 (copy of shipping order enclosed), I emphatically stated that the books had to be in my hands no later than Thursday, July 1. As a favor to my neighbor, Constance Contentious, I had purchased this large order for her as she was leaving for Europe. She wished to take the Picks as hostess gifts but does not have access to a computer.

When Mrs. Contentious arrived yesterday to take delivery of her promised order, she became very angry because it had not arrived. To my horror, she <u>spit</u> in my face and the drool dripped onto the collar of my expensive silk blouse. Not only have I lost a friend, but also my blouse has had to be dry cleaned.

I expect an immediate and thorough investigation into your company's shipping department's error. In addition, I anticipate immediate compensation in the amount of $9.50 for the dry cleaning bill.

Thank you, and I look forward to hearing from you within the next seven business days.

Sincerely,

Nell Neighbor

Enclosures

Before closing, I think it important to include some sort of Internet materials company as one of the best for which other like businesses should strive to copy. Advanced Micro Devices is one of America's largest semiconductor manufacturers. Its "people first" philosophy is probably what kept the company going strong through some pretty terrible financial upsets in the early 1990s. For instance, AMD did everything but develop wings and fly in order to avoid lay-offs. From spending a million dollars in job retraining to help displaced workers to sponsoring job fairs for any who absolutely had to be laid off, the company stood by its employees as best it could, even in the worse scenarios. But that's not all. Along with areas, such as tuition reimbursement, and continuing the climb up the perks ladder, we find that AMD even has a "dream vacation" program. Every seven years, this vacation is given to hourly employees; they

ellen*Ellen Phillips*

enjoy a week off with pay <u>and</u> $3,000 spending money. Move over, folks, Ellen's coming in!

In conclusion, as more and more companies open up their own virtual shopping malls, then by all means have fun and save your tired toes. Just remember to be a smart consumer first. And yes, while there are also many cases won by employing the vehicle of e-mail as the *Times* article reveals, I still cling to the old cliché, "It's better to be safe than sorry." So what's the safest, the best, and the most time-honored approach? An old-fashioned <u>letter</u>.

Helpful Agencies and Services

The **American Bar Association** has its own informational website to protect online shoppers, both before and after they purchase. Visit www.safeshopping.org.

The **Better Business Bureau** assists cybershoppers with binding arbitration. Contact the BBB at 4200 Wilson Boulevard, Suite 800, Arlington, VA 22203-1804 (800) 955-5100. The BBB Online provides a privacy seal on Web sites that will protect your personal information.

To avoid unwanted E-mail, contact the **Coalition Against Unsolicited Commercial E-Mail (CAUCE)** at www.cauce.org. The **Consumer Broadcast Group (CBG)** will assist in writing online complaint letters. Visit its web site at www.consumerbroadcastgroup.com.

The **Fair Credit Billing Act** protects consumers with problems with their charge and credit card accounts.

Contact the **Federal Trade Commission** to assist with warranty problems at Pennsylvania Avenue and Sixth Street, Room 240, Washington, DC 20580.

If you suspect Internet fraud practices, contact the **Internet Fraud Complaint Center** at www.ifccfbi.gov. This site is a new venture between the FBI and the National White Collar Crime Center. IFCC also may be contacted by writing to it at 1 Huntington Way, Fairmont, WV 26354.

The **Magnuson-Moss Warranty Act** requires online companies to make available to buyers copies of a full, a limited, and an implied warranty.

E-mail the **National Fraud Information Center** at www.fraud.org to file complaints and to read other complaints.

www.anonymizer.com provides a program to help defeat unwanted e-mail.

www.bizrate.com reports on more than 500 Internet businesses.

www.consumer.gov offers information by subject about complaining needs.

www.scambusters.org/scamcheck alerts us to Net merchant schemes.

www.seamless.com brings you a multitude of hints with regard to consumer assistance.

Chapter 5

Jobs, Jobs, Jobs

"Keep doing some kind of work, that the devil may always find you employed."
- St. Jerome

While many of us are contented with our chosen careers, others find themselves immersed in a cauldron of misery. The wake-up call of our alarm clock may find the perpetrator flung against the closet door, and we silently scream curses at everyone from the manager on down to the elevator operator. But, hey, it's a job; it's what puts the clothes on our backs and allows us some of the finer pleasures in life. We trudge on and outward each day and at the end of the week only find ourselves dreading the following Monday, dreading to begin the hassle all over again.

On the other hand, there are folks who, if unhappy in their current situation, search for another position. The following true example demonstrates a *Comedy of Errors*, which sometimes occur.

Betsy, (most names in *Fight Back and Win!* are changed to protect the innocent <u>and</u> the guilty), once found herself in deep doodoo — and I mean that literally! Her morning did not start off to be a successful one at all. She jumped out of bed at 5:30, heart palpitating because she had gotten the job-of-your-dreams interview to begin promptly at 9:00. Normally, before she got dressed for work Betsy would leisurely sit at her kitchen table with a relaxing cup of coffee and read the morning newspaper. The only fly in the ointment for the past three days to usurp this pleasure has been the sight of the neighbor's dog running blithely through Betsy's front yard, as he stopped, squatted, POOPed, and then ran carelessly away. More than shocked, appalled, and dismayed, on each of those three subsequent mornings this lady was also disgusted as, armed with a roll of paper towels, she gingerly picked up the POOP and deposited it in a plastic bag in the outside trash can.

The day before had been the last straw. Betsy had seen (and smelled) enough. She *calmly* walked across her own yard, *politely* knocked on the neighbor's door, and *firmly* (remember these three adverbs as they'll pop up later as three important adjectives) asked her to either keep "Stinky" on her own property or on a leash. This neighbor promised Stinky's sojourning would cease immediately. As Betsy turned to walk away, she heard a parting shot, "Yes, I'll keep my dog out of your yard but remember, it is biodegradable!"

In her mad rush to drink a quick gulp of caffeine and put on her new suit and shoes (after all, this prospective job would earn her an extra $15,000 a year so she's gotta impress the interviewer), the last thing on Betsy's mind was worrying about any "deposits." After all, she'd been promised no more trespassing on her land. Frantically hurling herself out the door (where had the time gone?) — **SQUISH!** Stinky had struck again, this time right beside the front door of Betsy's car! She gaped down at the mess that only a moment ago was her pristine shoes, fumbled for the house keys, ran back inside, grabbed wet paper towels, and scrubbed at the shoes and the POOP. Backing out of the driveway, she almost hit a parked car and then gunned the motor to make up for lost time. After a couple of miles, Betsy sniffed and realized she smelled something awful — in her haste she had forgotten to clean the soles of her shoes and the noxious aroma of Stinky's gift filled the car. If this odor was so evident to her, then Ms. Company President would surely gag when Betsy entered her office.

Making a quick U-turn (and almost colliding with yet another car), the marathon was on as Betsy sped home, each and every minute ticking away on her watch. When she arrived, she sprinted into the house, threw on another pair of shoes and began her own Grand Prix to the finish line. Oh, no! A truck overturned in her lane, spilling debris everywhere, and traffic barely crept along in the other one. Like an insidious mosquito crawling around in Betsy's brain, she later told me the line from Alice in Wonderland, "You're late, you're late for a very important date" spun faster and faster and louder and louder until she swore she experienced a mini-nervous breakdown each time the car slowly lurched forward.

<u>Finally</u> arriving at her past-appointed destination, her brain still in short circuit, Betsy wiped sweaty palms on her handkerchief, pasted a grimacing smile on her face, and the big moment arrived. As she strolled up to shake hands with Ms. Company, she couldn't help but notice a obvious crinkle cross the prospective employer's forehead as she peered at Betsy's feet. My poor friend glanced down and discovered to her absolute horror that in her race to change shoes, she had inadvertently thrown on one white pump and one navy. Gamely, she *tried* to

answer the questions with confidence and personality, but with each one her eyes were drawn to her mismatched feet, and she stammered out an answer that didn't make a whole lot of sense. Positive the job made in heaven would go to someone who knows how to better express himself or herself and certainly how to dress more appropriately than is apparent with *her* choice, Betsy slunk lower and lower into the chair until the trial was over. As she limply shook Ms. Company's hand in a farewell (for good) gesture, it was visible that this time the fake smile was pasted on the *executive's* face. Thoughts of Stinky – and his owner – whirled through Betsy's mind like a carousel as she vomited her murderous rage to each and every driver within eye contact on the way home.

Needless to say, "Betsy" didn't get her dream job, but she did more than explode traveling home on the highway or use that infamous middle digit. When she pulled into her driveway — no, she did not throw an arsenic flavored bone across the fence — and raced into her kitchen, she used her fingers much more effectively: she called *The Poison Pen*. Knowing of my charming and disarming (said tongue-in-cheek) methods, I became her hired gun, or as she later referred to me "The Pooper Police."

178 Sickened Lane
Champaign, IL 78932
June 12, 2000

Sally Squabble
180 Sickened Lane
Champaign, IL 78932

Dear Mrs. Squabble:

I have attempted on three different occasions to reason with you to attempt to solve the ongoing problem with your dog, Stinky. As I stated each time, your animal is running freely through my front yard, which, as you are aware, is against the law; he also takes that opportunity to use my grass as his personal toilet, which I have to then clean up myself. After your assurances of yesterday, imagine my appalled disgust when I stepped into his fourth installment this morning on my way to an important meeting.

I have tried to be both pleasant and reasonable about this distressing matter. However, as you have been totally uncooperative I must inform you that the very next time I see Stinky anywhere on my property, you will force me to call both the police and the animal control warden.

I regret that the problem has accelerated to this point, but you have left me with no other option. I trust that this will resolve the matter as of this moment.

Thank you.

Sincerely,

Betsy Stepin

While there were never any more cups of sugar borrowed or recipes exchanged or "hello's" either for that matter, Stinky never again lay a paw in my client's yard.

Fortunately for Betsy, she still had a job in which she excelled. The interviews she sought were of her own desire to try something a bit different. But what about people who don't already have a fond boss or who end up having to search for a job without first finding out the quagmire of such a venture?

Job Placement Agencies

While there are piles of opportunities out there in Job Land, unfortunately, there are also ads for firms that promise quick get-results-and-lots-of-money. Watch out. Some placement agencies may misrepresent their services, promise claims that can't or won't be fulfilled, promote fictitious offerings, or charge exorbitant up-front fees. The Federal Trade Commission warns the public about such companies as well as urging caution when responding to telephone or advertisements promising get home rich quick schemes, such as the ubiquitous envelope-stuffing business. The FTC suggests that when looking for a job or for an agency to assist in finding one, consumers should always

- **Be suspicious of any company that <u>promises</u> to obtain you a position**. First of all, there are usually more prospective workers than are jobs for them. Secondly, the promised position may be one for which you're under or over qualified or maybe one with which you just aren't comfortable. Look before you leap.
- **Be very skeptical if you're to be charged up-front fees and guaranteed refunds if you're dissatisfied.** Fees such as these are a real no-no. Additionally, if the refund isn't guaranteed in *writing*, then run - don't walk - to the nearest exit; otherwise, your "investment" is lost forever.
- **Get a copy of the agency's contract and carefully review it before paying any money at all**. It's one thing for you to pay for *information* such as executive counseling, resume writing, and job listings, but quite another to pay for promises (especially oral ones) that have little chance of materializing.
- **Absolutely do not give out your credit card or bank account information**. Unless you are knowledgeable about the company and have thoroughly checked it out with your local consumer protection office, the state's

Attorney General's office, and the Better Business Bureau, keep your mouth shut and your wallet closed.

- **Contact regulatory agencies if you believe you've been the victim of a job scam**. The Big Guns in this instance are the National Fraud Information Center (NFIC), the FBI, state and federal protection divisions, and the Federal Trade Commission itself. Even when writing about your misfortune, it wouldn't hurt to call the NFIC at (1-800) 876-7060 to lodge your complaint. This consumer hotline provides assistance in filing complaints against fraudulent businesses.

The FTC's consumer brochure **Help Wanted ... Finding a Job** is available from its Public Reference Branch, Room 130, Sixth Street and Pennsylvania Avenue, NW, Washington, DC 20580 or call (202) 326-2222. Also, to find out the latest news on both legitimate and fraudulent placement agencies, call the FTC **NewsPhone** recording at (202) 326-2710.

Ned Naïve frantically called me one evening, bemoaning that he had handed over $3900 to a job placement agency which falsely promised a great-paying position in the hospitality industry. He couldn't get back his money nor anyone to respond to his numerous telephone calls. My pen, sharpened to a razor-edged point, resulted in the following letter:

707 Scammed Lane
Baltimore, MD 21876
August 24, 2000

The Honorable J. Joseph Curran, Jr.
Attorney General of Maryland
Office of the Attorney General
200 St. Paul Place
Baltimore, MD 21202-2202

Dear General Curran:

An appalling problem has occurred with, what I believe to be, a fraudulent job placement agency. As I am a Maryland citizen, I trust you will launch an immediate probe on my behalf into this matter. The pertinent documentation follows:

- On Sunday, August 10, 1999, I read of You Pay-You Weep and Associates, 2111 Jobless Boulevard, Suite 700, Baltimore, Maryland 21222, (410) 351-9022, advertised in *The Washington Post*. Because I wished possibly at that time to seek a career move, I made an appointment with the company, and that is when this shocking predicament began.
- Fred Fraud, with whom I initially interviewed, promised me personal interviews with companies that would meet or exceed my then yearly salary of $60K. I was also assured that You Pay-You Weep would research and find applicable interviewers (see enclosed copy of contract). Unfortunately, I was naïve and did not investigate to ascertain that legitimate placement services should not require prior payment, and I concluded by paying this company $3900 at that time for their empty promises.
- By January 2000 I had no new position; in fact, from September 1999 to February 2000 I had no interviews at all with the exception of five <u>phone</u> interviews during September that achieved nothing.
- In January I spoke with Paula Pushy, complained about the lack of support from You Pay-You Weep, and requested a refund. The company refused to even consider my request but did assign Shawn Scam to be my new recruiter. Even I researched the newspapers to find companies with which to interview, resulting in personal meetings with Hyatt and Outback Steakhouse. Hyatt's proposition would have resulted in my making 33% less than my current salary at that time, and Outback, the only real source of interest to me, required

a test which they later stated I did not pass. Because I have always had problems in test-taking situations, I specifically informed Mr. Scam not to call Outback as I wished to do so myself to ascertain exactly why I had failed their test. He ignored my directive and called anyway.

- Mr. Scam did set up interviews with Kentucky Fried Chicken and McDonalds in mid-April 2000. Cognizant of the fact that neither could provide the salary or career move I sought, I explained to him that I could not afford to endanger my own job to meet unnecessary appointments. At this point, he became quite agitated.

- In May I spoke once more with Mr. Scam when he called me to inform me of my failure to pass Outback's test. I stressed my frustration about continuing these useless procedures and again expressed my dissatisfaction with his firm's practices. He <u>assured</u> me that You Pay-You Weep would provide me with an excellent position and that he would call me within two weeks to discuss the continuation of the contract. Unfortunately, I believed him, yet I am still waiting for this call. Once I realized that I had again been duped, I called Ms. Pushy on August 3, 2000 to demand a full refund but she, too, refuses to return my call.

I certainly should never have contracted with this service, especially with the exorbitant price attached and the demand for upfront money. Additionally, it is my error that I did not thoroughly research for the legitimacy of such companies and, specifically, You Pay-You Weep. However, after I discovered the full facts of this horrific situation and the on-going investigations by Attorney's General and the FTC of such organizations, I felt it imperative to bring this to your attention. Even though my present contractor's salary is quite comfortable, I believe it only fair and just that You Pay-You Weep reimburse me the full $3900, particularly in light of what has transpired.

Ellen Phillips

Thank you, and I look forward to hearing from you within the next ten business days.

Sincerely,

Ned Naïve

Enclosure

cc: Jodie Bernstein, Director
    Office of Consumer Protection
    Federal Trade Commission
    Pennsylvania Avenue and Sixth Street, NW
    Washington, DC 20580

    William Leibovici, Chief
    Consumer Protection Division
    Office of the Attorney General
    200 St. Paul Place, 16th Floor
    Baltimore, MD 21202-2202

    The Honorable Janet Reno, Attorney General
    United States Department of Justice
    950 Pennsylvania Avenue, NW
    Washington, DC 20530

    Louis Freeh, Director
    Federal Bureau of Investigation
    935 Pennsylvania Avenue, NW
    Washington, DC 20535-0001

    Aida Alvarez, Administrator
    Small Business Administration
    409 Third Street, SW
    Washington, DC 20416

Gregory Gotcha, President
You Pay-You Weep and Associates
2111 Jobless Boulevard, Suite 700
Baltimore, MD 21222

Luckily Ned was an ardent believer in the *Poison Pen Perseverance Plan* because he sure needed it in the end.

Let's now pretend that our defrauded fellow had walked a different direction down the job primrose path and written a resume to sell himself to companies. He, along with the person who wishes a new position, doesn't want to pay out the whazoo for a professional resume that can cost hundreds of dollars when created by this specialized service.

Several years ago, I had a severe case of teacher burn-out. It was no longer a treat to go into the classroom; children were more unruly and unwilling to learn, and it seemed as if parental support was more lacking than ever. I decided (being full of my own merits) that the business world beckoned with both hands full of money and success. The main problem I could see, however, is that after umpteen years in teaching, I felt I had no other skills. What to do? I asked around and for an exorbitant sum of money I found someone who could take my credentials and word them in such a way as to make me appear to be the Superwoman of All Fields. Even though I decided to remain in education after all, I learned a valuable lesson: words can definitely be reorganized to fit any occasion and to make anyone look good, and this is how the resume became part of my *Consumer Revolution* portfolio.

Just as in a letter, nothing is more important than how we express ourselves in the beginning. What we say initially is what makes us memorable. This is the time to plump out all achievements and make yourself sound even more accomplished than perhaps you really are, without fibbing. What key points do you want a prospective employer to instantly notice? Remember that the idea is to create interest and when you've got the proverbial foot in the interviewer's door, you'll sell <u>yourself</u>. Certain prevailing points should be followed when applying for any type of position. Just as I preach the best methods to grab a complaint-recipient's eye, similar principles can be followed for a potential employer's eye.

- **Include a one-page bio with your resume**. Write your chronological achievements in reverse order, beginning with your first position and ending with your most recent. Provide a brief explanation for each. Believe me, it will be an attention-getter when you write that you chaired a function that raised $100,000 for charity and the interviewer is looking to hire a fundraiser.

- **Ask the interviewer questions initially**. Not only will this give you a chance to catch your breath before *you're* placed on the spot, but it also affords you the opportunity to find out answers to "What is an average day like?" or "What skills would you like the ideal applicant to have?" and so forth.

- **Assume you'll present so well, you'll be asked to meet a higher muckety-muck**. That old "better safe than sorry" approach truly is appropriate if this scenario occurs. Be assertive. Tell the first man or woman that you wish to be as prepared as possible before meeting Mr. Next on the Ladder. Ask generic questions such as "What is his current pet project?" If you're fast on your thinking processes, you can turn this to your advantage when interviewing with the second person. What can *you* do to help guarantee the success of that pet project? If there's truly a way, then be sure to have a statement prepared along the lines of, "I understand your pet project is for [pill-free sweaters? soil-free diapers? Easter chipmunks instead of bunnies?]. I can help to ensure the success of the project by [and be specific, following your own credentials]." Not only are you establishing your qualifications but also your belief that Bigger Boss' plans are important ones. And for goodness sakes, don't dare to forget to write a thoughtful letter of thanks to the interviewer. It may just be the kicker that he or she needs to offer you that job, instead of someone else.

2020 Thanks Trail
Appleton, WV 74012
December 20, 2001

Mrs. Ellen Phillips
P.O. Box 265
Mt. Vernon, VA 22121

Dear Mrs. Phillips:

It was delightful meeting with you this afternoon. Your generosity of time, the information concerning *Ellen's Poison Pen*, and your expectations that fit my own credentials make me a viable contender for your staff specifications.

Again, I do appreciate your kindness. Certainly I promise that, given the opportunity, my pen can drip as poisonous as yours.

Sincerely,

Pauline Pen

"Courtney Capable" woke up one day and decided that her current position just didn't turn her on anymore. A jack-of-all-trades, she pittered and pattered as a housekeeper, a custom framer, a jewelry creator, and a chef. Courtney truly is an outstanding chef who actually had prepared food on one occasion for former President Gerald Ford, but now she ran from one part-time position to another. The purpose of our resume was to obtain the "job of her dreams." While I wasn't too sure of my abilities as a dream-catcher, especially because there was so much background to highlight as attention-getting generalities, I still gave it my best shot.

Courtney Capable
1234 Lookin Lane
Chicago, IL 60606
(870) 244-7799

FOR HIRE: <u>PERFECTION</u>

Career Objectives: Seeking a full-time creative and innovative position within the country where I can combine my education and experience in public relations, promotion, management, and marketing with my background in communications and education.

<u>Qualifications in Brief</u>:

- **Eighteen years progressively responsible work experience in the areas of public relations, marketing, communication, education, gold/silversmith, cabinet maker/carpenter, and master chef.**
- **Experienced in profit and nonprofit organizations. Works well with public in innovative approaches to creating, marketing, and selling products.**
- **Effective writer/editor. Knowledgeable about style, content, and English language skills.**
- **Enthusiastic representative/communicator. Comfortable with large and small audiences.**

<u>Experience</u>:
<u>Public Relations/Marketing</u>

Successfully managed and supervised catering services and was the chef for former President Gerald Ford at a haute cuisine restaurant. Meticulous attention to detail

provided for the service to become debt-free, realize a profit, and implementation of a smaller and better-run staff.

Managed employees, ordered supplies, set schedules and budget. Instrumental in employees receiving a profit sharing check.

Developed, owned, and operated a custom frames business and currently creates and sells original designs in the areas of cabinet making and finish carpentry. Products resulting from fine woodworking include such items as television cabinets, tables, wainscoted free form chairs, closets, etc. - all crafted from hardwood.

Innovated, created, and sold distinctive silver and gold jewelry, several pieces of which feature gem faceting.

Experienced in professional live-in housekeeping procedures: maintaining household and financial arrangements.

Directed choirs and was Music Coordinator for college and various church and civic choirs, orienting people to group process and goal determination.

Utilized position as Librarian Assistant for University of Illinois libraries to organize books and data, order books and supplies, and assist with administrative procedures.

Planned curriculum for Fine Arts Committee, which impacted upon hundreds of children and adults.

Experienced in receiving and recording orders, maintaining correspondence and records, and preparing administrative documentation.

Ellen Phillips

Training/Education

Secondary vocal music director. Girls' Assistant Basketball Coach, resulting in a State Championship title.

Substitute teacher at all levels with administrative duties related to attendance, reports, grades, and disciplinary matters.

Selected for Honors Award and Dean's List.

Selected as American Scholar, United States Achievement Academy; Outstanding Young Woman of America.

Received the Salute to Excellence Award, National Restaurant Association Educational Foundation, granted only to select individuals who actively demonstrate entrepreneurial superiority.

References available upon request

Courtney not only obtained a full-time position as a chef at a major university, she also has her own local television show – *Chef Courtney*!

One middle-aged gentleman who had been a piano salesman his entire adult life wished for a completely new career. His dilemma, though (and a true one for many of us in this age range) was that no one would hire a fifty-two-year-old man whose only experience was selling pianos. He explained to me that before he retired – or died – he wanted an exciting position, something about which he could be passionate and which would precipitate travel and a move from the small city where he lived.

This posed a dilemma for me, too. I really wasn't certain how to compose a resume that would factually provide his qualifications, yet make him appear more knowledgeable than he was about other areas (without stretching the truth too much). I asked him to send me any and all information he could accumulate about himself professionally, and I would see what I could do. I'm sure "Mr. Pianoman" doesn't mind me tattling that what he sent was sketchy, at best. He had been at his current job since he was twenty-two; he had been a store manager for the past seven years; he had assisted in writing advertisements for two local newspapers and a local cable television station; and once upon a time he was a committee member that set goals for state convention. Yep, I sure had my work cut out for me.

Paul P. Pianoman

6564 North Twenty-third Street
Columbus, GA 23089
Home: (881) 564-6632 Business: (881) 573-5755
E-mail: paul.p@pianoman.com

CAREER OBJECTIVE: **Seeking a full-time position with regular hours, pay, and benefits where I can combine my education and experience in public relations, promotion, management, and marketing with my background in communications and sales, allowing me to utilize my skills working in a positive environment to achieve a positive goal.**

Qualifications in Brief:

- **Thirty years progressively responsible work experience in the areas of public relations, marketing, communication, and management.**
- **Experienced in innovative public approaches to marketing and selling products.**
- **Enthusiastic representative/communicator; comfortable with large or small audiences.**
- **Effective advertising copywriter/coordinator.**
- **Negotiator with the general public and with large and small companies.**

Experience:

- **Successfully planned and implemented multi-media advertising budget and schedule.**
- **Motivated commissioned sales personnel to attain personal and company goals.**
- **Successfully mediated and facilitated conflict resolution.**
- **Experienced in dealing with diverse cultures.**
- **Successfully directed budget and staff to maximize profitability.**
- **Accomplished in daily attainment of sales goals and profit margins.**
- **Resourceful in completing projects in a timely manner.**
- **Works well under deadline limitations.**
- **Effective in appraisals and verifying bank documents.**
- **Experienced buyer and purchasing agent.**

References available upon request

After mailing out a slew of these suckers, Paul was thrilled to be offered a position in Atlanta as a traveling District Manager for, of all things, a piano and organ manufacturer!

Seeking the Job

Sometimes it seems as if there aren't enough jobs to go around. But what if a few (or many) *are* available, yet no one at the top seems to want to fill them? If you've had occasion to try for a position for which you're denied and then it isn't even filled by another prospect, then you can empathize with this lady's frustration. The problem had risen to stroke level, because she attempted many times to resolve her own difficulties with lots of documentation, yet she was repeatedly ignored. It was time for my entrance in the abbreviated version that follows.

9807 Persistent Place
Detroit, MI 48222
January 2, 2000

Ronald Ratfink, Commissioner
City Board of Hospitals
900 Cantankerous Center
Detroit, MI 48233

Dear Mr. Ratfink:

As one who wishes to work only for the welfare of this city's citizens, I turn to you with a shocking problem. I trust you will launch an immediate investigation into the matter.

- On October 3, 1999, I submitted an application to the Advisory Committee on Physician's Assistant for a waiver of education and examination for license in Michigan. I have continuously contacted Mr. Hardheart by telephone; I have sent additional information per his request. I might add that this department lost one of my job descriptions by a doctor. I was then told that I had not sent in a statement of performing the functions of a physician's assistant. I informed Mr. Hardheart that I had most certainly submitted this information, although the company for which I worked from 1983 to 1988 is no longer in operation at the site I was employed. I wrote a letter detailing my duties, which was notarized, and the company's owner also sent a letter of confirmation and a letter verifying my employment.
- On November 15, 1999, I mailed a letter to the Board of Medicine requesting a meeting with them for the purpose of defending my application for licensure as highly competent physician's assistant. To date, I have still received no response.
- On December 2, I physically visited the Medical Board on South Street and was told that I would receive a response within two weeks. I called Mrs. Excuse on

December 21, and she told me she would "get back to me," although she has failed to do so. At this point, I feel that I have exhausted all my resources. Many, many letters of recommendations and commendations have been sent in, not only by my previous co-workers, but also by physicians with whom I have worked in the past. It is obvious from all letters that these professionals deem me to be a superior physician's assistant. Therefore, I am puzzled by the lack of reciprocity, and certainly by the lack of response from the Medical Board.

What is ludicrous to me is that I have been told by many different employees that the Board has not yet met to make a decision. The Board will not acknowledge my calls or my efforts. It seems impossible that in this long span of elapsed time that the Board "has not yet met." There is no excuse whatsoever for what I believe to be totally inappropriate professional behavior, as well as a total lack of concern for someone who simply desires to help the citizens of Detroit. As many of these same citizens are moving into the suburbs, there are few who wish to work in an environment, which is painted so violently. I am one of the few. I wish to use those skills that God has given me to help others who need me, and I can think of no place that I am needed more than in this city.

Thank you, and I look forward to hearing from you by January 31, 2000.

Sincerely,

Nellie Nurse

Guess what? My letter didn't do the trick, but neither Nellie nor I gave up. Think back to when I stressed that sometimes we must try, try again.

[Nellie's heading]
February 8, 2000

[Ratfink's name and inside address]

Dear Mr. Ratfink:

As you have not seen fit to respond to my request of January 2, 2000 I have taken the liberty of mailing additional copies of that letter to a number of interested parties. (See enclosed list).

I find it appalling that you have not acknowledged nor responded to my request for assistance with simple, common courtesy. Even if there is some kind of a background check in the process in order for me to obtain my license, I cannot imagine why I have not received even a telephone call to that effect.

As I still wish to be licensed in Michigan, I hope that this time I will receive this certification immediately or the reason for its denial.

Thank you.

Sincerely,

Nellie Nurse

Enclosed

This one, too, resulted in nary an answer from Mr. Ratfink. By now, I don't remember who was madder — Nellie or me – but we did have a white (carbon copied) steed galloping to her defense.

[Nellie's heading]
February 26, 2000

Mary Francis Berry, Chairperson
United States Commission on Civil Rights
624 Ninth Street, NW
Washington, DC 20425

Dear Ms. Berry:

Thank you for your letter of February 24. Unfortunately, I have yet to hear one word from any person who received a copy of my letter, with the exception of Mr. Isler from your office and Congressman Conyers, who turned my letter over to Senator Levin. Mr. Isler stated that I had already contacted the necessary agencies.

By this point, it is obvious to me that Mr. Ratfink has little professional courtesy as I have not been afforded a response from him or from several others I have copied. I might add that when Ms. Excuse told me that she would let me know when the Board met, I later found out that it had already done so. Not only has there has been no response from the Board, I believe, too, that Ms. Excuse is guilty of fabrication.

I truly believe that this is a matter that falls into your area of investigation, and I will certainly appreciate you doing so at your earliest convenience.

Thank you.

Sincerely,

Nellie Nurse

Even though Nellie periodically gave out of steam, she didn't surrender. Her appeals were ultimately acknowledged and her license came through. This don't-give-up-til-hell-freezes-over lesson is one we should all remember.

But perhaps you're not a Nellie and you decide to trod the traditional path. Your resume is intact, you've learned your lesson with regards to job placement agencies, and you've placed yourself with a *legitimate* agency. You now find yourself sitting across from a Head Honcho as he grills you in an interview, but how will you get the job and a great deal? First off, be careful when talking money. Rather than saying you want a certain salary (which may be under his offer in which case you might become slave labor), slyly respond with something like, "I'm worth your best offer and will prove it once I get the job." If you consider the sum a low one, then negotiate a benefits deal that would enhance the salary.

A benefits package is often worth as much if not more than a higher-paying salary if you've got your ducks in a row. For example, more and more companies are offering day care for young children. If you don't wish your kids exposed to the germs of the other employees' little darlings, then ask about a swap for flexible time to work at home a couple of days a week, for instance.

Regardless of what you're offered and what kind of a "Let's Make a Deal" package develops, be sure to ask for a letter with all offers and their details. You don't want to be stuck after you've signed your name on the contract's dotted line. And certainly, *always* write a thank you letter promptly upon your return home, whether you take the job or not.

Job Performance Evaluations

Certain figures in authority often can be difficult. This can occur for a variety of reasons, such as one who is submerged in his or her own power, or a superior who is an habitual pain-in-the-neck, or one who is simply going through a difficult personal period. Whatever the reason, though, the employee may become the brunt of anger and hostility. This, then, necessitates strategies to help heave us out of the hole in which that irate boss has thrown us.

If someone gives you a hard time, the temptation is to strike back in full force. Don't. The old adage about catching more flies with honey than with vinegar is certainly applicable when dealing with someone who holds the purse strings to your livelihood. In order to respond effectively to this difficult person, you must act from *reason*, not from emotion. Watch for subtle signs of trouble, such as not being notified of a staff meeting or the like. Always ask for honest feedback before that finger points in your face and then act upon the advice. And for heaven's sake, remember that it's important to:

- **Not take it personally**. These people most likely behave in this manner in all situations and not just with you. Don't see yourself as the boss's target.
- **Use special techniques to control your own reactions**. Meditation or visualization can help. Picture yourself in a tranquil setting, such as at the beach watching the waves roll in. Deep breathing helps, also. As soon as you feel your own fury on the rise, focus on your breathing, exhaling slowly, until you feel you are calm enough to respond in a pleasant manner.
- **Think about your boss's inner needs**. Make sure you know what it is that Ole Bossy wants. Is there an underlying reason he or she is behaving towards you in this manner? Perhaps this person is insecure or feels threatened by you. After all, who ever said that the person in charge has to be the smartest one in the company? Try to focus on a problem-solving mode (such as strategies demonstrated in the forthcoming letter).

Don't forget that if someone bullies or blows up, resulting in your receipt of an inferior job performance evaluation, it's not the end of the world. By remaining cool, calm, and collected, and by *documenting everything*, you can come out the winner. Perhaps there are areas you are willing to concede. I do recommend this, as giving in on small matters often lead to your winning the more important points that truly affect your job security.

One day I received a call from a woman who had just that day been handed a truly nasty evaluation from her supervisor and had only three days in which to make a written response. Now remember, the whole key to handling any type of correspondence is to be as emotionally detached as possible. Three days didn't give her a whole lot of time for this exercise in composure. Assuring this lady that unless she had done something truly dreadful, such as calling a customer a fat bat with no more clothes sense than a street lamp, I could write a rebuttal for her to go to the head of human resources that just might save the day. My technique is to take only a few of the more conspicuous comments (remember to concede the lesser of the complaints) and then to refute these one by one. Again, make sure to document thoroughly. This is your "proof."

September 16, 2001

The following comments are made in refutation to the evaluation statements received from Ms. Bessie Boss on September 14, 2001.

1.   According to Ms. Boss, on August 25, 2001, I offered to sell a customer a larger size dress which was on hold for one of my colleague's own customers. Furthermore, Ms. Boss states that this practice is "in flagrant violation of company policy."

Comment: My colleague's customer had ordered the dress in question, but when it arrived, she changed her mind and did not purchase this garment. Therefore, I felt free to sell the dress to my own customer. In reviewing the corporation regulation book for *Dressing the Successful Women*, Article 3a states: "When a garment has been special ordered for a specific client and has not been

previously paid in cash or by charge, the client has five days to pay for said item or another store associate has the prerogative to sell the item." I must stress that this particular dress had been on the floor for more than the five-day waiting period.

2. Ms. Boss states that because a customer did not seem able to afford a Pendleton suit, I escorted her downstairs to the Sale Salon and said, "This lady cannot afford our department – she's better off down here."

<u>Comment</u>: Gina Girl, who was dismissed from our store, ostensibly repeated this. Not only is it difficult to understand why this suppositious comment was believed from a young woman who was fired, but also the customer in question will be happy to contradict the charge against me. Mrs. Samuel Shopper may be reached at 564-9008 between 9:00 a.m. and 4:00 p.m.

3. I was overheard by Ms. Boss telling my co-worker, Scottie Sales, that I "wish Ms. Boss would get off my back."

<u>Comment</u>: I did, indeed, make this statement to Mrs. Sales. However, on that particular morning I had just discovered I had been placed upon the 5-10 p.m. shift for the third week in a row. We all make comments in the heat of anger, but I was certainly in error by speaking thus to a colleague. [Here, she conceded her mistake and apologized]

It is a privilege and a delight to work for the *Dressing the Successful Woman* Corporation. The ten years I have spent with the company have been rewarding ones for me, and I believe that I have made a positive difference both in sales and with customer relations. There have even been a number of other department managers who have expressed a desire for me to work within their own

departments. I very much fear that these assertions which Ms. Boss makes will be taken at face value, unless refuted; thus, I will be unable to continue in this position that means so much to me.

Sincerely,

Ima Innocent

Within a few days, I received a letter from Mrs. Innocent that contained a glowing notice from the bigger boss. In it, he commended my client for her great service and noted the many commendations from satisfied customers found in her employee file. I expect "Ms. Boss" left Ima alone after that.

Job Firings
    Don't let the door hit you on your way out. The gist of these words, of course, is the ole' "We're downsizing … you're a troublemaker … you're incompetent." Whatever the reason, you now find yourself out of a job and the rent is due next week. Before you panic, remember you do have some options, just as Ima Innocent did earlier.

- **Discover the higher-up of the person who fired you**. The *firer* may be the CEO of a Fortune 500 corporation, but he or she still must answer to a Board of Directors.
- **Write to the higher-up**. If you have been dismissed unfairly, then document each episode that has caused any conflict with your boss and how you attempted to resolve the problem. If there has been no previous problem - perhaps simply a personality conflict or a perceived lack on your part - then you've really got a case for reinstatement.
- **Rebut each statement in the discharge letter**. If you've been savvy enough and maintained dates, events, and so forth, you have enough ammunition to clear yourself of each and every "charge."

- **Tell the head honcho what you wish done**. Just as in a complaint letter, don't leave this person second-guessing. Do you really wish this position back or do you simply want a glowing recommendation? Maybe you desire a transfer to another department or location or to another supervisor. Make your wishes clear.

Someone who once took my advice seriously because he had been having problems with his school vice-principal found himself on the "door-hitting" end of the stick. Compiling his information and documentation, we wrote the following rebuttal to his "You're fired!" letter.

October 13, 2000

To: Freida Firer
Vice-Principal

From: Daniel Dismissed
Custodian

Re: Job Dismissal

Dear Ms. Firer:

In response to your evaluation recommending employment dismissal effective October 8, 2000:

1.   "Inconsistent compliance with the administrator's request to come to your workplace properly dressed in a uniform throughout your sixty day work improvement plan."
Comment: I do admit coming to school on several occasions wearing my own clothing; however, I changed into my uniform before my workdays began.
2.   "In August, you were argumentative with Dr. Principal about your reassignment to Wrecked Elementary School to assist in cleaning that summer school site. You

failed to contact the school administration in the correct manner to alert them of your illness. Consequently, Wrecked Elementary was left without the appropriate number of custodians for cleaning."

Comment: This incident arose when Arnold Associate informed me that Mr. Brown, the custodial supervisor, sent word for me to go to Wrecked Elementary. Because I knew that Mr. Brown realized I had no car, I checked this request. In actuality, Mr. Brown had only sent a note requesting a custodian, and I was the one selected. I simply attempted to explain this to Dr. Principal, and I do not believe a simple explanation can be termed as argumentative. As for the day I did not report to Wrecked Elementary because of illness, I called and left a message on the answering machine since no one answered the telephone.

3.   "Your lack of consistent compliance concerning your beeper and, on the other hand, not wearing headphones while you work. Your failure to understand that supporting the custodial team by exhibiting positive and supportive behavior are expected of all school employees as part of the <u>Code of Conduct</u>."

Comment: After receiving a pager, I wore it at all times while at the job site. Also, as far as I am concerned, I cannot think of a time when I have been anything but supportive and positive. Please provide me with specific examples with regards to this allegation.

I truly do not understand the reasons behind my dismissal. Each of the instances you cite is not one with which I agree or even remember. Perhaps it is a matter of communication, as, for some reason, we seem to have been in conflict since I began working at this school. Whatever the <u>perceived</u> reasons, I certainly wish to maintain this position and I hope you will revoke your recommendation for dismissal.

Sincerely,

Daniel Dismissed

cc: Dr. Paul Principal, Principal, Hate-Me Elementary School

Department of Human Resources, Montgomery City Public Schools

David retained his job and received a transfer to another school where he is the darling of all.

Well, we've seen Betsy losing a prospective job due to unforeseen and unfortunate circumstances, Ned Naïve losing (and regaining) his money to a placement agency, Helena Hunting and Paul Pianoman finding their dream jobs, and Ima Innocent and David Dismissed maintaining their jobs in spite of their superiors' efforts.

So you see, whatever your career choice or the people for whom you work, changes *can* be made. Just as with a complaint letter, petition, or appeal, it's up to you to use words wisely to do the trick.

Helpful Agencies and Services

For information on finding a job and legitimate placement agencies, order the **Federal Trade Commission's** brochure *Help Wanted... Finding a Job* from its Public Reference Branch, Room 130, Sixth Street and Pennsylvania Avenue, NW, Washington, DC 20580 or call (202) 326-2222.

Call the **Federal Trade Commission's** NewsPhone recording at (202) 326-2710 for the latest news on both legitimate and fraudulent job placement services.

Call or write the **National Fraud Information Center (NFIC)** if you're the victim of a job scam. Reach this agency at P.O. Box 65868, Washington, DC 20035 and at (800) 876-7060.

Chapter 6
Your Right to Privacy

"If we're looking for the (fundamental ills of society)... we should test people for stupidity, ignorance, greed, and love of power."
- P. J. O'Rourke

The Fourth Amendment to the U.S. Constitution guarantees us our original right to privacy. Certainly when our forefathers drafted this great document, they never foresaw the out-of-control spin it would take in modern times. Our vital statistics, credit ratings, number and ages of our children, and the names of our pets – all seem to speed to some satellite in outer space which then beams the information back to earth for everyone else to view. Sometimes we simply feel like crawling into bed and pulling the pillow over our heads, but we know we cannot – and must not. We must have the courage to defy the odds and do everything in our power to retain our own privacy and that of others. Further, to help us with this situation (although I hope none of us comes in contact with the terrorists for which it's intended), late last year Congress passed and the president signed into law *The Patriot Act of 2001*. While the majority of this Act gives law enforcement more power to catch those specific bad guys, it also provides better tools to end financial counterfeiting. That section is certainly a boon to us consumers.

Mailing Lists
Each day most of us receive volumes of mail that promise a new and better credit card or excitedly alert us to the glorious vacation we've won. Twenty times a day telemarketers ruin a perfectly good dinner or an early-morning snooze in an attempt to sell us goods and services we don't need nor want. How can our names be on every worldwide list if not from that spy satellite? Well, thanks to the **Telemarketer Consumer Protection Act**, we now can eat – if not undisturbed – with the

knowledge that after dinner we are able to call these cretins back since their phone numbers won't be hidden any longer. Because we'll be able to reach them, rather than the telemarketers calling us and hanging up before we can yell, "Hit the Road, Jack," we're assured that if they do call again, we can sue and win. (The latter was already on the federal books, but how could we sue a hang-up or an anonymous number?) For telemarketers and other similar problem businesses, selling and buying is the name of this particular game, and I'm not talking about what you do within the parameters of your own personal or professional life, either.

First of all, not only is it imperative but also it's your responsibility to find out what happens to all that personal information you provide to mail-order companies, marketers, and government agencies. It may be as simple as these folks processing an order; they may use the info to let you know about other products, services, or promotions in which there may be an interest. What often happens can take on a more sinister vein, however. Even lawful businesses share these personal facts with others, and often the *others* aren't on the up-and-up. Zap! Our private life isn't private any longer.

So what do we do to avoid or to stop these unwanted intrusions into our lives? How can we stop companies from making a profit off of our names? The first order of business is to attempt to discover what companies are doing the selling (there's always someone willing and anxious to buy our mailing list). Do you enter contests? Well, you can bet your bottom dollar if you don't win the home of your dreams, its value has been purchased by loads of both legit and shady operations. Each time we fill out and mail in a warranty card for that new toaster or computer, the manufacturer most likely sells your name and personal information. Credit card companies are just as guilty and, often worse, are Departments of Motor Vehicles (and just when you thought the DMV was getting nicer).

The DMV in a few remaining states provides information for a fee (often as little as $5.00) to <u>anyone</u> who spots and tells it your tag number. This is a really scary scenario when one thinks of road-ragers, stalkers and other criminal types who then have access to your home address, telephone number, height, weight, etc. – all for a measly sum of money and thanks to your state agency. The following letter, seemingly an innocent one concerning a ticket, turned into a great deal more when the DMV decided to publish this fellow's name (whom I call "Larry-Learned-His-Lesson") and vital statistics.

You're merrily traveling down the highway, minding your own business and staying within the speed limit, when all of a sudden – *Whee Ooo, Whee Ooo* – the wrenching peal of a police siren bursts through the radio music. Uncertainly, you glance into the rear view mirror and, to your horror, the siren and the cop are after you. You pull over to the side of the road, fumble for your license, registration, and insurance information, only to find something's missing. As your tummy turns flip-flops, you try to explain to the dilemma to the officer (it's in your spouse's car, the dog ate it, and so forth), but he doesn't buy the excuse and proceeds to write a ticket for that very large fine. I once found myself writing an appeal for just such an unsuspecting young man, whose license subsequently was discovered to be suspended when his tags were run through the officer's computer. This was the least of all evils as my client later discovered.

884 Hostage Hideaway
Acton, MA 33388
December 18, 2000

Robert Roadway, Commissioner
Department of Motor Vehicles
569 Traffic Circle
Boston, MA 33880

Dear Commissioner Roadway:

On December 15, 2000, Officer Speedy stopped me for crossing the yellow line on Interstate I-195. When he

checked his computer, he discovered that my license had been suspended. I was shocked and appalled to learn this as I have never received any infraction whatsoever. The following then occurred:

- Officer Speedy impounded my car, which resulted in a great deal of turmoil and inconvenience. After losing a day's work while making a number of long-distance calls, I finally ascertained how the DMV's error transpired.
- In October 2000 your office mailed me a routine, spot-check inquiry to see if I carried automobile insurance, which I did. Unfortunately, the notice was mailed to my previous address and, therefore, DMV received no response. Because of my failure to respond to the mailing (of which I knew nothing), DMV suspended my license and then sent this notification to the <u>same incorrect address</u>.
- Because I did and do have insurance coverage and have committed no violation of a law, I would be so grateful if you immediately revoke this suspension. Otherwise, I will be fined $1000 when I appear in court on January 14, 2001.

I admit my error in failure to notify DMV of my new address, but I feel I have already paid for my oversight by losing a day's wages and having my vehicle impounded. However, I do not believe my sin of omission should result in a fine of $1000 and points on my driving record.

I appeal to you to grant the revocation of the suspension before January 14, 2001.

Thank you.

Sincerely,

Larry Learned-His-Lesson

While Larry did, indeed, learn his lesson and his appeal paid off, he later discovered that the Department of Motor Vehicles had made available his name, address, and telephone number to *lots* of other agencies for marketing surveys and solicitations.

And you think your local telephone carrier is innocent? Think again. For less than one dollar, many of them also sell your name and address; yet many customers pay the telephone companies a fortune for an unlisted number to protect their privacy and person.

"Okay, enough, enough!" you scream. Nope, afraid not. Your local pharmacy sells your data to drug companies, who in turn sell to medical insurance companies (maybe that's why your latest doctor visit wasn't covered). Or you could be like one of my clients who innocently answered an ad for a credit card only to decide almost immediately that he didn't want it after all. Because he refused to give out his social security number to the operator for fear of identity theft (more on this topic later), he found himself billed with finance charges for almost a year, even though he never activated the card, much less used it to charge anything.

1322 Angered Avenue
Springfield, IL 62707
September 21, 2001

Ivan Invasive, President
Credit Card Company
1099 Finance Parkway
Suite 300
Dallas, TX 45200

Dear Mr. Invasive:

In September-October 2000, I responded to your advertisement mailed to my home and sent in an application for two bank cards - one for my wife, Sheila

H. Stymied and for me (# 839007-1287937306). It was only after the cards arrived and I realized there had been no prior disclosure of certain fees that I immediately attempted to cancel the account. This is the point at which an appalling situation began and one in which I trust you personally will intervene.

- I called Credit Card and spoke with a representative on November 20, 2000 and instructed her to cancel the card as it was not what we had wished or even what it was advertised to be. She stated that in order to do so, I had to tell her my social security number. I was not willing to do this because so many consumers are victims of identity theft, and I feared this happening to me. Even after I explained my feelings with regards to this sensitive information, she informed me the cards (and the previously <u>hidden</u> fees) would continue.

- I continued in my futile attempts to cancel this account, which, it must be stressed, has never been used to purchase a single item. On November 23, I again spoke with one of your representatives as well as sent a fax to "Mary" asking for details of the terms and conditions. This, along with each of my subsequent requests, has also been denied, yet the finance charges continue to mount. The account has even been given to collection agencies, and my personal and professional reputation is at great risk.

- In March 2001, I applied for a home loan through Your Homes, a Chicago-based mortgage company. Because this so-called Credit Card debt was outstanding on my credit report, I experienced great difficulty in obtaining the loan. Even the loan officer, Heidi Helpful, attempted to negotiate with your company on my behalf but was met with rebuffs and the statement that I must "Pay up 90% of the debt or we're not interested." To add insult to injury, there is a current posting of the annual fee.

Presently, I owe finance charges in the amount of $192.26 as well as the annual fee, which I have thus far not paid under the circumstances (copies of all statements enclosed). I also noted on the agreement that "You don't have to sign this agreement, but you should sign the cards to use them" and "You may avoid Finance Charge on new purchases and on other charges by paying the total New Balance in full ..." These bank cards have <u>never been used to charge any purchases whatsoever</u>; therefore, there should not only be any "finance charge," but the transaction itself is not binding as it was never agreed to in any manner. I also never called to "activate [your] card at 800-768-2220 and unless [you] do this, the card is deemed unactivated and invalid." It is unconscionable that Credit Card refuses to honor my requests or its own agreement. In retrospect, perhaps I should have been less concerned with potential identity theft and more so with dealing with a corporation that, in my opinion, completely lacks integrity and professionalism.

I expect an immediate and thorough investigation into this matter so that it can be resolved to my satisfaction and I will no longer be the subject of unfair and harassing measures from Credit Card and its representatives. I also expect a letter of explanation to Equifax, Inc. so that my credit rating is no longer at risk.

Thank you, and I look forward to hearing from you within the next ten business days.

Sincerely,

Stuart J. Stymied

Enclosures

cc: E.J. Face, Jr., Commissioner
    Bureau of Financial Institutions
    P.O. Box 640
    Richmond, VA 23218

    Howard Beales, Director
    Office of Consumer Protection
    Federal Trade Commission
    Pennsylvania Avenue and Sixth Street, NW
    Washington, DC 20560

    Jim Ryan, Attorney General
    Office of the Attorney General
    State of Illinois Center
    100 West Randolph Street
    Chicago, IL 60601

    Jack Schaffer
    Commissioner of Banks and Trust Companies
    500 East Monroe Street
    Springfield, IL 62701

    Direct Marketing Association
    1111 Nineteenth Street, NW
    Washington, DC 20036

    National Action Financial Services, Inc.
    945 Concord Street
    Framingham, MA 01701

"Sam" received a swift answer in the form of an apology, deleted finance charges, and a copy of the letter to Equifax admitting error on the part of the credit card company. (As an aside, if you're a charge card spendthrift and get in over your head, there's hope on the horizon. Contact **Consolidated Credit Counseling Services, Inc.**, a legitimate non-profit counseling organization. Visit their website at www.debtfree.org or call a counselor at (1-800) 728-3632.)

Credit card scams abound as well and, seemingly, in the most innocent of situations (we think); if we're not really careful, we'll be the next victim. *Skimming* is the scam term to remember here. And as bad as I hate to admit it, more and more dishonest people have free access to our credit cards. I know I'm guilty of handing my own to the grocery clerk and running back to get that "one more thing." While I explicitly trust my folks, some others see a chance for some quick profit. Employees like these will double swipe through the store's reader and then use your number for their purchases. Unfortunately, you'll have no idea of what's occurred until your next statement arrives. But it isn't just supermarket employees, either. What about the waitress who takes your card as payment for dinner and comes back ten minutes later? Who knows, she may have colleagues who work at this site who are crooks also, and within that ten minute interval each of them has double swiped for his or her own corrupt purposes.

While there certainly are other methods of skimming and ways to avoid them, the best way to avoid paying those $10K charges next month is to save all receipts and carefully check them against your statement (the amounts are more important than the stores). If you notice a disparity, immediately call the bank that issued the card or the credit card company itself and you'll only have to pay $50 or less *if* these companies are notified within sixty days. (Don't forget reiterated words of wisdom, too. After checking each month's statement, put aside the receipts you'll need for the IRS and destroy the others. There are still crooks who love to go through trash to find those card numbers that are still readable – and usable.)

It's a real shame that bank debit cards don't offer the same protection. As you use this card, it automatically debits the necessary amount from your bank account balance without a signature. For instance, your bank account could quickly plunge to a zero balance if an unscrupulous pizza employee takes your debit card number over the phone and then flies first class to Paris. Usually, there's no fraud protection on this type of card so you can't dispute charges nor expect any assistance from regulatory agencies.

A type of fraud can continue with the mailings we receive. "ONE-OF-A-KIND-CREDIT CARD!! ONLY 3% INTEREST!!" If we sign, seal, stamp, and deliver without reading the very fine print, we've been suckered into perhaps 24% interest. This, along with other unsolicited mail, is what the **Mail Preference Service** is all about. MPS is designed to assist consumers in decreasing the amount of national non-profit or commercial mail they receive at home. When you register with MPS, your name is then placed on what is known as a "delete" file, which is made available to companies in January, April, July, and October. After registration, you'll probably notice a decline in this unsolicited mail after about three months. You will, however, continue to receive mail from companies with which you do regular business or from charitable or commercial organizations that don't choose to use MPS. And certainly, your postal carrier will continue to leave correspondence addressed simply to "Occupant." To register, send your name and address in writing to **Mail Preference Service, Direct Marketing Association, P.O. Box 9008, Farmingdale, NY 11735-9008**. One other juicy tidbit: for every unwanted piece of correspondence you receive, simple write "Return to Sender" on the envelope and put it back in the mail. Guess what? The sender then has to pay for the returned mail postage. Better yet, include your Sunday grocery ads in the pre-paid envelope. Evil, but it works!

While the Direct Marketing Association is the oldest and largest national trade association serving the direct marketing arena, it doesn't have lists or give names to any marketing company, except to remove the names of consumers who desire less of this kind of mail. If you specifically wish to be taken off Rotten Dog Food's mailing list, for example, then you must request Rotten to put your name on its in-house "suppress" file to ensure no further mailings.

Don't stop here, though. Write your state and national legislators and tell them enough is enough! Former President Harry Truman once remarked, "It's not the hand that signs the laws that holds the destiny of America. It's the hand that casts the ballot."

Another sensible idea is to contact the major credit bureaus to request that your name be removed from their distribution lists. A central toll-free number, **(888) 567-8688**, has been set up for consumers to call to "opt-out" of all pre-approved credit offers, or you can call each directly. The phone numbers are **Equifax (800) 556-4711**, **Experian (800) 353-0809**, and **Trans Union (800) 680-7293**. You can also order credit reports by calling (800) 685-1111 (Equifax), (888) EXPERIAN, and (800) 916-8800 (Trans Union).

For more information about how mailing lists are compiled, send a stamped, self-addressed envelope to **Consumer Services – Opening the Door, Direct Marketing Association, 1111 Nineteenth Street, NW, Suite 1100, Washington, DC 20036** for the booklet, *Opening the Door to Opportunity*. The FTC also publishes free brochures on credit-related issues and you can obtain a complete list of these publications; write *Best Sellers*, **Federal Trade Commission, Pennsylvania Avenue and Sixth Street, NW, Washington, DC 20580** or call the FTC at **(202) FTC-HELP, TDD (202) 326-2502.**

Identity Theft

Much worse and certainly more frightening than junk mail or telephone calls is the idea of identity theft. Once an unheard of phenomenon, this tragic name robbery has gained many victims in recent years. It can strike through various means, such as a misplaced wallet, someone literally going through the trash to find credit card receipts, or even mail stolen from your mailbox. If you inadvertently give out your social security number (perhaps even to one of those telemarketers mentioned earlier), you're fair game for months and even years of fraudulent bills and a wrecked credit rating. Reclaiming your identity can either be a nuisance or the most terrible nightmare of your life.

So just how much more easily is it possible for a criminal to steal your identity? While many of us refuse to give out our social security number as in the case of "Samuel Stymied," the number is still attainable by smart computer hackers, and in employee, bank and credit files. While the House passed HR 220 (which awaits Senate passage) that prohibits the use of social security numbers for identification by government agencies, don't think the other organizations are sacred cows. Anyone with a little ingenuity can access files to gain your number. This valuable piece of information provides access to your checking, savings, and investment accounts, and so forth. There have even been instances where robbers have deliberately obtained a menial job with a bank or other financial institution that enables them to access your social security number, sometimes for their own benefit or as part of a ring of identity thieves. What are some ways you can avoid the theft of your identity? The Federal Trade Commission and I offer the following tips:

- **Guard your identifying information with your life**. Find out how it will be used and whether it will be given out to any other party. If a third party enters the picture, then either opt-out of having the information shared or high tail it out of this particular Dodge City.

- **Check with your insurance company about ID theft protection**. As we go to press, only two insurance companies offer an attachment to their homeowners' policies. One is Chubb, which offers free crime protection, and the other is Travelers, which charges $25. The fortunate folks who belong to these two companies are breathing a sigh of relief since both will pay much of their members' legal expenses if the member should become a victim. I strongly urge the rest of you to do as I have done and am doing: deluge your own insurance company with demands for such protection and, hopefully, we'll all rest a lot easier.

- **Dispose of any items containing personal information received through the mail**. These items could be copies of credit applications, credit offers (don't forget the earlier advice about opting-out through the Big Three agencies), expired charge cards, and so forth. Be sure to cut or rip them to shreds before throwing them away so that no part can be identified.

- **Carry only credit cards and identification that you actually and regularly use**. It's bad enough if your wallet's lifted and you later discover your one bank card and gas card have been used for a spending binge. Far worse, however, is if two credit cards, five department store charge cards, and three gas credit cards got into the thief's hands as well. If your wallet is stolen, *immediately* alert your creditors by phone and call the credit bureaus so that they can place a "fraud alert" in your file. This should keep your false charges to a minimum.

- **Pay strict attention to charge card billing cycles**. If your bills don't arrive on time, call the companies. Criminals may have sent in a change-of-address; their charges to your cards can be misdirected and you won't even know it. Along this same line, keep *all* receipts to check against your monthly statement. Destroy those you're not saving for the tax man and, in fact, it wouldn't hurt to invest in an inexpensive shredder to make sure no one sees anything of value in your trash but the (honest) trash collector.

- **Place a mail slot in your door**. If you're an apartment dweller or so forth, certainly the post office has master keys for their carriers to place mail in mailboxes and, unfortunately, there's not a whole lot you can do. Remember what happened a few years ago in Seattle when a crook somehow obtained this master key and unbelievable amounts of checking accounts were emptied as well as personal information about anyone who used either these mailboxes and the so-called secure "Big Blue Boxes" found on street corners. The really scary part of this story was that the postal officials *knew* these thefts were going on for *several years* but notified no one to be cautious! Don't depend on others for protection – protect yourself first and, if possible within your postal area, have a mail slot in your door or even rent a post office box for further protection.

- **Prevent check fraud**. A regularly increasing problem, check fraud can be prevented by using some common sense tips. For example, order checks from your bank instead of cheaper mail-order companies. By doing so, checks are harder to alter. Always review your cancelled checks. Make sure the checks are still made out to and endorsed to the intended party, and if there's a problem, then notify the bank ASAP (even though you have thirty days to do so). Hang onto your deposit slips. Scam artists are prone to deposit worthless checks into your account *but* they do so in order to get back some of the "deposit" as cash.

- **Order a copy of your credit report at least once a year**. If you are paranoid like me, then order more frequently. The reports will cost around $8.00 each, depending on which state in which you live, but it's money well spent. Make sure you have at hand the telephone numbers (which I've already provided) and addresses of the Big Three: **Equifax, Inc., P.O. Box 740123, Atlanta, GA 30374-0123; Experian, 701 Experian Parkway, Allen, TX 75013;** and **Trans Union Corporation, P.O. Box 97328, Jackson, MS 39288-7328**. If you become a casualty of identity theft, be sure you call the Big Three's fraud report phone numbers and have them place a "Fraud Alert" on your credit reports. The fraud report numbers are: Equifax (800) 525-6285, Experian (888) 397-3742, and Trans Union (800) 680-7289. An even quicker way to ascertain your rating at Experian is to visit **CreditPage** (www.creditpage.com). In less than a minute and for an $8 fee, CreditPage delivers this single report for a routine credit check. If you need to check further (for example, prior to applying for a mortgage), then CreditPage offers a merged report from the Big Three for $29.95. This combined report arrives via mail, however.

- **Visit the FTC online for help.** www.consumer.gov/idtheft is the site to report identity theft and to get help on restoring your credit.

Lucky for us, the Congress passed the Kyle Bill in the fall of 1998, which *finally* made identity theft a crime that law enforcement officials must now recognize as such and attempt to solve, just like other criminal acts. Senator Jon Kyle, the sponsor of the bill, tells us that "While ID fraud costs financial institutions approximately $2 billion a year, ID fraud theft victims can spend hundreds of hours and thousands of dollars to clear their name and restore their credit." The Federal Trade Commission suggests the following if your purse or wallet is stolen, even though self-knowledge and self-help is still the best prevention.

- **File a police report immediately.** You'll also need a copy of the report if your bank, credit card company, or insurance company needs proof of the theft.
- **Cancel each credit and charge card**, and then get new cards with new account information.
- **Report the missing cards to the "Big Three."** Ask them to flag your accounts and add a "victim's statement" to your file.
- **Notify your bank.** Cancel checking and savings accounts and open new ones. Don't forget to stop payments on outstanding checks. Get a new ATM card, account number and PIN or password.
- **Call your utility companies**, including the phone company. This will prevent the thief from getting new service using your ID.

(More advice follows, beginning on page 129.)

"Priscilla Panicked" called me in a panic to report her victimization. While on vacation her wallet was stolen, and she immediately contacted the charge card companies. Because Federal law limits consumers' liability for credit card fraud to

$50.00, she felt pretty safe from that standpoint. However, when she alerted the credit reporting agencies (after having earlier requested the flagging of her files), Priscilla discovered that the flag had not been picked up by the credit-scoring system; thus, all seemed to be lost. She even reported the crime to her local police to no avail. Even with the new law, sometimes law enforcement officials don't even recognize victims of identity theft, and usually consumers have little to no real proof to provide to the officials.

To make matters even worse, her credit application for a loan to finance her daughter's first year of college had been denied based on "her" poor credit rating. You see, Priscilla forgot the most vital piece of information that was now in the hands of a nasty crook - her social security card. In the interim, this person had requested <u>four</u> credit cards and then maxed out the limit of each to the total tune of almost $30,000! The poor woman began receiving dunning calls from collection agencies, which was her first inclination that something was terribly wrong. She immediately contacted the Social Security Office, but by then it was too late. Her credit was in tatters. In addition, the loan she requested several months later for her daughter's first year of college was turned down because of Priscilla's credit standing, and the young woman was not able to return to school for the spring semester.

To further exacerbate the problem, Priscilla couldn't be sure that in future months or even years the thief wouldn't set up other fraudulent accounts for which she would be responsible *and* would further jeopardize any gains she had made to clear her name and credit history. Under the circumstances, her mental and emotional state was shot to pieces, too. I honestly didn't know if I could help her at all but all we can do is try.

133 Desperate Avenue, #11
Salem, NH 03899
November 25, 2001

The Honorable Philip McLaughlin
Attorney General of New Hampshire
Office of the Attorney General
State House Annex
25 Capitol Street
Concord, NH 03301-6397

Dear General McLaughlin:

I am frantic because I am the victim of identity theft and no one else seems to care about my shocking situation. Please help me by investigating immediately and thoroughly on my behalf.

- My wallet was stolen on November 1, 2000, while I was vacationing in North Carolina. I reported the theft to my credit card companies and to Equifax, Experian, and Trans Union, as well as to the local police. I did not realize at that time, however, that the loss of my Social Security number should have been my primary concern.
- On January 15, 2001, I began to receive telephone calls and letters from You're Caught and Jailtime collection agencies. Of course, I had no knowledge of the $29,000 worth of charges for which they said I was responsible. I quickly contacted the four credit card companies [here I named each one and the persons with whom she spoke] and subsequently wrote a letter explaining my predicament. I mistakenly believed that the matter was then resolved and especially since I also reported the theft to the Social Security Office and received a new number.
- On October 29, I requested a re-finance loan from my lender, We Have Your Home Loan, Inc., in order to finance my daughter's freshman college year. To my horror, the loan was denied because my credit report was sullied by reports of the thousands of dollars in unpaid bills. My daughter will now have to forego her

educational dreams in order instead to work the first semester, hopefully to save enough money to attend the local junior college in January of next year.

I realize that identity theft is one of the hardest cases to prove and, certainly, the possibility of the other "Priscilla Panicked" making other charges and opening new accounts is a strong likelihood. However, the theft of my good name and all that it entails must be both recognized and acted upon by public officials who have the authority and willingness to come to my defense. Please join with me in this horrific battle to clear my name and credit standing. By using the powers of the Office of Attorney General, you will not only assist me but will also send a clear message to criminals everywhere that New Hampshire protects its innocent citizens at all costs.

Thank you, and I look forward to hearing from you within the next two weeks.

Sincerely,

Priscilla Panicked

cc: [I also wrote a short cover letter to each of the ccs]
   The Honorable John Ashcroft, Attorney General
   United States Department of Justice
   950 Pennsylvania Avenue, NW
   Washington, DC 20530

   Robert S. Mueller, III, Director
   Federal Bureau of Investigation
   935 Pennsylvania Avenue, NW
   Washington, DC 20535-0001

   Kenneth Huntley, Chief Postal Inspector

Ellen Phillips

United States Postal Service
475 L'Enfant Plaza, West, SW
Washington, DC 20260

The Honorable Jon Kyl
United States Senate
SH-724
Second and C Streets, NE
Washington, DC 20510

The Honorable Judd Gregg
United States Senate
Russell Building, SR-393
First and C Streets, NE
Washington, DC 20510

The Honorable Robert C. Smith
United States Senate
SD-307
First and C Streets, NE
Washington, DC 20510

The Honorable Dianne Feinstein [a big advocate for privacy rights]
United States Senate
SH-331
Second and C Streets, NE
Washington, DC 20510

The Honorable Charles Grassley [another big advocate]
United States Senate
SH-135
Second and C Streets, NE
Washington, DC 20510

The Honorable George W. Bush, President
United States of America
1600 Pennsylvania Avenue, NW

Washington, DC 20500

Margaret LaMontagne, Domestic Policy Council
The White House
1600 Pennsylvania Avenue, NW
Washington, DC 20500

The Honorable Jeanne Shaheen, Governor
State of New Hampshire
State House, Room 208
Concord, NH 03301

[The next three ccs went to Equifax, Experian, and Trans Union]

Priscilla's case is still pending, as we go to print on *Fight Back and Win!*, although she did receive a quick reply from a number of sources. An investigation is currently underway, and she has hope that sooner than later her <u>own</u> identity will be hers once more.

Identity theft or fraud is an issue on which you must be persistent. Even though it takes a terrible financial and emotional toll on your life, don't ever give up the ghost. Make sure you

- **Maintain careful reports on your each and every action**. Remember, documentation is the most important key.
- **Continue to be in contact with the Big Three**. Also, know that the law now mandates that insurers, retailers, banks, and other industries that gather financial information on you must obtain your express permission before credit reporting bureaus be allowed to sell that confidential data to marketers. Insist that no credit or credit records should be granted to *anyone* without first calling you at home or at work for your okay (and preferably with a *written* okay, if you can get away with it). Not only will this law help to protect your privacy, but it also should help your junk mail problem.

- **Alert your banks**. Replace any credit cards and ATM numbers, and put new passwords on these accounts. Do not use your mother's maiden name or your social security number (the villain that probably landed you in this pile of dog doo in the first place). It's also a good idea to cancel your checking and savings accounts and to open new ones. Stop payments on outstanding checks, too.

- **Keep calling the police to check on your case**. Be certain the report(s) lists any fraudulent account numbers. Police reports will also help to strengthen your cause. Even if you're told there's nothing they can do, perhaps if you log in enough calls they'll resort to some kind of action just to get you off their backs.

- **Get a new driver's license**. Don't take a chance that the impostor "you" isn't using your old one. In addition, it wouldn't hurt to get a copy of your driving record (no, not to check how many stoplights you've run and been caught); because a license is one that is always requested for identification and your records will show up any questionable information. Immediately report such items to your local Department of Motor Vehicles. (And as an aside, write Congress members that you think the so-called "smart card" is a great idea. If you're unsure, then talk to members of the military who use these cards for just about everything.)

- **Notify any government official/agency and consumer agency you can think of**. Start with the U.S. Postal Inspector, the Secret Service and, if you think someone may be either using a lost or stolen passport or may attempt to obtain a new one in your name but at the scammer's address, then contact the passport office. Two Web sites that may help are **Consumernet** (www.consumernet.org) and the **Privacy Rights Clearinghouse** (www.privacyrights.org). Consumernet is an organization that provides consumer access to privacy advocacy issues, and the Privacy Rights Clearinghouse provides us with in-depth information on a variety of privacy issues, as well as tips on safeguarding our personal privacy.

In fact, more of us need to realize just how risky the Web is, too. If we're wary about our neighborhood grocery clerk, then how much more cautious should we be regarding our privacy when dealing with potentially-billions of onlookers? Consumers should always check out a site's privacy policy (usually found on its home page). Readers who have kept abreast of my site's "Consumer Tips of the Week" will recall my push in demanding that online stores not sell, trade, or rent a person's personal information and that this policy be stated on store sites. Not only will our opting out protect our personal information, but also it will help to avoid junk e-mail (spam). As I discussed in Chapter 3, both the Better Business Bureau Online and the Internet Fraud Watch are both valuable protection resources.

- **Write a form letter that can be mailed or faxed when you receive a question about fraudulent checks written on your bank account**. Briefly describe what happened, note your bank's name, account number and the name and phone number at its customer service office, as well as the check manufacturer, the case number assigned to you by police, and the name of the officer handling your case.
- **Change your locks if keys were stolen**. Depending on which or both, change the locks on your home and car. Deny this creep any further access to your personal property or information.

The Financial Privacy Act of 1999 requires federal regulators to issue rules to protect consumers, including the following:
1. Federal banking regulatory institutions defines "confidential information" to include all data in checking and savings accounts, certificates of deposit, securities holdings and insurance policies.

115

2. Financial institutions must tell customers what information it would sell or share, and to whom, when, and why.
3. Customers have the right to say no or to "opt out" to the selling or sharing of this information.
4. The customers would have to give his or her consent before an unaffiliated third party could view this confidential information.

If we kick, scream, fight, and deluge Congress with letters and calls about *all* forms of privacy protection, we'll be a safer society. But in the meantime, don't forget two important tips. Be smart. Stay alert. By doing both you'll protect yourself and your identity from theft and fraud.

Helpful Agencies and Services

Consumernet (www.consumernet.org) and the **Privacy Rights Clearinghouse** (www.privacyrights.org) are both good sources to assist with identity theft questions and concerns.

Send a stamped, self-addressed envelope for the booklet *Opening the Door to Opportunity* at Consumer Services - Opening the Door, **Direct Marketing Association**, 1111 Nineteenth Street, NW, Suite 1100, Washington, DC 20036.

The **Federal Trade Commission** publishes free brochures on credit-related issues. Write *Best Sellers,* FTC, Pennsylvania Avenue and Sixth Street, NW, Washington, DC 20580 or call at (202) FTC-HELP; TDD (202) 326-2502. Also visit its site www.consumer.gov/idtheft to report identity theft and obtain information on how to restore your credit.

Write the **Mail Preference Service** at the Direct Marketing Association, P.O. Box 9008, Farmingdale, NY 11735-9008 to register to remove your name from national profit/non-profit lists or from commercial mail.

Contact the major credit bureaus to request your name be removed from their distribution lists. Call **Equifax** at (800) 556-4711, **Experian** at (800) 353-0809, and **Trans Union** at (800) 680-7293. To order a copy of your credit report, write Equifax, Inc., P.O. Box 740123, Atlanta, GA 30374-0123; Experian, P.O. Box 2104, Allen, TX 75013; and/or Trans Union Corporation, P.O. Box 1000, Chester, PA 19022. Also **CreditPage** (www.creditpage.com) can get you a copy from Experian for $8.00 with no wait time. "Fraud Alert" numbers to call are (800) 525-6285 (Equifax), (888) 397-3742 (Experian), and (800) 680-7289 (Trans Union).

Chapter 7

Is There a Doctor in the House?

"Trust yourself. You know more than you think you do."
- Unknown

Sometimes we wonder if a competent doctor is anywhere to be seen in our generic "house": the hospital, the office, the lab, the X-ray facility. More than likely (and I *am* being facetious), we'll see him or her on the golf course, in the gym or, even easier to spot, pushing that wheelchair filled with our cash all the way to the bank. Alert! Alert! Alert!

Your medical reports may be just as important as your credit reports. Each time we visit our physician or check into the hospital for even out-patient surgery, we leave a paper trail that not only gets longer and longer but often has incorrect information found within. The idea that our medical experts descend from the right hand of God is old-fashioned, yet it is a doctrine in which many folks still wholeheartedly believe. We assume our medical records are the doctor's or the hospital's or our health insurer's property, and we also mistakenly believe that the files are up-to-date and always accurate.

Granted, most health providers and their staff do their damnedest to ensure the accuracy of patients' files but, on the other hand, others aren't quite as careful. Doctors may be in a hurry to write their findings (and even when they're not rushed, how many of us have ever been able to actually decipher their scribbles?). Secretaries are only human, too. Not only are they faced with oft-illegible notes, they may be understaffed and transcribe the wrong information because four phones are ringing at once.

Some health care providers are highly protective of *your* records, perceiving them as private property. They do *not* belong to the provider, however; the records are yours and belong exclusively to *you*. Most doctors' offices will provide copies for you when you pay copying expenses, usually through an independent medical service. If they refuse to furnish you with a copy, then contact your state's department of insurance and loudly complaint in writing. In addition, while health insurers and hospitals may not copy for you, you have the right to go in and inspect your records. If you note a discrepancy or error, then you can order a copy (again, check with your department of insurance for your state's guidelines in this area.)

So what's the big deal over medical records? Just why should you go through the hassle of coercing, paying for copies, spending perhaps hours searching through them and possibly alienating Dr. Goodfeel who's been your family doctor for the past twenty-five years? Let me relate a personal example that will certainly illustrate the importance of the process.

A couple of years ago, my husband and I decided we needed long-term health care insurance. I researched possibilities, narrowed my choices, and blithely mailed off the application and the three months premium. Imagine how *shocked, appalled, and dismayed* I was to receive a letter from the insurer denying me services. It seemed that someone in my physician's office had made an enormous error on my chart after a routine visit for back pain. Because it was known that I had had polio as a child and that I had "guinea-pigged" myself out several years before to the National Institutes of Health's Post-Polio research program, my chart now read that I suffered from Post-Polio Syndrome. Had this truly been the case, any insurer would be stupid to offer long-term care for me.

I immediately called and wrote my physician and explained the error to him, and he equally as quickly wrote a letter negating the findings in my records, taking full responsibility for the mistake. (On the heels of that fiasco, while further studying my husband's records, I discovered a file of another patient who was being treated for a sexually transmitted disease. Name, address, Social Security number, you name it. Boy, wouldn't he have cried "LAWSUIT!" if he knew of this mess?) It took awhile to straighten everything out, but I finally received permission for the policy, and the erroneous information was purged from my files. I might add that, at my insistence, both my letter and his were then included in my records to avoid any further problems – at least with this specific diagnosis.

Close to the end of former President Clinton's term of office, he issued a ruling designed to prevent misuse or unauthorized disclosure of medical records. Consumer groups hailed this action, but, naturally, the health care industry and a number of large employer groups decried the privacy rules.

So what do we get with an enactment like this? People will have the right to see and change (a lá my *post-polio* example) their records and to restrict the release of medical information (Again, it's not your employer's business if you're being treated for depression as long as your job isn't negatively affected and, frankly, not even under those circumstances.) The rule also requires providers and health plans to develop policies that protect our privacy and (this is one of my personal favorites) to require them to obtain a patient's <u>written</u> consent for the use of medical information, especially in non-emergency situations. Unfortunately, it still takes two years from its February 26, 2001 effective date for those that it's aimed against to comply with the decree. And to add insult to injury, a little tally to be tucked away in your brain is that health care costs are expected to rise this year to $1.37 **trillion** so we all better be extra careful with our health and our pocketbooks.

Physicians

Just remember, even though you're not the doctor, you <u>are</u> the one who must live with the consequences of any errors he or she might make with regards to your health. It's up to each of us to be an informed patient *before* treatment becomes necessary. And it's also important to know that there's no room for the paternalistic attitudes of yesteryear – you and your physicians must be partners in the decision-making process. Be your own advocate initially and, hopefully, an outside activist will never be necessary. What do you need to do in order to either find a new doctor or to ensure that your present one stays abreast of current medical practices?

- **Check <u>The Best Doctors in America</u> books**. This five-volume set is based on research and reviews and features physicians from all over the country, including both family practitioners and specialists. For information on ordering, call (888) 362-8677.

- **Examine the prospective doctor's qualifications**. This is much easier than it sounds. A good Internet source is the American Medical Association's Web site <u>www.ama-assn.org</u>). Physician Select cites information about physicians' education and specialty for over 650,000 licensed doctors. (It's important to know, though, that a large number of superb physicians don't belong to the AMA; so don't let this be your sole deciding factor.) To burrow even further into their secret lives, contact the organization **Medi-Net** at (800) 972-6334, which can access anything from licensing and certifications to any disciplinary action taken against this person. Be prepared to pay $15.00 and an additional $5.00 for each extra doctor. It's money well spent. Visit the Web page of the **Association of State Medical Board Executive Directors (DocFinder)** at <u>www.docboard.org</u> to dig even deeper. These organizations even reveal criminal convictions and state penalties for disciplinary action taken against a particular physician, as well as addresses and phone numbers for most state boards. <u>www.sanctionsearch.com</u> is also a good tool for this kind of discovery purpose. And don't forget the most obvious source of all - your family and friends. Their recommendations (or not) are free and readily available. Ask and even grill them about their own experiences with a prospective physician.

- **Make an appointment to "interview" a prospective physician**. Don't fear being blunt. Tell him or her what you're looking for in a doctor (your life could be in these hands). Are you more comfortable with one who takes the time to sit down with you and give his or her undivided attention? If so, check out the waiting room; how crowded is it and are patients moved (too) quickly through like a herd of goats? Get his opinion on homeopathic practices if these are important to you. If he or she isn't one of the many doctors today who understand that homeopathy can go hand-in-hand with more conventional medicine, you probably want to look elsewhere for a physician. Along this same line, be familiar with osteopathic physicians (DOs) who are fully licensed to practice medicine. If you're under the care of or looking for one of these specialty doctors rather than using a conventional MD, contact the **American Osteopathic Association** (800-621-1773) for information concerning the physician's certification status.

- **Ask if there's any objection to printed prescriptions along with "regular" ones**. No one is infallible, and if you can read the prescription before you leave the doctor's presence to check its accuracy and your own understanding of the treatment, dangerous mistakes can be avoided.

Let's say your own personal Dr. Feelgood has slipped up in some way. Not a life-threatening screw-up, but a mistake nonetheless. "Carol Cough" had a beef with the physician who had taken care of her for many years. She liked and respected him, but on this one occasion after verbally attempting to get results and not getting any, she decided a letter was a necessity.

8710 Teed-Off Terrace
Juneau, AK 99811
October 11, 2001

Nathan Nonchalant, M.D.
8101 Physician's Parkway
Juneau, AK 99811

Dear Doctor Nonchalant:

I am absolutely appalled at the current lack of efficiency with your practice, which has adversely affected my health this past week.

- **I began to feel quite ill on Monday, October 1. As you are aware, each year at this time I develop a cold and a cough, and you always simply place a call to the pharmacy for my prescription. I had no idea that this year would be so different and such a hardship for me.**
- **On Friday, October 5, I called your office for this medication but was informed that you were not available to take my call or even to return it. I was assured, however, that one of your associates would contact the pharmacist at the Healthy Hall Drug Shoppe that same day. That assurance was a false one.**
- **On Saturday, October 6, I still had received no word that my medication was forthcoming and, in fact, even the pharmacist continued to call your exchange for the promised prescription to no avail.**
- **On Monday, October 8, I once again made a futile attempt to reach you. This time, the receptionist, Paula, informed me that you were "gone." She was of no assistance whatsoever, even when I questioned why one of your associates could not contact the pharmacy <u>as previously promised</u>. Once again, neither the pharmacist nor I were called regarding the medicine, either then or today.**

This is an egregious situation. You have been my physician for almost twenty years and to be treated in such a horrific manner is, in my opinion, totally unprofessional. One simple telephone call would have initially solved the problem; instead, I have suffered for almost a week because of the lack of attention on the part of you and the other doctors in your practice.

at 779-8541 as well as one of explanation to me.I expect an immediate telephone call to my pharmacist

Thank you.

Carol Cough

cc: American Medical Association
1601 Broadway
New York, NY 10019

The Honorable Michael Mangano
United States Department
Health and Human Services
P.O. Box 23489
Washington, DC 20013-1133

The Honorable Bruce M. Botelho
Attorney General of Alaska
Office of the Attorney General
P.O. Box 110300
Dimond Courthouse
Juneau, AK 99811-0300

Not only did Carol receive an immediate phone call from the doctor, but also her prescription was ready before she had time to drive to the pharmacy.

So what happens if Dr. Feelgood or some new physician screws up and you feel any particulars of your health are going to hell in a hand basket? My earlier anecdote regarding the medical record-keeping problems within my own chart made me somewhat of an expert on this type of situation. In addition to my previous advice, if there's a potential (or, even worse, a *real*) problem, then consider the following once you've obtained your medical records:

- **Check for missing information**. For example, an initial or recent physical exam should cover your family history, lifestyle, past and current health and any complaints, a listing of allergies (including drug or allergy sensitivities), and any changes to the above since your last physical.

- **Records should always mirror your current and specific problem**. Why were you visiting the doctor in the first place? There also should be some documentation of history and whichever exam you were given. Certainly, the diagnosis and treatment must be included, too. Has the doctor noted any and all prescriptions from other health-care providers as well as his or her own? Are you asked about over-the-counter medications you're presently taking? Sadly, not only do some physicians fail to keep current with the latest findings, but also their inadequacies may prevent your wellness or, worse, severely exacerbate your problem. Also, be sure to check out the doctor's policy or attitude with regards to referring to specialists if necessary. Unfortunately, some folks like the power of having their patients all to themselves and jealously guard this privilege. They also may not like to admit they don't have the answers to help you, or he or she simply may be unaware that the prescribed treatment isn't working, as it should. No one physician knows all the solutions about every condition, but it is this person's responsibility to refer you to another who can help you with your particular illness.

- **Ask the right questions**. Are you sure the records recall what happened with this particular visit? *Be very careful.* If your complaint has to do with crying jags, for instance, resulting from the death of a parent or a mean and nasty boss, you may later find the doc has labeled you as mentally ill, as "evidenced" by your symptoms. And just wait 'til the big boys at your HMO get a hold of that burden – and don't think they

Ellen Phillips

won't. So be sure to request firmly that your doctor allow you to personally review any requests for information about your health. If there's any particle that you wish to remain private, insist on an attachment to these sections that states: "Not to be released without my personal permission in writing."

- **Write the Medical Information Bureau (MIB) to find out if information about your medical history is stored in the insurance industry's database**. The address is P.O. Box 105, Essex Station, Boston, MA 02112 or call at (617) 426-3660. When you receive this report, thoroughly check it to ensure its accuracy. If you do find an error, challenge it in writing with a back-up statement from your doctor. While this is a necessity as I found out when incorrect information was posted in my own physician's files, there's another and equally important reason for doing so. Nullify any past medical waivers and unequivocally inform the Bureau not to release any information about you and yours without your *written* consent. Take this one step further: when you're asked to sign any waiver, make sure it covers only the specific information the doctor, hospital, and so forth need and states that this waiver is good for normally no more than a couple of months. A nice plus is that the MIB will reinvestigate when disputes arise.

- **Do something quickly if you discover an error in your physician's file**. Call Doc immediately and explain that his records and yours don't match. Tell him or her what you wish deleted and also what needs to be inserted in its place. Don't stop there, however. Follow up your conversation with a written (of course) request/demand for action. Be sure you include a sentence such as "I expect this letter to become a part of my medical records" and later check to see if his or her office complied. Send a copy of the letter to your insurer's records department to provide further documentation.

- **Always ask for a written copy of the doctor's notes before leaving**. In addition, it's best to keep your own records, too. Detailed notes on each conversation or visit to any physician will not only keep information and questions fresh in your mind, but when you whip out your own medical journal, the doctor (or anyone else, for that matter) will realize you're a savvy medical consumer.

- **Use your own common sense**. Let's say you hop over to your local supermarket for a free blood pressure check. Do not fill out any questionnaire or even have the procedure done until you discover who will have access to the collected data. The same principle applies when filling out any questionnaire, even those seemingly innocuous ones that accompany free aspirin and the like and which ask if you experience migraines, diarrhea, and so forth. There actually have been instances where HMOs and drug companies have "discovered" (this *is* the technological age, after all) these so-called problems and subsequently hassled lots of folks. Don't allow any form qualifications. While many fabulous doctors are not necessarily board-certified, they do have other medical knowledge of "Big Brother" to find out problems that may come back to haunt you in the future. And for heaven sakes, don't forget that miscommunication is usually the major source of irritation – or worse – between patient and physician. The following illustrates this all too well and makes you wish to fight hard to eliminate the stereotypical but oft-very real HMO chain of command that stymies physicians and patients alike. (Heads up, Doctors Paulo Franco, Ian

Gordon, Donna Hurlock, Michael Lieberman, Stephen Rex, and Leslie Williams – I don't mean you!)

We also need to be *verrrry* careful when scheduling office surgery. Thirteen percent of all surgical procedures are now performed in physicians' offices. While office surgery certainly can be safe and effective (and let's not forget cheaper!), problems may exist, such as having no crash carts or other sophisticated items to use for emergencies in the office. And if something unforeseen does happen, you really have no agencies to which to appeal, as state or national organizations usually don't regulate office surgery. So before you choose office over hospital, ask the doctor questions such as:

1. **Are you board-certified?** If not, then you better check further into his or her recommendations to replace this specialized training. If you find few to none at all, then you better run, don't walk to the nearest exit.
2. **Who will administer the anesthesia?** This person *must* be either a board-certified anesthesiologist or a certified nurse-practitioner-anesthetist.
3. **Are you prepared for emergencies?** Again, the barebone minimum for any surgery problems that may arise in office surgery is a crash cart with a defibrillator and airway resuscitation equipment.

These are only a few of the questions you need to ask and have answered to your own personal satisfaction. Then and only then should you decide that office surgery is the best option for you.

Once upon a time, a man walked into a doctor's office and the receptionist asked him his problem. He replied, "I got shingles." She told him to fill out a form and to supply his name, address and medical ID number and after he was done, to please take a seat.

Fifteen minutes later a nurse's aide came out and asked the man his problem. He answered, "I got shingles." So she took down his height, weight, and so forth and then told him to change into a gown and wait in the exam room.

A half hour later, a nurse came in and asked him his problem. He answered, "I got shingles." So she took his blood pressure, gave him an electrocardiogram, and told him to wait for the doctor.

An hour later the doctor came in and asked him his problem. He responded, "I got shingles." The doctor checked him out thoroughly and then looked very puzzled.

"I just checked you out to a fair-thee-well, and I can't find a sign of shingles anywhere."

In exasperation, the man replied, "They're outside in the truck. Where do you want 'em?"

Pharmacists

Believe or not, as this book goes to print I've received not one single request for a complaint letter to a pharmacist. This doesn't mean, however, that we should sit idly by and trust him or her to do what is best for us with regards to filling our prescriptions. Just as we need to make it our business to be knowledgeable about the person who prescribes the medication, we also must be vigilant about the person who hands us our bottle of pills to swallow every four hours. In fact, according to the *Washington Post* (July 2, 2000), most pharmacists don't have to report their errors – even if these resulted in someone's death. Additionally, not only are there no limits on the lengths of pharmacists' shifts but the technicians who help to fill the prescriptions rarely even have to be certified. Very scary...

But, on the other hand, maybe because so many of us are losing faith with the medical industry as a whole, we find ourselves depending more and more upon our pharmacist (whom, for whatever reason, we tend to regard as outside the conventional fold). There are still questions to be answered by these professionals, too, and I'll share some with you. First, though, a crucial point: *try to always fill your prescriptions with the same druggist*. With a touch of the computer, this person can then view all your medications history and, much more often than your doctor, inform you if there will be possible adverse reactions with a new medicine. Pharmacists also tend to keep more abreast about accurate and up-to-date drug information on the market than your doctor, which, of course, is in your best interests. On to the fill-in-the-blank answers you require:

- **What is this drug?** Make sure you get all the ends-and-outs, such as brand and generic names (and if one works as well as the other) and if it works well in conjunction with any other prescriptions and OTC medicines you're currently taking. Tell the pharmacist why you're taking this medicine; sometimes doctors inadvertently prescribe the wrong drug for what ails you. Be sure to find out when and how it should be taken. Some medications require a full stomach. Know any restrictions before you walk away and make sure the bottle is clearly labeled with the information. It wouldn't hurt to check out the FDA's Internet site www.fda.gov for information on prescription drugs, medical devices, and a whole lot more.

Back in the spring of 2000, the national news told the story of a five-year-old Virginia boy, who died so unnecessarily and so tragically. The child wasn't suffering from a terrible illness; he just needed a prescription filled for a minor problem. Unfortunately, the youngster's death resulted solely because of an error in dispensing a prescribed medication. This wasn't your run-of-the-mill "fast food" pharmacy, either, but one of the most progressive in the state, if not in the whole country. Indeed, the owner/pharmacist (who was out of town when the mistake occurred) even spent $175,000 a year earlier on an automated pill counting machine so that he and his colleagues could spend more time talking with patients. If a tragic error like this can occur in the best of pharmacies, then it can happen anywhere.

- **Am I allergic to any of the drug's ingredients?** Remember your druggist's magic computer *if* you stick to one pharmacy. And it's a given that if anything strange occurs, such as a rash, upset stomach, or so forth, you contact your doctor immediately.

- **Are there any side effects?** If your pharmacist is as good as he or she should be, then this person should be able to provide a comprehensive explanation of any possible side effects and what to do if you experience them.
- **How should this drug be stored?** Certain medications must be stored in a cool dark place (and not in your bathroom medicine cabinet). Find out the best location since some drugs may lose their potency very quickly if improperly stored.
- **Are there special situations to avoid with your medications?** Notwithstanding the medicine cabinet scenario, some drugs need to be absented from alcohol and/or taken with milk, and so forth.

Even when we explicitly trust our pharmacist, however, there should be warning labels attached, just as on the prescription bottles that person gives to us. No, not for the pharmacist himself, but for an entity called the *pharmacy benefit manager*. Those who belong to HMOs (and more on these darling organizations shortly) can find themselves on the fast road to Screw-You-to-Hell because of PBMs and their oft-perceived methods of entrapment and real methods of throwing doctor-patient confidentiality out of the door. Here's how it works.

You carry your prescription to the pharmacy and pay your share of the bill with your HMO's prescription card, whereupon the pharmacist keys in the information into his or her database. The information is then immediately transmitted to a PBM who checks to ascertain if the drug is covered by your health plan and is safe for your use. If all is okay, the PBM transmits back and your pharmacist is allowed to fill the prescription. So far, so good, right? Wrong! The PBM doesn't stop there. Now, *Big Brother* comes out to play, and what happens next is downright creepy and we must all be aware of the potential and terrible consequences.

From the initial permission, the PBM's computer pathway speeds forward, downloads information on you, stores it in various computers, and certain developments can occur. For example, now the PBM can send PBM-employed pharmacists to talk with your doctors about your care and you don't even know about it. And even though they "promise" removal of patients' identifying information, these folks can make tons of money by selling *you* to a number of health industry companies. The problem just gets worse, too.

Let's go back to the physician section in which your doctor's records may reflect you as clinically depressed because of your (well-deserved) weepies over certain traumatic situations in your life. Little do we realize that the infamous PBM (as well as the Medical Information Bureau) can zip out news of the "confidential" visit you had with your doctor. The next thing you know, your employer receives a letter with the notification that you're being treated for depression and then the proverbial you-know-what really may hit the fan. An enormous number of pharmacists and physicians alike are concerned over this issue, and so should you be as well. Write your senators and representatives about this issue. Contact the **National Association of Boards of Pharmacies** at www.nabp.net. Explain your fear of benefit management companies intruding into your personal and medical lives - and do it now.

One final word to the wise. While reputable online pharmacists offer concern, convenience, and competitive prices, even those professionals may do more harm than good. First off is that many may not accept your insurance. In addition, if the onliners aren't affiliated with retail stores or chains, it could take a week or longer to receive your meds by mail. Furthermore, some health-related Websites can't keep your personal information on a private basis, leading some undesired sites (or even hackers) "permission" to use your information as they wish. You know how Ms. Paranoia feels about that!

Even more dangerous, there are some online drugstores that pose the risk of real harm to consumers. Whether the medicine is a weight control substance – either OTC or in prescription form – or any other kind of drug, cheaper is definitely not necessarily better, especially without your own physician's okay. We don't know the possible and even probable effects some drugs will have on us, and you don't want to find yourself pushing up daises because you had a brief surge of insanity and took some dangerous medication simply because you fancied yourself a size smaller. Before buying from any Internet drugstore, check them out, too, with the National Association of Boards of Pharmacies. If the suspicious site doesn't have the Verified Internet Pharmacy Practice Site seal, then run for the hills!

Most of us believe that the Honchos who work in the pharmaceutical industry are all out to wring our wallets dry with their high-priced medicines. I leave that discussion to others, but I suspect that the companies most supportive to employees are also those more supportive of their customers. Take Pfizer, for example. First of all, there's no wait whatsoever for full vesting (most companies in Corporate America have a wait time of from one to five years) as well as a wealth of other financial extras. And any pregnant employees are assured that they will be paid nine weeks salary when off for childbirth and, when the new mama returns to work, she can leave Junior at any of Pfizer's onsite day care facilities. The company's adoption reimbursement is $5,000 and adoption for a special-needs child is reimbursed in the amount of $6,000. Moreover, any unpaid leave for both childbirth and adoption for moms and dads stand at twenty-six weeks. These generous benefits don't even include other amenities such as company gyms, discounted products, and so forth. Pfizer is truly a grand place to work, and consumers/patients can reap the benefits.

In closing this particular section, Gary E. Benes, R.PH of Alexandria, Virginia, shares some of his thoughts about the responsibilities of being a community pharmacist.

"Pharmacy technicians must receive standard and thorough training and be licensed by a governing authority. Third party claims must be pre-approved upon reaching the pharmacist. Maybe the number of pharmacies should be reduced so that pharmacists can be centralized in order to support each other. If this were to occur, one pharmacist could concentrate in dispensing without interruption while another pharmacist counseled patients and handled telephone calls. Changes like this would remove much of the stress from the workplace, allow the dispensing pharmacist to document his/her work more thoroughly and, subsequently, to reduce dispensing errors.

It would also be helpful if all prescriptions were presented to the pharmacist in printed form with no handwriting involved except for the practitioner's signature. [Amen, brother!] If prescriptions were typed, typed and faxed, or sent by e-mail to the pharmacist, much time could be saved in trying to decipher the intent of the physician and errors would be reduced."

Hospitals

When we're told a hospital stay is imminent, whether for an emergency or for scheduled surgery, fear naturally zooms throughout our veins like ice water. There are ways, though, to combat the apprehension, and one of the best is to ask the right questions *before* entering those sterile hallways. Hopefully, you've asked your doctor for a second or even third opinion (usually your HMO requires this). Then if the hospital stay is a must and if you have the time to do so, then consider the following:

- **Be sure the hospital is accredited "with commendation."** The non-profit organization **Joint Commission on Accreditation of Healthcare Organizations (JACHO)** tells us that "regular" accreditation means squat. If your local hospital doesn't have the JCAHO ranking, then go to the nearest university's teaching hospital. They frequently have much better care to offer than those in small towns and often in small cities. For a free hospital report, write JCAHO at 1 Renaissance Boulevard, Oakbrook Terrace, IL 60181 or call (630) 792-5800.

- **Check the hospital's surgery records**. Usually the more operations a hospital performs, the lower its complications rate. Also, the more Registered Nurses on the premises, the better. RNs, as opposed to nursing aides, are trained for the best patient care. Too bad more and more of the latter are being utilized because of cost-counting factors. And let's face it, wouldn't you really rather accept an unknown pill from a knowledgeable professional instead of someone with just a high school diploma (no insult intended)? Thoroughly check the number of available RNs at the hospital that you're considering.

- **Investigate the surgeon**. What is this doctor's death rate and complications rate? What is the number of times this person performed your particular surgery? Surgical errors account for about half of all medical mess-ups, ranging from (literally) an instrument left inside your body to a physician who doesn't wash his or her hands properly, leaving you with a raging infection. Better make sure your doc is the best he or she can be. If not, then it's your right to switch to another one.

- **Investigate the anesthesiologist**. Sometimes this professional is more important to your well-being than the surgeon. We've all heard horror stories about a patient who supposedly was given the correct amount of anesthesia and awakens during the operation only to find the medication isn't working. More horrible is that the patient feels every slice of the knife, yet is unable to speak because of the anesthesia. Make sure the person who puts you out is board-certified, knows your health history and anything else about you that might cause a problem during the operation.

- **Be careful when signing hospital consent forms**. Make sure you both understand and agree with what you're *John Henry*ing. Many hospitals these days are obtaining consent for videos to be shot while you're under anesthesia, especially if your surgery is unique or you're in a teaching hospital. Another clause to watch for is a statement that your operation will be performed "under the direction of" your doctor or, perhaps, by others "selected by him/her." If you don't want either of these, then cross out that portion of the consent; even better, write on the document that you expressly do not wish either provision.

And when the surgery is (successfully) completed and you're back in your room, still stay diligent. If you have no family member or friend to stay with you, then make a quick friend of the hospital's patient representative. Don't think that once you're recovering you can let your guard down because mistakes can still happen at your expense (both financial and health).

- **Insist that anyone who comes in contact with you has clean hands**. While this should be a given, it ain't necessarily so. Doctors, nurses, and the like are often in a hurry and don't take the time to wash from one patient to another or even to wear gloves as they should do, plus hospitals are notoriously the germiest places around. A health care professional once told me that if you're not sick when you are admitted, you surely will be while you're there, especially if you're afraid you'll insult your caretakers about germy hands.
- **Don't just swallow any medication given to you or blithely go along with any test**. Insist that you know specifically what the medication or test is for, who ordered it and why. Be sure the hospital pharmacist works directly with hospital personnel to lower the risks and that the pharmacist receives a <u>copy</u> of the doctor's orders rather than just a verbal communication. If you

develop any new symptoms upon taking the new medicine, notify your doctor or the hospital pharmacist. And don't let Nurse Needle ramrod you into continuing the dosage until it's approved. Also, be aware of dangers a test may pose, especially with regards to nuclear medicine and radiation, which can be particularly dangerous. It wouldn't hurt (pardon the pun) to get a second opinion on tests interpretations as well. Misreading of tests is a very common occurrence in hospitals.

- **Always ask questions**. If you're uncomfortable, uneasy, or unsure about any procedure, question it with your last breath. (Who knows, if you don't, it just might be!)

If you have the opportunity when you're sick or contemplating surgery, be sure to choose a hospital like Baptist Hospital of Miami. One member of many "Baptist" hospitals throughout the country, this one can't be beat for patient concern and employee contentment. For instance, Baptist Hospital of Miami opened one of the very first staff child-care centers, dating back to the early sixties. *Friendly* is the everyday term around its corridors with each person treating others like best buds. Employees enjoy benefits such as a fitness center, a car wash, and a dry cleaning service. Out of many other perks, one of the better ones around is that employees are permitted to borrow vacation time from other staff members. One item that <u>really</u> appeals to me is Baptist's wallet card, issued to all employees. I think you'll agree that this is about the most consumer/patient-friendly piece of literature you've ever seen in this lifetime.

"YOU ARE BAPTIST HOSPITAL

- You are what people see when they arrive here.
- Yours are the eyes they look into when they're frightened and lonely.

137

- Yours are the voices people hear when they ride the elevators, when they try to sleep and when they try to forget their problems.
- Yours are the comments people hear when you think they can't.
- Yours is the intelligence and caring that people hope they'll find here.
- No visitors, no patients can ever know the real you – unless you let them see it. All they can know is what they see and hear and experience.
- And so we have a stake in your attitude and in the collective attitudes of everyone who works at the hospital. We are judged by your performance. We are the care you give, the attention you pay, the courtesies you extend.
Thank you for all you're doing."

Health Maintenance Organizations

You feel a twinge of apprehension as you read the cover of your managed care packet and notice the company's logo. It features a hand tightly squeezing a turnip. Then, while pouring through the packet, a number of statements catch your eye, such as *'The use of antibiotics will be deemed an 'unauthorized experimental procedure'* and *'Your twenty-four hour claims line is 1-800-TUF-LUCK.'* While I'm trying to pull a funny here, unfortunately with the experiences that many of us have had, these "funnies" aren't too far off the mark. Even though I discussed HMOs in *Shocked, Appalled, and Dismayed!*, there are still many issues I didn't cover, some of which have come more recently to my attention and of which everyone needs to be made aware.

Please don't think I'm getting my jollies at the expense of sacrilege, but the following Biblical illustration, while funny, in many cases also appears tragically true. Entitled "In the Beginning," it goes like this.

"In the beginning God created the heavens and the earth. And the earth was without form, and void, and darkness was upon the face of the deep. And Satan said, 'It doesn't get any

better than this.' And God said, 'Let there be light,' and there was light. And God said, 'Let the earth bring forth grass, and the fruit tree yielding fruit,' and God saw that it was good. And Satan said, 'There goes the neighborhood.'

And God said, 'Let us make Man in Our image, after Our likeness, and let them have dominion over the fish of the sea and over the fowl of the air and over the cattle, and over all the earth, and over every creeping thing that creepeth upon the earth.' And so God created Man in his own image; male and female created he them. And God looked upon Man and Woman and saw that they were lean and fit. And Satan said, 'I know how I can get back in this game.'

And God populated the earth with broccoli and cauliflower and spinach, green and yellow vegetables of all kinds, so Man and Woman would live long and healthy lives. And Satan created McDonalds. And McDonalds brought forth the 99-cent double cheeseburger. And Satan said to Man, 'You want fries with that?' And Man said, 'Supersize them.' And Man gained five pounds. And God created the healthful yogurt, that Woman might keep her figure that Man found so fair. And Satan brought forth chocolate and Woman gained five pounds. And God said, 'Try my crispy fresh salad.' And Satan brought forth Ben and Jerry's. And Woman gained ten pounds. And God said, 'I have sent thee heart-healthy vegetables and olive oil with which to cook them.' And Satan brought forth chicken-fried steak so big it needed its own platter. And Man gained ten pounds and his bad cholesterol went through the roof.

And God brought forth running shoes and Man resolved to lose those extra pounds. And Satan brought forth cable TV with remote control so Man would not have to toil to change channels between ESPN and ESPN2. And Man gained another twenty pounds. And God said, 'You're running up the score, Devil.' And God brought forth the potato, a vegetable naturally low in fat and brimming with nutrition. And Satan peeled off the healthy skin and sliced the starchy center into chips and deep-fat fried them. And he created sour cream dip also. And Man clutched his remote control and ate the potato chips swaddled in cholesterol. And Satan saw and said, 'It is good.'

*And God sighed and created quadruple bypass surgery.
And in response Satan created HMOs."*

- Anonymous

All laughs aside, in a number of instances many HMOs
have become the demon that denies expensive treatments,
restricts our choice of physicians, limits referrals to specialists,
and cuts hospital stays. We're told that if rising costs for 2001
weren't high enough (and they certainly were), then the
anticipated rate hikes that managed care companies will pocket
for 2002 will at least equal those costs (to us) from last year.
Unfortunately, too many of us blindly turn over our health -
good or bad - to health maintenance organizations without
thoroughly checking them out. Some people don't have a
choice, however. The companies for which they work have only
one HMO from which to choose, and you're really stuck with its
plan unless you have a spouse with a different plan.

If you're lucky, though, you have a range from which to pick.
Carefully eyeball any open enrollment offers your employer
may provide and then compile a list that assesses your own
needs. Also make a list of comparative payments, co-
payments, deductibles, yearly cost of prescriptions, ease of
information, and so forth. What is your life style? If you're newly
married and plan to have children, check out each plan's policy
on different factors, such as what it pays for cesarean sections.
Take *all* possible situations into perspective and then, before
making your decision, you need to ask some pertinent
questions and make sure you can live with the answers (and I
literally mean *live*).

- **Can any prospective plan be rated**? Yes, it most
  certainly can. Before you find yourself in deep doodoo,
  obtain an Accreditation Status List. This list compares
  information on all the health plans that the **National
  Committee for Quality Assurance** has reviewed. NCQA
  can assist you in two areas. First, call the organization at
  (800) 839-6487 to receive its free brochure, *Choosing
  Quality: Finding the Health Plan That's Right for You.*
  Then call (888) 275-7585 and you'll be sent an

Accreditation Status List - a report card - on the quality of HMOs. Pull up NCQA's Web page at www.ncqa.org if you prefer to go that route. A word of warning, however: health care organizations are becoming more and more secretive (I wonder why?) about their services. While some of the providers may share this information with the employers who carry the plans, in many cases they slap policyholders on the wrist and tell us to "Hit the road, Jack" if we dare ask for ourselves. NCOA can help here, too. It tracks companies' performance and disclosure data. If your plan is involved in a hush-hush venture, then you'd better demand the reason why it's hiding its scores. Secrecy is O.K. in some situations, but not when your healthcare is concerned.

- **How does it define an "emergency"**? We're all told that in the case of a suspected heart attack, for example, to call 911 for an ambulance. But what if you get to the hospital only to discover you're really experiencing a bad case of gas from eating a whole Peking duck? Some HMOs won't pay for this false alarm and you're probably stuck with a couple of thousand dollars to ante up. Make sure your coverage exists on what you believe to be an emergency - with terrible symptoms and doesn't depend on the final diagnosis.
- **What hospital(s) are you allowed to choose**? Some HMOs allow any hospital the patient wishes, while other plans mandate a specific one. If this is the situation, then check out their list of hospitals available for your use. I don't think you want to drive a hundred miles each way to use any hospital service.
- **Who is the primary care doctor**? For those of you who don't need this type of doctor for HMO purposes, then hurrah for you! The rest of us must have a doctor from the "allowed list" as well as specialists, dentists, and so forth. The primary care doctor must write a referral for you to see another doctor or to have other medical services, such as a mammography. Hopefully, your own Dr. Feelgood is on the list and you'll have no problem

with referrals. If he or she isn't, however, you better check out the physicians thoroughly before you make your selection. Even Congress is aggressively checking out a more direct access to specialists. Check your state laws since some states require HMOs to have certain procedures about referrals. For example, if you have a chronic condition that necessitates regular visits to your specialist, then, hopefully, your state has a "standing referral." If your plea for this type of referral is denied, then here is another reason for an appeal. Just remember as always to have those documented "ducks-in-a-row." Contact **Doctor Finder**, **Medi-Net**, and the **Association of State Medical Board Executive Directors** as well as your state health department. For help. Another source to investigate is **Healthfinder** (www.healthfinder.org), which is the federal government's site. Among other links, Healthfinder can connect you some of the largest private information providers.

- **What if you're out of the service area or in an extreme emergency you go "out-of-network"?** This may be the most important question of all to pose to prospective HMOs. Emergencies <u>do</u> occur in areas not around your home or the base areas covered by a plan. Perhaps you're on a European vacation and that "gas" problem turned out to be the real thing. Maybe a life-threatening emergency situation exists and you must go "out-of-network" in order to receive care or possibly to save your life. Make sure you know the HMOs policies on this up front; otherwise, the likelihood is greater of *you* being responsible for all medical bills. Congress agrees that we need a standard for emergency coverage instead of depending on what our health providers tell us we *must* do. Scream loud and long (in writing) to your senators and representatives; otherwise, you might find yourself in the following boat.

"Sly Survivor" is one memorable person for a number of reasons. Just over four years ago, he was diagnosed with a rare form of esophageal cancer – one so uncommon that only fifty to hundred cases are diagnosed each year and, worse, only a tiny percentage of these patients survive. Determined (there's that word again) not to be one of the latter statistics, Sly sought advice from oncologists who informed him of one of their number at Memorial Sloan-Kettering who specialized in this particular cancer. Sly didn't take the time to go through the doctors in his HMO; he knew he had to have the best if there was a chance of survival. I'm happy to say that he is alive and well today because of his decision, but that choice left him bereft of thousands of dollars that his HMO refused to pay because he went "out-of-network." The following letter swooped out to (as I termed them in *Shocked, Appalled, and Dismayed!*) the ivory-tower tyrants.

101 Determined Drive
Mt. Vernon, NY 11375
April 3, 2001

Darryl Disgraceful, President/CEO
Diseased Healthcare
119 Madison Avenue, Suite 1309
New York, NY 10003

Dear Mr. Disgraceful:

Because of the appalling lack of concern from anyone within your organization, I turn to you for assistance as one human being to another. I have survived the rarest form of esophageal cancer, one that strikes only 50-100 persons a year, with the survival rate of less than one percent for most of them. Certainly, I am most fortunate to be one of these very few and will have been in remission for three years this June. If, however, I had depended upon the in-network system of treatment mandated by Diseased, in all probability I would have

143

died within the first few months of the cancer's onset. Therein lies my problem and the one for which I turn to you for your personal intervention.

First and foremost, I appreciate Diseased's agreement to allow my oncologist, Dr. Carl Caring, and the attending surgeon, Dr. Perfect Person, both of Memorial Sloan-Kettering Cancer Center (MSK) to continue with their treatment as in-network services (enclosed correspondence regarding this approval). However, the horrific events leading up to this acknowledgment is another matter altogether.

The cancer was first diagnosed in June 1997 at MSK, and Dr. Perfect performed the surgery in late August. It was highly recommended to me by medical personnel that he provide the procedure and subsequent treatment, as he was the best-known thoracic surgeon with a special surgical technique that other colleagues did not practice at that time. Not only has this rare form of cancer been Dr. Perfect's field of expertise for twenty-five years, but also the pathologists at MSK have a much better understanding of the cells' test results. Therefore, MSK was the facility where there was first-hand knowledge of the disease and where I could be treated accordingly. Even after this aggressive approach, Dr. Perfect could not guarantee my having more than a few months of life remaining. Furthermore, after a preliminary investigation into the list of Diseased's in-network physicians, I knew that to have any chance at all, there was no choice but to place my life in the hands of MSK's oncologists. I had no time to shop around the list of your approved physicians, even if they did have the unique knowledge necessary to treat me. My prognosis was poor at best, and all of the doctors with whom I consulted agreed that the care I would receive at MSK could save my life but could not be duplicated at other facilities, nor with other specialists anywhere within my area (i.e. in-network care).

New York law requires all health maintenance organizations to provide access to "non-network" physicians if there are no in-network physicians with the appropriate training and experience to meet the patient's needs. Because I was diagnosed and treated just prior to this law being passed, Diseased now refuses to pay these pre-existing bills. It was even explained to your company that this disease and the subsequent medical care constituted an emergency. Yet, it continued to hide behind a cloak of indifference and defensiveness, stating that its policy on emergencies included "... a sudden unexpected onset of a bodily injury or a serious illness which, if not treated <u>immediately</u>, may result in serious medical complications, loss of life or permanent impairment to bodily function. Mr. Survivor clearly did not present with any of the immediate life threatening situations as described above." (See November 26, 1999 letter from Dr. Daniel Despicable, Medical Director of Diseased Healthcare of New York.) It is certainly evident to me and I am sure to you as well that this statement is nothing short of ludicrous. If the rarest form of cancer exists, one in which only a minute number have a chance for survival, and treatment must be given immediately to attempt to save a life and Dr. Despicable does not believe this to be an "emergency," then perhaps I need to remind him and Diseased that assisted suicide is illegal in the state of New York. Had I waited on in-network physicians and/or the new law to pass, I would certainly be dead.

Dr. Despicable continues with his position that several of Diseased's oncologists had the expertise to initially treat me. I find it quite strange, however, that even though the Assistant Attorney General, Troy Oeschner (letters enclosed), requested a list of these physicians who would have had "the expertise to diagnose and treat metastatic small cell cancer of the esophagus in June 1996" and the number of patients diagnosed with and treated by any in-network doctors, Dr. Despicable did not reveal this information at that time or ever. I also find it interesting that there was no address or telephone number on Dr. Despicable's' letter so that any concerned party could respond to his claims.

MSK physicians all sent letters of necessity to Diseased (copies enclosed). All were ignored. These doctors are as baffled as I as to the <u>true</u> reasons behind the denial of the initial claims.

I realize that your company has an enormous amount of subscribers and I am only one of them. Yet, I have been a loyal policyholder through my employer for four years, and I expect that loyalty to be reciprocated. With HMOs and the many problems concerning them strewn within the media on a daily basis, I would think that something as catastrophic as my ordeal would be dealt with fairly and justly. It is simply unconscionable that I have been treated in such an intolerable and abhorrent manner by certain people within your organization who should thank God every night that <u>they</u> have not endured what I have. Perhaps some people in a position of power have forgotten what it is like to have to depend upon others who should care what happens in a life-and-death situation. I truly hope <u>you</u> are not one of the latter and will investigate this matter thoroughly and promptly.

Thank you, and I look forward to hearing from you by April 30, 2000.

Sincerely,

Sly Survivor
Patient ID # 555509990-9
Group # 4533-98

Enclosures

cc: The Honorable Tommy Thompson, Secretary
United States Department of Health and Human
Services
200 Independence Avenue, SW, Room 615-F
Washington, DC 20201

The Honorable Elaine L Chao, Secretary
United States Department of Labor (covers all health
plans)
200 Constitution Avenue, NW
Washington, DC 20210

The Honorable Charles E. Schumer
United States Senate
Second and C Streets, NE
Washington, DC 20510

The Honorable Hillary Rodham Clinton
United States Senate
Second and C Streets, NE
Washington, DC 20510

Troy Oeschner, Assistant Attorney General
State of New York
Office of the Attorney General's Health Care Bureau
The Capitol
Albany, NY 12224-0341

Neil D. Levin, Superintendent
NYS Department of Insurance

Ellen Phillips

Agency Building 1-ESP
Empire State Plaza
Albany, NY 12257

Physicians Who Care
10615 Perrin Beitel, Suite 201
San Antonio, TX 78217

Cancer Legal Resource Center
919 South Albany Street
Los Angeles, CA 90015-0019

Raul Reprobate, CEO
Diseased Healthcare of America
298 Sickened Street
Chicago, IL 66676

While his HMO did finally agree to pay for treatment following this letter and subsequent investigations, it refused to accept the charges for the initial surgery. My client continues to fight to this day.

So let's say your HMO won't pay for certain medical services, just like Mr. Survivor's, but you do have the time to try to resolve the problem. Insist upon a second opinion outside of the "network." Sometimes a respected medical expert can change the HMO's mind. Additionally, contact agencies that take an interest in citizens being denied appropriate care (remember all my advice about regulatory agencies in *Shocked, Appalled, and Dismayed!*). Tell your HMO that you are filing an immediate complaint with the state Department of Insurance, members of Congress and the U.S. Department of Labor. As for the latter, it has proposed regulations for all employee-sponsored health plans. According to Labor officials, health providers would have to respond to patients' compelling appeals within seventy-two hours. Seek advice from Physicians Who Care and the other organizations mentioned earlier. The key point to remember is to *keep good records*. Document each and every dealing you have with all individuals. This includes all telephone conversations and the names of those with whom you spoke, referrals to other physicians, any comment - good or bad- from your physician, all office visit dates, any medical procedures and prescription medications. All of this documentation is in your favor if you have to do battle with your HMO.

Speaking of battle, the **Patient Advocate Foundation** (PAF) is a really great organization whose mission is to help people who are facing or are involved in a medical crisis. A nationwide network, PAF deals with everything from job discrimination for the ill to helping with getting insurance companies to pay medical bills. Private donors, university medical centers, cancer groups and drug companies fund PAF, and it has a staff of full-time caseworkers and a state-by-state network of resources. This non-profit advocacy/activist organization first tries "nice," then comes out swinging on our behalf if all else fails. In addition to being an ill person's champ, PAF offers lots of free printed material and, sometimes, even financial assistance. Contact the organization via its Web site (www.patientadvocate.org) or call (1-800) 532-5274. It just may be the key to what the doctor ordered.

HMOs demand that even participating physicians feel the squeeze. They're buried under an avalanche of health-care paperwork, which usually results in hiring more secretaries and bookkeepers. Doctors must keep abreast of complicated and changing rules on billing, practice patterns, and referrals. Their waiting rooms become more and more filled as ill people are forced to find a "primary care" physician. The upshot is the loss of precious time that we *deserve* as we sit shivering in a thin gown frantically trying to explain our symptoms before Dr. Disorder rushes out. More and more physicians are even opting out of managed care plans these days. Even though their patients may have to pay more for an office visit than for a standard co-pay the insurance companies allow us, these doctors have found much-needed relief from the constraints and bullying of HMOs. And patients are willing to fork over the fee in order to receive the time, care, and compassion of the past.

Too bad, the insurance industry doesn't give a flying fligger and continues to be a royal pain in the you-know-what; however, its indifference shouldn't stop you from continuing your letter-writing campaign. Make a formal appeal to your HMO as well. If you can get an outside review board to hear your case, there's a good chance the odds may favor you. Many states currently have this process on their books and, indeed, research proves that about half of the cases taken to state appeals boards win. If, for some outside reason this doesn't work, then consider contacting your local newspaper and try to find a reporter interested in publicizing your story. Believe me, your HMO does not wish your predicament to be advertised and might be provoked into paying for the medical service. Be cautious, though. Name-calling and other forms of <u>unprofessional</u> words and behaviors could land a libel suit in your lap. Stand up for your rights - but in the *right* way.

Another little-known secret is when challenged, an HMO will often overturn its own decision. And let's don't forget the most important ammo of all — a lawsuit. We're now able to do so via last year's so-called *federal* Patient's Bill of Rights. Yes, you heard me. If you have the means to do so, then sue the sleazebags for the outcomes of their medical decisions. While experts are of two minds about this avenue and many cynics believe the process will only pile up health care costs to consumers, there have certainly been a rash of state lawsuits won against HMOs that haven't done enough to protect their insurers' health. For instance, the length of acceptable hospital stays (in the HMO's eyes) has shortened so dramatically that it often borders on the insane.

Speaking from personal experience, when I underwent a hysterectomy, I was dismissed within forty-eight hours only to return home with a raging infection. This meant re-admittance to the hospital for another three days! Saving money? I think not. What I should have done and what you must do in a situation such as this is to follow the advice of medical experts. Tell your doctor that you're not well enough to be dismissed. A little known tidbit is that physicians can challenge discharge policies of insurers and hospital administrators. If this doesn't work, tell the person who's trying to discharge you that you'll hold him or her personally responsible if something happens to you as a result of this early discharge – then do it. Unfortunately, under some managed care programs, physicians actually can be *penalized* if their patients' stay in the hospital is longer than the HMO thinks necessary. Scream loudly and long both verbally and in writing for your rightful care, and if this doesn't work, reconsider the lawsuit.

Advocacy groups and even many physician groups think that these managed care corporations *must* be liable; after all, their decisions are the reasons why we receive the care we get (and I use the term "care" rather loosely). If enough of us take this avenue - a lawsuit - assuming our letter-writing campaign doesn't do the trick, then perhaps some of managed care's more arguable programs may be dropped. So if all else fails, then haul the tyrants into court for "negligent denial of care."

There may be light at the end of this very dark tunnel, however. Even though our esteemed members of Congress often appear to enjoy partisan bickering rather than truly helping their constituents, there's still agreement between the parties that health care is in a state of shambles. But even though many states have now passed some sort of a patients' bill-of-rights, President Bush still holds the key to federal law, however, since he specifically wants a cap placed on the amount for which we can sue our insurance companies. (Can anyone say, "Big business"?) More on his plan shortly.

In July 1999 the Senate voted on its version of the "Patient's Bill of Rights." Unfortunately, there were key differences between it and the bill passed by the House in October of that year. Some important contrasts between the two include:

- **Who is covered?** The House covers all Americans with private health insurance, while the Senate provisions apply only to forty-eight million people who are in plans regulated by federal law. They do include greater access to emergency rooms, specialists, and medications, but only for that reduced number of folks.

- **The right to sue your HMO.** The House lifted the federal ban on lawsuits by people in health plans that fall under federal regulation. Injured patients could sue in state or federal court for unlimited damages. The Senate, on the other hand, mandates no new rights to sue.
- **Obstetricians and gynecologists.** Under the House approval, women can see these specialists without approval but can't choose them as primary care doctors. The Senate's Bill is similar but it only applies (again!) to federally regulated plans.
- **Emergency room treatments.** The House requires HMOs to make payment for reasonable services, while the Senate applies only to federally regulated plans. (Anyone getting tired of the term *federally regulated*?) House and Senate negotiators agreed to two sections of the mutual Bill, which are:
- **Appeals.** Both House and Senate require health plans to allow patients to appeal denials to experts outside of the plan.
- **Tax changes.** Both allow self-employed people to deduct the cost of health insurance and create a new deduction for long-term care. Both also allow more medical savings accounts, tax-free, to pay for routine care, if they purchase a high-deductible insurance policy in the event of an emergency.

Now this where President Bush's disagreement with members of Congress comes into play. His ideas, while somewhat shared with the other side of the coin, do disagree on some pertinent points. He believes (as do the rest of us) that patient protections should apply to all Americans. Patients also should have a rapid medical review process for denials of care, and the process should ensure that doctors are allowed to make medical decisions and patients receive care in a timely manner. Litigation is allowed but *only* as a last resort. Mr. Bush's bill wants Federal remedies expanded to hold health plans accountable, including the right to sue in federal court, but, most importantly, the damages cap cannot exceed $750K.

On the other side, however, the <u>bipartisan</u> proposal, sponsored by Senators Teddy Kennedy, John McCain, and John Edwards, proclaim that protections must cover every American with private insurance. It also would establish a speedy independent external review process, if internal review fails; however, patients must exhaust internal and external appeals before going to court. Federal courts would have jurisdiction over cases of injury or death involving administrative decisions, while state courts would hear cases involving medically reviewable decisions. One of the biggest disagreements, as previously mentioned, is the amount of damages. Bush's plan refuses to exceed $750 thousand, while the opposing plan caps damages at $5 million. Humongous difference, huh? As I edit this book, my mother is in the hospital, and we believe that her doctor of a week ago probably made a terrible error during her treatment *and* her insurance company refused to allow more than a single overnight after the operation. If Bush's proposal passes, how long do you think his $750K will last with a person, such as my mother, who could require 24/7 care for the remainder of her life?

If we care about potential life-and-death matters, we should seriously think of casting our vote at <u>www.patientadvocate.org</u>. Certainly, writing immediately to our own members of Congress, both Republican and Democrat, about issues that so extremely affect us is the only way to make our opinions (and their votes) heard one way or the other. Those powerful wealthy folks have all *their* healthcare provided by us, the taxpayer, leaving us the ones who have to worry about health protection for our loved ones and ourselves. The least they can do is defend our rights to have some of the same.

So **please** write the President and all your Congresspeople. Tell them your expectations concerning the passage of a Patient's Bill of Rights and demand that they vote accordingly!

And on an even worse note, regrettably, while states still allow patients' rights to sue doctors and hospitals for medical malpractice in state courts, and we will continue to be able to sue HMOs under certain limited circumstances in federal court, the Supreme Court placed a severe limit on us in June 2000. Our esteemed justices decided that HMOs couldn't be sued in federal court for offering bonuses to doctors who hold down costs *even if patients are harmed* when a physician withholds care because of this. It's too bad consumers can't sue the members of the High Court who voted for the HMOs and against the American patient. (My point of view alone, not that of my publisher!) Since Congress passed the measures that protected managed care in the first place, then it must be up to that august body to pass preventative measures that would now protect consumers.

"Hope Hurt" phoned me one day, full of outrage. Even though her managed care provider had pre-approved a surgical procedure, just before she entered the hospital (and in a great deal of agony, I might add) they pulled the plug, so to speak. Filled with anger and indignation, Hope wished a strong letter to the insurance company.

7277 Angered Avenue
Dallas, TX 77792
February 26, 2001

Terrance Tyrant, President
Hurting Insurance Company
175 Ignore Parkway
Cambridge, MA 02227

Dear Mr. Tyrant:

An appalling travesty of justice has occurred with Hurting Insurance Company in conjunction with an automobile accident in which I was involved, the injuries I sustained, and the subsequent surgery. I am sure you do not condone the types of practices demonstrated to a loyal policy-holder of over eight

years and will immediately investigate this situation. The chronological order of events is as follows:

- On August 6, 2000, I was the passenger in an serious automobile accident. I suffered a broken nose and injuries to my left shoulder, left knee, and lower back. After receiving treatment from emergency room staff, I then contacted Dr. Sam Smelly, who provided the initial nasal consultation and Dr. Kenneth Kind who specializes in neurology. Of course, I also immediately contacted Hurting's claims adjuster, Angela Authorize, who filled out the necessary paperwork and approved it when it became evident that surgery on my fractured nose was essential.

- She confirmed and approved Dr. Oscar Operation's surgical diagnosis on September 20, and surgery was then scheduled for October 16. Three days prior to the operation, Ms. Authorize informed me that Hurting would not pay for this procedure unless a company-approved physician sanctioned it. Because I was in so much pain and was literally unable to breathe, I felt I had no choice but to proceed with the October 16 surgery. Ultimately, of course, I was forced to pay the $8,000 hospital and doctor bills.

- Afterwards, I contacted Hurting Insurance in an attempt to be compensated for this amount. Special investigator Michael Meany harassed me both before and after my surgery with repeated telephone calls and visits. Even after I told him I could not meet with him until my pain subsided, he continued these tactics. Finally, my attorney demanded that he cease badgering me.

- My PIP is for the amount of $10,000, which would pay for my medical expenses. I certainly did not choose to suffer from these injuries, the ensuing surgery, nor from my lost wages while I was unable to work. I am still undergoing physical therapy five days a week as prescribed by Dr. Operation and have had to receive nerve shots: two in my shoulder and one in my lower back. Because Hurting, under the auspices of Ms. Authorize and Mr. Meany, ignored my justified claims after I have paid for a policy to cover just such eventualities, I then hired an attorney to fight this inequity.

I am not sure why the matter of the reimbursement has been such a problem. The only solution on which I can decide is that it is based on gender discrimination. Perhaps Hurting Insurance Company only sells policies that, in my opinion, are useless ones to people not of female gender and if and when the occasion arises for someone such as I to need its services, the claim is denied - even after initial approval.

I truly do not wish to go through the litigation process. However, I have the means and the complete determination to do so. My claim is a fair and just one; not only do I expect reimbursement of the $8,000 surgical expenses, but also lost wages in the amount of $6,500 from the almost four months I have been unable to work (total amount $14,500). I am certain that after careful review of this problem, you will concur with me.

Thank you, and I look forward to hearing from you within the next thirty days.

Sincerely,

Hope Hurt
File # AR99-99999-01
Policy # ATH 223 684444-01

Enclosures

cc: The Honorable Tommy Thompson, Secretary
United States Department of Health and Human
Services
200 Independence Avenue, SW
Washington, DC 20201

Kenneth L. Jost, Assistant Director
Office of Consumer Litigation, Civil Division
United States Department of Justice
624 Ninth Street, NW
Washington, DC 20425

Kim Stokes, Associate Commissioner
Department of Insurance
P.O. Box 149104
Austin, TX 78714-9104

The Honorable Kay Bailey Hutchison
United States Senate
SR-284
First and C Streets, NE
Washington, DC 20510

Lawrence Lawyer, Esquire
Lawsuits & Lawsuits, LLC
Courthouse Office Center
789 Courthouse Road, Suite 146
Dallas, TX 99005

While Ms. Hurt never received the full amount she demanded in his letter, she did carry the torch right on into the courtroom. You betcha, Hope's *piece de la resistance* was a lawsuit and she won the costs of the surgery itself.

"Salinda Sleepless" experienced a horrible problem with her HMO. Now before I state her tale of woe, how many of your spouses snore? You kick, you punch, you try earplugs and pillows, but nothing works. The snorer continues to blast your eardrums, even if you move to a separate bedroom (which can play havoc with your love life!). Before you throttle your mate or seek a divorce attorney, make sure he or she doesn't suffer from sleep apnea. This is a severe medical problem whereby the sleeper actually loses his or her breath and, in documented cases, can even die while asleep. Salinda had been diagnosed with this disorder, but the HMO could have cared less (and probably gleefully thought this would be one less patient for whom to pay medical bills).

218 Trance Avenue, SE
Spokane, WA 99880
April 19, 2001

Steven Sham, CEO
Mistreat Managed Care, Inc.
5908 Dastardly Drive
Suite 1322
Newark, NJ 68421

Dear Mr. Sham:

I am both appalled and outraged by the most recent response I received from Mistreat (see copy of March 24, 2001 letter). It is unconscionable that my health – and possibly my life itself – is in jeopardy because of the qualifications, or possible lack thereof, by the person(s) reviewing my claim. I trust you will immediately and thoroughly investigate this situation.

- **On February 2, 2001, I received an overnight Polysomnography Test (see enclosed results). Dr. Paul Practitioner, who is board-certified in the area of sleep medicine, conducted the test and certified to its outcome. Dr. Practitioner's diagnosis was obstructive sleep apnea.**

- After so many sleepless nights and often awakening gasping for breath, I was certainly relieved to know there was a <u>confirmed</u> medical reason for these debilitating episodes and that I would finally obtain relief and assistance. Dr. Practitioner faxed a Certificate of Medical Necessity to Mistreat on February 15 prescribing a CPAP Rental for me to be used in my home (see enclosed copy). Needless to say, my fears were abated that I would stop breathing during the night and be unable to help myself.

- On February 22, Mistreat's representative, Edith Edict, informed me that the request for home medical equipment was denied (see enclosed). Mistreat's opinion was that my sleep apnea was not severe enough for the company's coverage. I subsequently spoke with Marcel Merciless at Mistreat Case Management on February 23, 24, and 25. He informed me that the reviews for CPAP devices were performed and, subsequently, denied by a physician who was not board-certified in sleep disorders.

- On March 24, as noted previously, the letter arrived from Mistreat stating that my condition did not meet its medical criteria for payment issues for the CAPAP. I am still in a state of shock from this decision as is Dr. Practitioner. Additionally, I am very skeptical of this decision since the original paperwork from Mistreat indicated the determination was made by non-medical staff, much less staff trained in sleep medicine.

It is incomprehensible that someone with no certification in sleep disorders can justifiably deny the prescriptive orders of a sleep medicine specialist with over thirty years experience in this field. Even though I have been well satisfied with my coverage until this egregious situation occurred with Mistreat Managed Care (my employer's benefit plan), the circumstances around this recent incident has been nothing short of horrific. I am certain once you investigate and approve the CPAP device, which

Ellen Phillips

is a medical necessity, I will once again feel secure with my health insurance.

Thank you, and I look forward to hearing from you within the next ten business days.

Sincerely,

Salinda Sleepless

Subscriber ID: 045YOUSUCK66
Group Number: 14521

Enclosures

cc: **The Honorable Tommy Thompson, Secretary**
United States Department
Health and Human Services
200 Independence Avenue, SW
Room 615-F
Washington, DC 20201

The Honorable Elaine L. Chao, Secretary
United States Department of Labor (covers all health
plans)
200 Constitution Avenue, NW
Washington, DC 20210

The Honorable Maria Cantwell
United States Senate
SH -730
Second and C Streets, NE
Washington, DC 20510

The Honorable Patty Murray
United States Senate

SR-11
First and C Streets, NW
Washington, DC 20510

The Honorable Christine O. Gregoire
Attorney General of Washington
Office of the Attorney General
P.O. Box 40100
Olympia, WA 98504-0100

Hope Tuttle, Director
Consumer Resource Center
Office of the Attorney General
900 Fourth Avenue, Suite 2000
Seattle, WA 98164-1012

Deborah Senn, Insurance Commissioner
Insurance Building Capitol Campus
P.O. Box 40255
Olympia, WA 98504-0255

Dr. Paul Practitioner
Helpful Hospital
Sleep Disorders Center
1100 Attention Avenue
Spokane, WA 99990

Edith Edict
Mistreat Managed Care, Inc.
5908 Dastardly Drive
Newark, NJ 68421

Marcel Merciless
Mistreat Managed Care, Inc.
5908 Dastardly Drive
Newark, NJ 68421

[I also cc'ed her employer as the health plan was company-provided]

Salinda soon found much-needed relief when the rental for her apparatus was approved.

This person and others were able to obtain what they wished, and you may as well if you follow this chapter's advice. One important piece of advice, though, about medical insurance: if you know a child who doesn't have any, please beg his or her parent or legal guardian to enroll the small one in the **Children's Health Matters Program**. This program assists with uninsured kids' enrollment in Medicaid so that they have access to quality health care. Go online to www.childrenshealthmatter.org for more information.

I almost fell out when I learned of a special relationship between national consumer advocacy agencies, Consumer Action, the National Consumers League, and a real live HMO – California's PacifiCare Health Systems. My primary intention was to research PacifiCare as one of the outstanding companies for the New Rules of Business highlights. Never did I dream that the company far outshines its competitors and is considered a model by consumer groups.

In 1997, PacifiCare paid the Consumer Action advocacy organization to create, print, and distribute "It's Your Health: How to Get the Most Out of Your HMO," which, truthfully, could be part and parcel of my Web site's Tips of the Week. With mounds of research provided by Yankelovich Partners, the sixteen-page brochure offers great advice on what makes a better program, how to choose and to continue a rapport with primary care physicians, the best methods to resolve disputes, and so forth. (I particularly like the *Checklist for Coverage.*) In other words, readers are told how to best act as their own advocates with regards to their health. Can you believe that an HMO – generally the nasty of all nasties – actually placed its reputation on the line in order to play footsies with consumer groups? I think we can definitely take PacifiCare out of the latter category.

I realize I'm taking up more space than with some other exceptional corporations, but with health care such an issue for all Americans, I think it's important to touch on PacifiCare's philosophy. Its involvement with consumers stems, in large part, from its corporate values and a practical decision based upon its business model. As one of the nation's first, and now largest Medicare HMOs, the company realized it had to effectively communicate with its clients/patients. PacifiCare believes that the better their members understand the company's "product," the more satisfied the members will be with it. To this end, the HMO uses member education and outreach campaigns, simplified enrollment materials, and town hall meetings where management and members review concerns and issues affecting the health plan. PacifiCare went one step farther, however. Its commissioned research in 1997 found, among other concerns, that just fourteen percent of Americans spent only one hour reviewing their enrollment materials and believed that they understood their benefits. So what happens to the other eighty-six percent? These folks became the focus for subsequent research and, finally, the "It's Your Health" brochure. As a matter of fact, it became so successful that PacifiCare originated a second brochure, printed in 1998 and entitled, "It's Your Choice: Are Medicare HMOs Right for You?" In addition to Consumer Action, the Gray Panthers and the National Consumers League involved themselves in this venture. And for those folks who aren't quite as literate in the English language, the booklets are also available in Chinese, Korean, Spanish, and Vietnamese.

Even as the economy of 2001 took a dive and PacifiCare, among others, was forced to drop many of its Medicare clients, the company continued to maintain consumer support and rapport, as well as to make long-range plans to help its insured. One of its plans entails a major health initiative strictly for women. The big five-year plan calls for PacifiCare to double the size of its commercial health plan benefits, expand big-time its pharmacy benefit management operations, and the company will also offer many new services to seniors. Which of its members would say "no" to housekeeping assistance and financial planning? I surely wouldn't.

PacifiCare prides itself on its continual collaboration with physicians, patients, special interest groups, employees, pharmaceutical industries' representatives with regards to issues surrounding drug affordability and effectiveness, mental illness and managed care and the chronically ill. All of these activities allow the company to dialogue with important parties that will stay attuned to PacifiCare's consumer interests and sensitivities. According to Ben Singer, Corporate Public Relations Vice President: *"It's given us a legitimate bridge to cross with consumers and special interest groups during a time when many feel a gap has widened. We have a level of credibility that is tangible and people know we will listen to them. As an organization, that's benefited us and allowed us to question what we do and how we do it, and ultimately seek a better way in running our business."*

And believe you me, after reading the tons of information that Mr. Singer was kind enough to send me, I lead the cheerleading advocacy squad that screams accolades for PacifiCare.

Dentists

According to the American Dental Association, the *average* dentist makes in excess of $100,000 yearly. But even as other medical costs continue to rise, so do those of the folks in this profession and, all too often, the consumer ends up once again swinging from the noose of the financial rope. From overcharging and sometimes even overtreating, dentists and dental specialists are making, in many instances, a grand profit off our aching teeth and mouths. And there are now sophisticated procedures that promise to enhance our looks that really cost a pretty penny if we're willing to foot the expense, such as laser whitening (which the American Dental Association is reluctant to sanction as an effective treatment).

So what do we do to make certain we have reputable fingers in our mouths?

- **Explain expectations**. The dentist himself or herself upon consultation should always ask pertinent questions with regard to teeth problems, including taking your health history and medications currently prescribed. Then tell this person what <u>you</u> want in a dentist and be specific. Are you interested in tooth-colored fillings and bonding? Is the throbbing pain in that left molar the beginnings of an abscess, which will surely result in a more expensive and complicated procedure? What are routine costs? Again, it's your money and your mouth - put them both to work where it does you the most good.

- **How often are x-rays taken?** While x-rays should only be repeated every two to three years, some dentists like to redo them on a more frequent basis. Unless you're subject to a lot of tooth decay, this is simply an unnecessary and medically unsound expenditure. Check to see if the dentist provides digital radiography, a replacement for the more traditional x-ray. By placing a small plastic sensor in the patient's mouth, when connected to a computer, these images reduce our radiation exposure by close to 90%!

- **Is the dentist a general practitioner or will you need a specialist?** My own problems are such that I go to my own dentist and to the periodontist every six months, for a total of four visits a year. It's worth the extra expense to me, but you may feel differently. Be sure, though, to see that whoever does the work checks for potentially suspicions conditions, such as oral cancer and gum disease, and be wary of a dentist who balks at second opinions over expensive proceedings like crowns or dental surgery.

- **Is tooth cleaning part of your regular check-ups?** This is most important and, if not performed by the dentist, should be done by a licensed and trained dental hygienist.

In order to avoid complaints about Dr. Fingers, be sure to ask specialists and friends whom they recommend, just as you did with physicians. In the event you still need to write a complaint letter later on, then contact your state dental association. These nice people will either refer you to a local dental society or handle the review themselves – free. If you do encounter a "professional" whose dental skills equal those of Attila the Hun, then perhaps a letter such as the following one might do the trick.

8907 Upset Avenue
Montgomery, AL 36103
October 23, 2001

John Anderson, D.M.D., President
Alabama Dental Association
836 Washington Avenue
Montgomery, AL 36104

Dear Dr. Anderson:

An appalling situation recently occurred with one of your members, Dr. Sarah Snaggled, Tooth & Snaggled Denistry, 1431 Southern Bypass in Montgomery. I am certain that upon reading of this matter, you will personally investigate on the behalf of the Alabama Dental Association.

- **On October 16, 2001 I took my daughter, Terry Toothache, to Dr. Snaggled for an examination. As this was our first visit to this office, I had ensured that this dentist was on your roster of members. Unfortunately, what transpired makes me wonder what the qualifications for membership actually are.**
- **Terri is just five years old and the area around one of her baby teeth was infected. Imagine my horror when Dr. Snaggled recommended pulling the inflamed tooth as well as the ones on either side, for**

a cost of $699. When I objected, this dentist terrified my already-frightened daughter with the remark, "If we don't pull these teeth today, then we'll have to pull *all* the top ones." (This conversation was in the presence of the dental assistant, Sally Shocked.) Needless to say, my daughter and I immediately left Dr. Snaggled's office never to return.

While Terri should have received regularly scheduled exams from a pediatric dentist who would then be apprised of any subsequent problems, even I know that Dr. Snaggled's diagnosis was a bizarre one. If she earns her living by terrifying children and their parents into unnecessary procedures, then she must be stopped from these practices.

I trust the Dental Association will censure Dr. Snaggled, and I look forward to hearing from you with a verification of such by November 30, 2001.

Thank you.

Sincerely,

Tesa Toothache

By following the advice in "Is There a Doctor in the House?", you'll take all aspects of your health into your own hands and, by doing so, you'll become even healthier and happier in the future.

Helpful Agencies and Services

Call the **American Dental Society** at (312) 440-2500 to find out the address and telephone number of your state association.

The **American Medical Association's Physician Select** Website (www.ama-assn.org) provides detailed information on over 650,000 doctors.

Contact the **American Osteopathic Association** at (800) 621-1773 for certification status.

Visit the Web page of the **Association of State Medical Board Directors** (www.docboard.org) for information on disciplinary action taken against doctors and to obtain addresses and telephone numbers for most state boards.

Check the **Best Doctors in America** books and order from (888) 362-8677.

Children's Health Matters program helps uninsured kids with enrollment in Medicaid. Visit CHM's site at www.childrenshealthmatters.org.

Log on to **Doctor Finder** at www.ama-assn.org, which cites information about education and specialties.

Investigate **HealthFinder** (www.healthfinder.org) to provide information on large private health providers.

"It's Your Health" brochures may be ordered from Consumer Action at (800)-929-1606 or by sending an SASE ($.55 and legal-sized) to Consumer Action-HMO, 116 Montgomery Street, Suite 233, San Francisco, CA 94105.

Ellen Phillips

The **Joint Commission on Accreditation of Healthcare Organizations (JCAHO)** sends out reports on commended hospitals. Call (630) 792-5800 or write to 1 Renaissance Boulevard, Oakbrook Terrace, IL 60181.

Write the **Medical Information Bureau**, P.O. Box 105, Essex Station, Boston, MA 02112 or call (617) 426-3660 to find out where your medical history is stored and who has had access to it.

Call **Medi-Net** at (800) 972-6334 to access information about specific physicians.

For questions regarding your pharmacist or pharmacy, log on line to www.nabp.net and "speak" with someone at the **National Association of Boards of Pharmacists**.

Obtain an Accreditation Status List on health plans by calling the **National Committee for Quality Assurance** at (888) 275-7585. To receive the free brochure *Choosing Quality: Finding the Health Plan That's Right for You* call (800) 839-6487. NCQA's Web address is http://www.ncqa.org

The **Patient Advocate Foundation** assists consumers after HMOs refuse to pay for care, among other problems. Contact this group online at www.patientadvocate.org or by calling (1-800) 532-5274.

Contact **Physicians Who Care** at (800) 800-5154 for advice on grievance procedures and for an advocate to help with appeals to HMOs.

Order *The Best Doctors in America* books by calling (888) 362-8677.

www.fda.gov provides accurate medical information, especially pertaining to prescription drugs and medical devices.

Chapter 8

Home Sweet Home

"Everybody wants to build, and nobody wants to do maintenance."
- Kurt Vonnegut

Novelist Kurt Vonnegut's quote is probably more true today in connection with the "home" industry than at any other period in history. We take risks when we trust others at their word regarding their products or services because we want to believe them. All too often, however, to our *shock* we must suffer the consequences.

The arena of such businesses is not limited to "building" as the title implies. It can also encompass other types as well, such as mortgage lending corporations, brokers, and settlement agencies. So heads up if you're planning to re-finance your home, to remodel or simply to make some much-needed repairs, to build a new home, to have your furniture moved, or perhaps to buy that vacation timeshare you've always envisioned owning.

Mortgages

Before you (don't) look and leap, you'd better find out the entire life history of your mortgage broker and how and who pays this person. Your best choice is the broker who not only agrees to represent you (as will literally hundreds of others if your credit is good) but also one who can deliver the best rates and terms. It's this person's job to scout around to discover what's best for *you.* And what's best for you may depend upon what's best for the company's employees.

Providian Financial maintains its happy staff in a variety of ways, such as stock options, and profit sharing abounds for all employees. On the one hand, while Providian doesn't provide paid leave for childbirth, it does make available onsite day care. Dependent care is matched up to $1,000 a year, and child and elder care referrals are available. Because looking to our future (make that *old age*), is more imperative than ever these days, it's nice to know that Providian's 401K eligibility begins after only 2.5 months on the job with available stock options.

An even better program is that of the Fannie Mae Corporation. Employees pay zippo for the medical plan and the company subsidizes dependents' coverage costs. There's onsite childcare, paid leave for mothers <u>and</u> fathers, and up to $6,000 reimbursement for adoption expenses. Fannie Mae allows for flexible work options, including teleworking (at home) and flex-time. There's an employee-assisted housing program and a forgivable loan if the money is used for the purchase of a primary residence. One of the perks that I particularly like as a Baby Boomer and habitually worrying about my elderly mother is that Fannie Mae provides full-time elder care consultants. I could point out even more examples of why Fannie Mae personnel sing and smile during work hours, but I'll leave the rest to your imagination.

So let's say the first person you'll probably talk with is a real estate agent (if buying a new home) or a broker as previously mentioned. Whether you're getting a loan through Fannie Mae, Providian, or another loan company, be very careful when buying a home to ensure that the agent serves your interests as the buyer. It's also safe to assume that if the same agent is acting for you <u>and</u> the seller, the agent will concentrate on obtaining a higher sale price since this means money in his or her pocket but less in yours. Shop around, get recommendations from friends and colleagues, and find an individual who'll represent only *you*. Here are a couple of hints to remember before you settle:

- **Ask what this person will do and for what fee**. Make sure this is up-front information so you don't get stuck later on with any hidden agenda. For instance, some brokers use transaction or document fees for as much as $150 in order to offset the cost of paperwork. Find a company that doesn't charge this fee or ask to have it deleted from the contract.
- **Compare costs and services with what's recommended**. Even though the broker or real

estate agent usually recommends a lender, title company or settlement attorney, you don't have to accept any of this bunch sight unseen. Compare costs. They could be substantial.

- **Shop around for a no-cost mortgage**. These mortgages can be a great deal if you don't have enough money for closing costs. You'll pay no points or closing costs and they'll be added to the loan balance. There are two schools of thought to this advice. One is that the buyer comes out ahead initially since these fees don't add a bunch of moolah to your monthly payments. However, on the other hand, if you've got a thirty-year loan and you're not planning to move anytime soon, these additional costs will definitely be expensive over the long haul. One source to aid you is the **Federal Reserve Board**. While we normally think of the FED as stocks and bonds-oriented, it provides information about the **Truth in Lending Act and the Equal Credit Opportunity Act**. Contact the agency at Twentieth Street and Constitution Avenue, NW, Washington, DC 20551 (http://www.bog.frb.fed.us).

- **Complain loud and long**. The **Real Estate Settlement Procedures Act (RESPA)** should protect you from unfair or unethical practices. If your complaint doesn't work with the broker, lender, settlement agent, and so forth, then write to RESPA at the **Office of Fair Housing and Equal Opportunity, U.S. Department of Housing and Urban Development**, 451 Seventh Street, SW, Washington, DC 20410. You may also contact the office (and maybe even receive instant information for your own specific complaint) at http://www.hud.gov.

"Lenore Lynchu" followed much of the advised procedure but when it came time for settlement, she found her husband and herself frustrated with this particular can of worms. Even

Ellen Phillips

though the sum of money was minute, to Lenore the letter was a matter of principle.

> 90073 Frustrated Street
> Columbia, MO 65211
> February 27, 2001

Bob Biggest, President
Idiot Mortgage Corporation
555 Idiotic Parkway, Suite 322
Dallas, TX 77761

Dear Mr. Biggest:

I finally find myself in the position to write of an appalling circumstance that occurred with your personnel at Idiot, 1000 Gimme Street, Suite 248, Columbia, Missouri. I trust you will immediately investigate this matter so that I may then receive a letter of explanation about the fiasco.

- **We were originally scheduled to close on our re-finance on November 10, 2000. This loan was approved through Refinance Mortgage Company with settlement taking place at Ye Old Settlement and Title Services in Columbia (with the lock expiration of November 18). Because my husband was to be out of town, he signed a Power of Attorney on November 9. I went to Ye Old on November 10 only to discover that the loan officer, Susan Schedule had failed to schedule for closing with Idiot personnel.**
- **I traveled again to Ye Old for the second scheduled closing on November 13. When I arrived, Ms. Schedule informed me that Idiot had called to say that my broker, Angela Agent, had "left something out of the paperwork." I knew this was incorrect, as Ms. Agent**

would certainly have called me that day so as not to make a trip to Ye Old. I called Idiot from Ye Old's office, left a message to have someone call me immediately within thirty minutes, which allowed me the time to return home. That request was blatantly ignored. In fact, I later learned that <u>Idiot</u> was at fault because its personnel deliberately delayed the closing due to its volume and more time available to close because of the lock extension negotiated by Ms. Agent. (See bullet #4.)

- I immediately contacted Ms. Agent who assured me that the message to Ms. Schedule was an error; her processor called Idiot and spoke with Lindy Loony who informed her that all the paperwork was, indeed, intact. Obviously, the person with whom Ms. Schedule spoke on that date made an inexcusable mistake, resulting in a waste of my time, my husband's trip to sign the Power of Attorney, and the forfeiture of the $50 we paid for this. While the lock was then extended for thirteen days, this meant an additional 1/8 percent of the loan amount equaling $243.75 which Ms. Agent paid from her own pocket and, additionally, by the end of the ordeal she also failed to make her commission.

- On November 17, Ms. Agent spoke with David Dummy in Idiot's Columbia's marketing department. His only response to her queries was to place her on hold to run back and forth to speak with the manager, Daniel Dishonorable. When Ms. Agent finally became irritated enough to demand to speak directly with Mr. Dishonorable, she was placed on hold for <u>two hours</u>. When she realized he had no intention of talking to her, Ms. Agent faxed him a message (copy enclosed), which he totally ignored. This was her attempt to extend the lock at Idiot's expense because of its failure to <u>twice</u> close on time and its error in not waiving the three-day recession period at Idiot's expense. Therefore, Ms. Agent extended the lock at 1/8 % at her own expense. When I called Idiot myself, I was curtly informed that it was against "policy" to discuss the situation with me and the reasons why this company continued to make these mistakes. Needless to say, I was infuriated at what I perceived to be a total lack of assistance and professionalism.

- Once again, the closing date was extended - this time to November 24. My husband and I finally closed on that date (loan # 1333338). I might add, too, that the attorney, Lawrence Lawyer, charged us an additional and erroneous 25 % of the closing costs, $487.50 (I assume at Idiot's behest). Ms. Agent and Refinance Mortgage did not realize we had been overcharged until she received the paperwork and the check on December 4. Refinance then refunded this sum to us.

This entire matter, while now resolved, was an egregious situation from start to finish. Not only did Ms. Agent forfeit her commission and have to pay personal out-of-pocket expenses, my time was squandered going back and forth to Ye Old Settlement Company, as well as calling Idiot only to encounter rudeness and ineptness. I did have detailed notes with times, dates, and persons with whom I spoke but, unfortunately, these have been misplaced or thrown away by my cleaning service. However, this entire process makes me realize anew just how many companies need a course in customer relations and proficiency.

Not only do I trust you will investigate this affair promptly and thoroughly, I expect a letter of explanation as well as reimbursement for the $50 paid to Ye Old for the Power of Attorney. After all, it was Idiot's mistake that the closing did not occur as planned; hence, the wasted money.

Thank you, and I look forward to hearing from you by no later than March 16, 2001.

Sincerely,

Lenore Lynchu

Enclosure

cc: Stephen Brobeck, Executive Director
Consumer Federation of America
1424 Sixteenth Street, NW, Suite 604
Washington, DC 20036

Mortgage Bankers Association of America
Consumer Affairs
1125 Fifteenth Street, NW, 7th Floor
Washington, DC 20005

Jeremiah W. Nixon, Attorney General
Office of the Attorney General
Supreme Court Building
P.O. Box 899
Jefferson City, MO 65102

Doug Ommen, Chief Counsel
Consumer Protection and
Trade Offense Division
P.O. Box 65102
Jefferson City, MO 65102

Lawrence Lawyer, Esquire
Ye Old Settlement & Title Services, Inc.
979 Barrister Boulevard
Columbia, MO 65223

Daniel Dishonorable, Manager
Idiot Mortgage Corporation
1000 Gimme Street, Suite 248
Columbia, MO 65212

Adam Aboveboard, President
Refinance Mortgage Company
144 Consumer Court, Suite 100
Columbia, MO 65212

Carla Clever, President Central Region
Refinance Mortgage Company
900 Realtor Road, Suite 1900
Columbus, OH 43215

Angela Agent
Refinance Mortgage Company
144 Consumer Court, Suite 100
Columbia, MO 65222

Mrs. Outraged was reimbursed her $50 and "Idiot's" manager probably received a new and not-so-nice addition to his personnel file.

- **Carefully eyeball the contract, especially if you're building a home from the ground up**. Too many folks are screwed when they *think* they're getting items as part of the contract, yet when the home is built or otherwise becomes their property they discover differently and sometimes with little recourse. Furthermore, when you buy a home from an existing owner, make sure that the homeowner allows inspection or provides disclosures. If not, the seller may be hiding serious problems so your best bet is to hit the road. Along these same lines, if the owner wants to sell the house "as is," this, too, is a danger sign since it means the seller won't fix anything that's wrong. (Okay, maybe you don't mind having an upstairs leaky toilet that drips down the walls of your three-story house and leaves smelly and unsightly gunk in its path.)

Let's take the case of Scott Runkles. He and his wife had saved for years to build the home of their dreams. What they didn't realize, though, is that the dream would become their worse nightmare. The resulting letter is an abbreviated form because *much* more was wrong with the "dream house."

2030 Duped Drive
Annapolis, MD 21012
February 26, 2001

Carl Callous, Regional President
Ruined Homes, Inc.
1098 Difficult Drive, Suite 233
Baltimore, MD 21099

Dear Mr. Callous:

As president of Ruined Homes, only you can assist us with the shocking and horrific problems we have recently experienced with the purchase of our new Ruined home at River View Estates in Annapolis. Therefore, I must turn to you for your immediate and personal intervention.

- In April 2000 we were the very first contract on a new home to be constructed in River View. Unfortunately, because of an unforeseen dilemma in September, we were forced to either cancel our contract or choose another lot in the development. The sales representative, Sam Shyster, informed us of a "wonderful" lot that had just become available. He assured us that lot #18 was a much better one and, in addition, much larger than the ¼ acre lot #29 that we had originally contracted. An extra lot premium of $5000, added to the $3000 premium already paid for #29, certainly seemed indicative of a larger "better" lot. However, we were still somewhat skeptical; we only could visually observe a substantial area where several homes were to be constructed, and there were no corner markers to indicate the boundaries of lot #18.
- After sharing our concerns with Mr. Shyster, we were assured that there were <u>no</u> home sites in River View under ¼ acre. We were not only impressed with what we believed to be the reputation of Ruined Homes, but also with Mr. Shyster's informative and convincingly knowledgeable input. At the date of signing the addendum for the lot transfer (see enclosed copy), we also requested a site map or plot plan and a contour map of #18. This was promised to us in "a couple of days."
- Two weeks later, after receiving nothing, we again asked for the plot and contour map; we received an apology and a further (false) assurance that the information was immediately forthcoming. This scenario continued to repeat itself until December, *two*

months later. Because of our frustration with what we felt to be Mr. Shyster's inefficient and misinformed role as your liaison, we then contacted the Ruined Homes Regional Office (see enclosed copy of letter) and finally received the information, almost three months after signing the addendum for lot transfer.

- We were never offered any pre-construction lot "walk-through" to explain the property boundaries. The Ruined Homes Homebuyers Guide states, "If you have any questions, the first place to start is your sales representative. If he or she does not know the answer, your question will be directed to the appropriate Ruined team member." This is what we did by discussing our concerns with Mr. Shyster. Most certainly, if he was unsure about <u>any</u> of the property details, he should have directed the questions to a knowledgeable source from Ruined. This did not prove to be the case in any fashion whatsoever.

- Imagine our horror when we subsequently discovered that our lot was <u>*not*</u> the promised at least ¼ acre, much less the assured larger one. In fact, our "bigger better" lot, which carried a substantial $8000 premium is a mere 1/6 acre, <u>*only 198 square feet over the county minimum*</u>. We believed this was surely an error and discussed our shock and anger with Mr. Shyster during the pre-construction meeting on February 3, 1999. All we received was his apology if we thought the property had been misrepresented. Additionally, we also discovered during this "pre-construction" meeting that the foundation had already been constructed <u>prior</u> to the meeting.

- After personally contacting Anne Arundel County to verify the plot details, we were further appalled to learn of an almost ten foot county easement located in the back of our property. This easement will prevent us from constructing a fenced yard to ensure the safety of our small children. Ruined <u>never</u> communicated any information at all with regards to an easement and, in fact, it is not even specified on the plot plan supplied by Ruined.

We are in a state of disbelief and outrage over this egregious situation. Our current home has been purchased, and we are forced to settle on this Ruined home that was, in our opinion, deliberately misrepresented from the very beginning. Our eagerly awaited dream house has evolved into a terrible nightmare, solely because of the actions of your employee. Our impression of Ruined Homes has understandably been terribly marred, and we would not wish for any of our family, friends, or colleagues to experience any similar experience with Ruined Homes.

To attempt some resolution, we will consider a significant decrease in the contract price as well as an additional credit towards the contract price. We will also consider credit towards closing costs in the amount of the increased lot premium we paid for our "bigger better" lot – the one that does not even allow space for a small, fenced back yard. I am confident that you will remedy this matter by March 9, 2001.

Thank you.

Sincerely,

Scott L. Runkles

Enclosures

cc: The Honorable Donald Evans, Secretary
United States Department of Commerce
Fifteenth Street and Constitution Avenue, NW
Washington, DC 20230

Howard Beales, Director
Office of Consumer Protection
Federal Trade Commission
Pennsylvania Avenue and Sixth Street, NW
Washington, DC 20580

The Honorable J. Joseph Curran, Jr.
Attorney General of Maryland
Office of the Attorney General
200 St. Paul Place
Baltimore, MD 21202

Steven B. Larsen, Commissioner
Insurance Administration
525 St. Paul Place
Baltimore, MD 21202

Robert Hergenroeder, Jr., Commissioner
Bureau of Financial Regulations
500 North Calvert Street
Baltimore, MD 21202

The Honorable Robert Butterworth
Attorney General of Florida
Office of the Attorney General
The Capitol PL 01
Tallahassee, FL 32399

National Advertising Division
Council of Better Business Bureaus, Inc.
845 Third Avenue
New York, NY 10022

Thomas Downs, Director
National Association of Home Builders
Consumer Affairs Division
1201 Fifteenth Street, NW

Washington, DC 20005

Ralph Repugnant, CEO
Ruined Homes, Inc.
8088 Builders Boulevard, Suite 300
Miami, FL 33130

David Dimwit, Regional Manager
Ruined Homes, Inc.
1234 Devious Drive, Suite 666
Severna Park, MD 21010

Michael Meany, Production Manager
Ruined Homes, Inc.
1234 Devious Drive, Suite 666
Severna Park, MD 21010

Nathan Noodlehead, Sales Manager
Ruined Homes, Inc.
1234 Devious Drive, Suite 666
Severna Park, MD 21010

Sam Shyster, Sales Representative
Ruined Homes, Inc.
1234 Devious Drive, Suite 666
Severna Park, MD 21010

While Mr. and Mrs. Runkles' letter did result in a credit to apply towards closing, once they moved into their "dream home," it became evident that the lies about the acreage and so forth were just the bottom layer of a twelve-layer cake from "Ruined Homes" — the company that *ruined* theirs. I thought it particularly odd, too, (actually, I loved it!) that soon after all the investigations that developed after agencies received this letter, "Ruined" Homes moved out of the state of Maryland for good.

Remodeling

Lordy, what a nightmare! Having been through the process twice (and each time making a promise it'll be the last one), I've definitely learned some valuable lessons that I'll pass on, as well as what experts have to say. Contractors are the first issue that comes to mind. One third of all American homeowners spent over $180 *billion* on renovations in 2000. (The figures for 2001 aren't completed by publication.) So with this colossal figure in mind, whether you're building that dream house like Mr. and Mrs. Runkles, making repairs that I'll discuss later on in the chapter, or remodeling your existing home, the *contractor* you select is the prime ingredient to a smooth(er) process. It's your right to be assured that your man or woman is a quality professional who delivers on promises.

- **Get a referral**. While this may sound like really stupid advice that anyone with a grain of sense should know, there are lots of folks who leap first and are appalled later. While the majority of builders are well qualified, there are fly-by-night operators just waiting to pounce on naïve homeowners. In fact, even the ones who have been around for a long while need to be checked out. (Being bonded and insured or having the proper license is no more important than discovering if past customers would use this contractor's services in the future – and why not.) Don't just stop with asking friends and colleagues, although they're a great source of information having been there themselves, but also inquire of companies or suppliers as to whom they would recommend. Once you've narrowed the list, then ask the contractors for names of at least three references you can contact and then head on down to inspect those homes. Rely on your own eyeballs, please. A super little eight-page brochure to help you in your search can be obtained by writing **The National Association of Home Builders, 1201 Fifteenth Street, NW, Washington, DC 20005-2800, Attn: Member Service Center**. Be sure to include a stamped, self-addressed envelope.

- **Check that the contractor is licensed and insured.** This may sound like silly advice as well, but it'll be to your financial sorrow if something goes wrong with the job or if one of the workers falls down a just-dug hole and breaks his neck. Don't take the big guy's word, either. Get the proof in writing and then call to make sure he's telling the truth *before* you end up in court. Also, don't dare just hire the person who throws in the lowest bid. This is usually a sign that he or she uses inferior materials or that the "contractor" isn't subcontracting out the work to licensed professionals — a plumber, for example (remember that leaky toilet?). And horror of horrors, numerous states have no licensing or registration requirements at all. The Remodelors Council of the National Association of Home Builders tells us that in many states all one has to do is pay a fee for a business license. No qualifications, no regulations, nothing.
- Call the **Better Business Bureau** in the state where the contractor is located to see if any complaints are on file. Then call the **State Licensing Board** to verify that the contractor's license is current and no action is pending against the company.
- **Get a detailed written estimate of the work you want done**. These folks should tell you if, when, and why prices might change, what's really required for this job, ensure their work is to code, and a whole lot more. The estimate should also include such items as the following: the contractor's name, address, and phone number; his license number; and the beginning and completion dates of all work. Be sure to check out warranties, guarantees, and assurances, including verbal ones; quantities and qualities of all materials; brand names, model numbers and specifications of all materials. Certainly don't forget to find out when final payment is due. We often tend to overlook little items that may just become big headaches later on if we're not careful. For instance, if you're spending the money for a new roof, then specify the kind, the brand, the color, and anything else you can think of. Don't leave anything to chance.

- **Expect quality work**. Too bad that many homeowners don't oversee the work as they should. While our expectations are obvious, the reality can sometimes be very different. How about a door that hangs crooked or a toilet that doesn't properly flush? Keep a careful eye on developments and lasso those suckers in if things aren't going as you anticipated or as they should. Along this same line is to avoid intimidation. Sure, the contractor wants you to think he or she is the greatest invention since ice cream, but it's *your* money he's spending. Keep tabs on costs and materials, how current subcontractors' licenses are, and so forth. You may have to periodically remind the contractor who the boss really is - - you!
- **Make your down payment as small as possible**. The best rule of thumb is thirty percent down upon signing the contract for major renovations, another third when the job starts, and the final payment when it's completed to your satisfaction. Once the balance is paid, insist that the contractor give you a letter stating that you've paid in full. This statement protects you if the contractor doesn't pay his or her subcontractors or suppliers. Generally, you can call on the contractor for a year following completion of the job to return and fix anything that goes wrong. Get this in writing, too; otherwise, you may find yourself contacting the Better Business Bureau and the State Licensing Board after all – this time for your own complaint.

And how can you be sure your contractor is getting materials that will endure for the lifetime of your house? Rest assured everything's under control if purchases come from Lowe's Companies, Inc. Even though this company is humongous and growing by leaps and bounds, employees still enjoy a family-type atmosphere. Why, even those on the lowest rung of the staff ladder are assured that folks as high up as Chairman Robert Tillman would stop to shake their hands when visiting the stores.

Entry-level employees who receive a card listing the seven steps needed to become a customer service manager know it will take them less than four years to complete the steps. (And during this time their salaries will double!) Happy personnel also know that Lowe's buys back its own stock and redistributes it into employee accounts. These ESOP accounts either can be sold back to the company upon the individual's retirement or the person can keep it. I've heard lots of stories about the hundreds of thousands of dollars earned by this stock plan by boo-coos of Lowe's employees over the years. Is there any wonder that Lowe's folks do their darndest to make us happy consumers? (In fact, an executive with the Metropolitan Washington Better Business Bureau recently told me that, in his opinion, Lowe's is the very best customer relations company around.)

An additional trap to avoid when you decide to remodel your home is being ripped off by one of the workers. When we've carefully done our homework and are satisfied that we've got the best man or woman for the job, vigilance is still an important guide. Don't leave money lying around; lock up your jewelry; hide Grandma's sterling silver flatware. If you're still too trusting and valuable items disappear, the first recourse is to call your insurance agent. The agent's investigators will contact the police and talk with the contractor. If this person is bonded and insured (and I trust you've made sure of that long before now), then your insurance company will deal with the contractor's insurance company.

Too bad "Jackie Jewels" didn't know what to do when she found herself in this situation. Yes, she followed all the rules regarding her contractor who was in the process of adding on a kitchen and a sunroom. And yes, she was careful to hide anything that might scream out "Take me! Take me!" to a potentially dishonest worker, except for the morning she rushed off to work so fast that she forgot to put on her emerald drop necklace. There it lay on the bathroom counter, but not for long. When Jackie realized her mistake, she raced back home only to discover the necklace had gone bye-bye. She was so upset (as she should have been) that she and her contractor got in a screaming match over his thieving throng of workers. While she finally did contact her insurance company, she wanted a letter to the builder and that's where I came in.

787 Hysterical Hideaway
Gretna, LA 70055
June 23, 2001

Mike Mastermind
Masterful Designs Company
79 Builders Boulevard
Gretna, LA 70054

Dear Mr. Mastermind:

While I do regret my outburst at you when I discovered my missing necklace last week, I still am appalled at the incident itself. When we contracted for you to build my addition, I assumed that you employed dependable and honest people to work at my home. Obviously, I was in error.

While I will receive compensation from your insurance company for the loss of the necklace, the sum is depreciated. The necklace's last appraisal (copy enclosed) was $2200; however, I am promised only $850 from Builders' Liability Insurance Corporation.

I trust you agree to either pay the difference of $1350 or to deduct this amount from the $15,000 balance of what I owe to you. I look forward to your decision by the end of this week.

Thank you.

Sincerely

Jackie Jewels

Enclosure

cc: Thomas Downs, Director
National Association of Home Builders
1201 Fifteenth Street, NW
Washington, DC 20005-2800

Peter Payer, President
Builders' Liability Insurance of America
7099 Negligent Lane
Baton Rouge, LA 78864

Jackie received a check by week's end.

Home Repairs

Your deck has collapsed. The roof is crumbling. The wallpaper is stuck and hell or high water won't get it unglued. All of us need repairs to the homestead on occasion. Many of the same rules apply, regardless of whether we're utilizing the services of a contractor or a handyman. Some of my sources say to use a handyman if the project costs less than $10,000. If it were I, though, for that amount of money I'd find someone a bit more skilled. Regardless of the amount of the repair, we don't have to pay as much down as when we're dealing with a contractor. Ten to twenty percent of the total is a suggested sum. And if we're working with a company, such as an electrical or plumbing service, usually the charge comes after the problem is fixed. But beware. Handymen-for-Hire or, as we know them around my parts, *The Street Urchins*, are a dime a dozen and most aren't worth the additional nine cents. These are the people who knock on your door and sing you their version of "Let's Make a Deal," such as *Only $99.95 to re-asphalt your driveway*. Because you have noticed a few pits and uneven parts and the price sounds right, you carefully watch the process before handing over the money. (After all, you are one smart cookie, aren't you?) But before you have time to slap your back in self-congratulation, the nice, new, smooth driveway looks pretty awful. Flushed that $100 bucks down the 'ole tube, didn't you? What you didn't foresee as you oversaw was that these *Urchins* used cheap and inferior materials and then moved on to another neighborhood to find another sucker. Hey, I've been a prime sucker myself a time or two.

Maybe you're a wiser judge of character and you hire a capable person for that repair - the gasping air conditioner, for example. He comes, he fixes (sort of) and leaves with your money in hand. Too bad his "repair" work leaves with him. But he comes back when you call him, ready to do the job again. Doesn't he need a refresher course by this time?

While your repair problems might not be as specifically severe as "Wanda Wheezing's," the following letter is still applicable in many instances.

946 Breathless Way
Oxford, MS 39415
August 16, 2001

Frank Fixit
Fixin-for-U
132 Handyman Street
Oxford, MS 39415

Dear Mr. Fixit:

Because you did not repair my air conditioner on two separate occasions as promised and for which I paid $236.50, my health is in appalling jeopardy. (See enclosed statement by my physician, Dr. Frederick Feelgood and copies of paid invoices.)

As you will note from Dr. Feelgood's letter, my medical condition makes it imperative that I live in a climate

controlled environment. Unfortunately, since the air conditioner failed, I am unable to do so within my own home. Both times when you failed to repair the unit I had to stay with my parents who live twenty-five miles away for a total of five nights. This was a terrible inconvenience for me.

The discomfort and bother of this mal-functioning unit would be horrendous enough for someone with no health issue, but it exacerbates and can be even life threatening for a person with extreme respiratory problems such as I have.

While I am sure you performed as best you could to repair the air conditioner, it simply does not work properly. I have had it repaired by another company and, therefore, I wish an immediate reimbursement of the sum I paid to you.

Thank you, and I look forward to receiving the $236.50 no later than August 24, 2001.

Sincerely,

Wilma Wheezing

Enclosure

cc: Leyser Q. Morris-Hayes, Director
Consumer Protection Division
Office of the Attorney General
P.O. Box 22947
Jackson, MS 39225

Julie McLemoil, Director
Bureau of Regulatory Services

P.O. Box 1609
Jackson, MS 39201

Money paid, case resolved.

Or maybe you've found yourself more like Debi Deceived, who faithfully patronized one plumbing company for years. When members of this *smelly* operation tried to put one on over Debi, she didn't stand for it, just as I wouldn't expect you to do.

107 Robbery Road
Hot Springs, AR 99001
August 15, 2001

Paul Putrid, Owner
Putrid Plumbing Company
10610 Stench Street
Hot Springs, AR 99003

Dear Mr. Putrid:

As a loyal customer of your company for many years, I am certain that you wish to be aware that, in my opinion, certain members of your personnel – specifically, I. R. Inmate and Danny Devious - have recently victimized me. I trust you will immediately and thoroughly investigate this appalling situation.

- **The problem first arose in February 2001 when I moved into my new home. Water accumulated in the laundry room so I called *Putrid Plumbing*. Mr. Inmate snaked the laundry tub drain and, in addition, performed two minor repairs for a cost of $307.75 (copy of invoice enclosed). Less than two weeks later the laundry tub overflowed again; Mr. Inmate returned to my home on March 1 and determined** that roots in the drain were the problem. This visit cost me $237.10 (copy of invoice enclosed).

- On March 5, Mr. Inmate attempted to solve the problem with a stronger snake but to no avail. This time the bill was $98 (copy of invoice enclosed). He returned to the office to check with you about installing a simple drain but learned that simple drains were no longer to code with the county. It seemed that the only alternative left was to install a sump pump and to re-pipe to connect with the main stack. He informed me this was the <u>only</u> option and it would cost $3500. Additionally, there would be holes in my ceiling's drywall. When I informed Mr. Inmate that I simply could not afford this added expense (I had already paid $642.85 in less than two months), he assured me he could repair the drywall on his own time for only $200.

- By March 8, Mr. Inmate completed the work for which I paid him $200 (see enclosed copy). I was alarmed, however, when he informed me that he was presently on work release from the county jail. (No one from *Putrid Plumbing* had apprised me of this fact.) He did agree that the flooding problem most likely was covered by my homeowner's policy and that he would write what was necessary for my reimbursement. In spite of his prisoner status, but because he seemed to be so helpful and the flooding ceased, I even wrote a commendation letter concerning Mr. Inmate.

- I mailed a letter to Homeowners Insurance Company on March 14, 2001 and enclosed what I thought were the necessary forms (copy enclosed); however, some information was lacking in order to process the claim, specifically the itemization of the costs to repair the pump. Homeowners' office in Little Rock called and left a message for Mr. Inmate on April 10, but he did not return the call. Even after I spoke with him on April 17, he still did not contact Homeowners.

I attempted to reach him again on April 27, May 3, May 4, and May 7. Finally, on May 15, I called to speak with you directly but was informed that I must talk with the service manager, Danny Devious. Mr. Devious promised he would "try to get everything worked up" and to call him the following Monday before he called Homeowners. On May 21, I did as directed, but Mr. Devious stated that he was "unable to get through to Homeowners."

- I spoke with Al Agent in Little Rock on May 23, and he informed me that he had received no call from either Mr. Inmate or Mr. Devious. He did authorize a transfer of my case to Catlin Claims at the Hot Springs field adjuster's office. On June 1, Ms. Claims inspected my basement and drafted an estimate for repairs. Unfortunately, the sump pump itself would be considered an improvement unless she could obtain clarification from either Mr. Inmate or Mr. Devious. At approximately this same time, the condenser on my furnace/air conditioner broke and flooded two other basement rooms. Needless to say, I did not contact *Putrid Plumbing* for this repair.

- In early June I spoke with Mr. Devious and he informed me that Mr. Inmate had left the state with possessions belonging to your company but that he himself had attempted to call Ms. Claims. I certainly doubt the veracity of his assurance as the latter never heard from him, even after repeated messages from both of us and a letter sent by Ms. Claims (see enclosed copy dated June 11, 2001). I was able to recoup some of my losses, less $1900 for the cost and labor to install the sump pump. Even though my claim was then closed, Ms. Claims stated that it would be reopened if she had the opportunity to speak with either Mr. Inmate, Mr. Devious, or you (see copy of letter dated July 2, 2001). Mr. Devious continued to refuse to return my calls. He did send a letter to the attorney I retained, but it was only a description of the work and not the explanation required by Homeowners. My attorney wrote again on July 24 and on August 7, 2001 (copies enclosed), but Mr. Devious refused to respond.

This entire fiasco is both outrageous and inexcusable. Your company willingly hired a <u>prisoner</u> to work in homes and did not reveal this important information to me (nor to anyone else, I assume). Secondly, your service manager is, in my opinion, highly unprofessional given the lack of courtesy and response to Homeowners, to my attorney, and to me. As owner of *Putrid Plumbing* it is ultimately your responsibility to ensure that I am reimbursed the $1900 loss; I assume you are aware of the shocking transgressions of your employees. As I stated previously, I have been a loyal customer for many years, and I expect that loyalty to be reciprocated.

Thank you, and I look forward to hearing from you and to receiving the full $1900 compensation by no later than August 31, 2001.

Sincerely,

Debi S. Deceived

Enclosures

cc: Shelia McDonald, Deputy Attorney General
    Consumer Protection Division
    Office of the Attorney General
    323 Center Street, Suite 2000
    Little Rock, AR 72201

Office of Consumer Protection
United States Department of Commerce
Room 5718
Fourteenth Street and Constitution Avenue, NW
Washington, DC 20230

Howard Beales, Director
Office of Consumer Protection
Federal Trade Commission
Pennsylvania Avenue and Sixth Street, NW
Washington, DC 20580

Catlin Claims, Claim Specialist
Homeowners Insurance Companies
4404 Resident Road, Suite 4
Hot Springs, AR 99008

L. L. Lawyer, Esquire
Attorney Attorney Lawyer & Associates, P.C.
8732 Courthouse Square, Suite 112
Hot Springs, AR 99001

Mrs. Deceived soon pocketed the entire $1900 from Danny Devious, no thanks to her own attorney.

Rentals

You signed your lease, paid your deposit and think you're set for the next several years. Then you meet Prince (or Princess) Charming who wants to move you into a real live house. Hey, you've paid on time each month for your apartment and, in fact, have been a model tenant for a long while. It shouldn't be a problem to get out of your lease, especially since the area in which you live may be a college haven with lots of students who need apartments. Unfortunately, you run into a surfeit of excuses and downright hostility, just as "Beth Bride" did before she sought out the *Poison Pen*. The following letter may be used for most any situation dealing with apartment management.

2303 Poorer Parkway
Pierre, SD 57502
February 16, 2001

Diane Dummy, President
U-Owe-Us Management, Inc.
546 Monied Avenue
Boston, MA 62458

Re: Beth Bride Lease
Meanly Apartments

Dear Ms. Dummy:

I have met with no success from my father's letter [a former attorney] **to Hortense Hateful, Property Manager at Meanly Apartments in Pierre, South Dakota (see enclosed copy and her subsequent response). This situation is nothing short of egregious, and I trust you will personally and immediately investigate on my behalf.**

- **Prior to my sixty-day notice on October 2, 2000 regarding the necessity to vacate 1546-A Old Maid Lane, I had lived at Meanly since 1995. During that time I was a model tenant, even when I was denied reciprocal loyalty. In fact, there was only one occasion during all these years where I was late on my monthly payment - <u>one day</u> late for which I was accessed a hefty $35 fee. In addition, when I moved to this address in June 1995, not only was my prior approval of the apartment rejected, the apartment was also to be re-carpeted and new kitchen and bathroom floors added** prior to this move. The carpet was <u>not</u> replaced at all and the kitchen floor was <u>not</u> replaced until the summer of 1997. Many other problems occurred with the apartment, and I was frequently forced to wait for repairs for weeks at a time, if anyone came at all. Even when repairs were "completed," the problem usually reoccurred within a few days. These, however, are almost unimportant when faced with the remaining travesties that occurred with Meanly.

- As a single mother with a limited income, I lost my job both in 1995 and 1997 because of company downsizing; this meant a significant drop in yearly income. Additionally, each year the lease was renewed the rent increased between $50-60 monthly, which meant negotiations with the Leasing Office so that I could pay only $20-25 extra per month. Our research proves that most apartments in that area increased their rents to their current tenants only $5-10 a month during that period. My only leverage in negotiations was that the carpet had not been replaced as promised and, therefore, I should not have to pay "market" price. The last increase of $70 was in June 2000, but after conferring with leasing agent Tessa Trader we agreed upon a monthly rent of $736 - $20 more than the previous amount.

- This lease was renewed for July 2000-June 2001. In September 2000, I informed Ms. Hateful of my intentions to marry and to vacate the apartment. Ms. Hateful explained that the apartment should be rented by December 2000 and I might be responsible for the December payment. Ms. Hateful never noted any financial obligation through June 2001 and, thus, I gave two months notice on October 1, 2000. As a matter of fact, she agreed to my placing ads at my workplace, in stores, and so forth, and also agreed that I could use her name as a contact for prospective renters.

- Subsequently, I advertised my apartment throughout the area, but both the high rent and the fact that Meanly raises the price each year trouble potential tenants. I have called Ms. Hateful on many occasions, but the other agent, David Discord, always gives some excuse as to why I am unable to speak with her. My calls are never returned, but I assume it is because Mr. Discord fails to give the former the requests.

- On the morning of January 15, 2001, after personally traveling to the leasing office to request a copy of the lease, I was informed it was unobtainable at the time. Even when I stated my intent to return at 3:00 p.m., it was not available then, either. After speaking with Mr. Discord concerning the status of the apartment and a rental date, he abruptly and, in my opinion, rudely and unprofessionally informed me in no uncertain terms, "Because you broke your lease, we will rent your apartment last." Obviously, this is true as there was only one unit to be rented before mine in October and by January there were <u>three</u>.

- To further exacerbate matters, Meanly refuses to allow me to sublet. Even if the apartment was rented at $736 per month, I would be glad to pay the excess $52 for the current $788 payment. I might stress, also, that my father's request for your name and address was refused, and I had to research on the Internet to obtain the information. This further demonstrates the type of attitude of which I write.

On February 10, 2001, a friend called Meanly after another friend had called the previous week. Both specifically asked for the apartment I described in my ad, and both were told there was no three-bedroom unit on the second floor. This is a blatant falsehood. Moreover, my friends were informed there could be no rental unless the advertisement originated with Meanly. This is untrue as well since Ms. Hateful agreed to my doing so and even placed her name on my advertisement. I simply cannot understand why Meanly refuses to rent this apartment rather than letting it stand vacant, especially with the $52 monthly increase. Even though I have personal knowledge of these same inequities against other tenants, I still believe this situation is nothing more than a vindictive measure on the part of certain personnel within Meanly to ensure I suffer needless financial hardship. Therefore, I expect either a refund of payments that I have made since December 1, 2000 plus interest or the right to sublease the apartment, <u>under the contractual terms of the June 1, 2000 lease</u>.

I appreciate your prompt attention to this shocking matter, and I look forward to hearing from you by February 28, 2001.

Sincerely,

Beth Bride

Enclosures

cc: The Honorable Mark Barnett
    Attorney General of South Dakota
    Office of the Attorney General
    500 East Capitol Building
    Pierre, SD 57501-5070

    Timothy Bartlett, Director
    South Dakota Consumer Affairs
    500 East Capitol Building
    Pierre, SD 57501-5070

    Hortense Hateful, Property Manager
    Meanly Apartments
    878 Greedy Drive
    Pierre, SD 57504

David Discord, Leasing Agent
Meanly Apartments
878 Greedy Drive
Pierre, SD 57504

April Authority, Regional Manager
U-Owe-Us Management, Inc.
117 Devour Drive
Boston, MA 10106

It took one more letter, but our new bride was able to cancel her lease, thereby saving quite a bit of money and, even better, "Meanly" returned her initial deposit.

And even though Amway Worldwide Corporation isn't a mortgage company, a builder, or so forth, millions of consumers purchase products for their home through this company. We're reminded that its Satisfaction Guarantee is one of the best in the business.

"Listening to and responding to consumers' needs are fundamental here at Amway.

Their comments and concerns are taken very seriously; after all, they are our lifeline. We look at challenges as a 'window of opportunity.' It gives us a chance to improve something that is not quite right, and to show our customers how important they are to us.

[Our guarantee] assures customers that they are getting what they expect and what they pay for, and if for some reason they aren't satisfied, we'll do whatever it takes to make it right." [*]

Moving Companies

Your new home is built and it's time to transfer your existing belongings to the site or you've bought new furnishings for that great addition to your old home. It's now time to avoid another trap—moving companies. This albatross is listed among the top five in areas of complaint and deservedly so in many

---

[*] Robin Horder-Koop, Vice President, NABR Customer Service and Distribution, Amway Corporation

instances. So what are our choices? Some folks will move themselves. They'll pack everything, load it on a rented truck, unload it, unpack it, place items where they need to go, and then lie abed for the next month with a backache and chronic exhaustion. Others will hire a mover and think everything will be hunky-dory because the movers will treat the homeowner's possessions like gold. Unfortunately, this isn't always the case so we need to ensure we're getting the best service possible.

- **Get at least three estimates**. The estimates should include the weight of your goods and a non-binding estimate of the total cost of the move. The cost of the move is first based upon the total weight of the truck's occupied space added to the mileage. Certainly a three-room apartment will be much less expensive than a full household because of these two factors. It's also important for a non-binding estimate (which movers don't like) since you can then see the difference in cost if you have a yard sale, for example, or give Great Grandma's piano to your daughter before the move. This, of course, makes the weight and space much less for the total sum.
- **Find out what services cost extra**. Do you have a split-level home with lots of stairs? Do you wish the movers to hook up your appliances? Be sure these variables are included in the cost of the estimate.
- **Be very careful about guaranteed delivery**. Get the specific pick up and delivery dates and times *in writing*. Check the estimate for destination charges. If there are none, then make sure it's because none apply. If the charges are listed and you believe they're too expensive, then check the interstate-move rate book, *Tariff 400-M*. If the company tells you they don't have a copy, they're lying and trying to overcharge you.
- **Check the mover's credentials.** Contact the **Surface Transportation Board of the Federal Highway Administration**. If your mover isn't licensed by this organization, toss them out on their ears. Call (202) 366-0450 to obtain the verification. Be sure to check, too, that

the mover is a member of the **American Mover and Storage Association (AMSA)**. You can get this information by calling (703) 683-7410 or going online at AMSA's Website http://www.moving.org.

- **File a claim if there's a dispute**. You can't mess around, though. The claim must be filed within nine months of the delivery date. Federal law dictates that a company must make a settlement offer or deny your claim within 120 days. If the claim is denied, once again (as always) you've got a chance at some recourse. Because I'm sure you checked out the moving company's membership in AMSA, you can request arbitration with the organization if your claim is $1000 or less. This service costs $150. Contact AMSA at its Dispute Settlement Program, 1611 Duke Street, Alexandria, VA 22314.

But maybe you didn't follow the above steps. Instead, you simply went to the phone book, called some moving companies, and chose the cheapest one because it quoted you a reasonable price for your pocketbook. However, when you arrive at your new home and before the guys start unloading, you're presented with a bill that bears no resemblance whatsoever to the original price. You argue with the foreman, only to hear that unless you pay up, your possessions will be held hostage forever. That is what happened to "Patty Possessions."

**610 Hot Springs Road
Jamestown, TN 87012
June 15, 2001**

**Horace Hostage, Owner
Hostage Moving, Inc.
7901 Residences Road
Memphis, TN 33398**

Dear Mr. Hostage:

I turn to you personally for your intervention with the shocking problem I recently experienced with your company.

- When I moved to Jamestown from Nashville on April 30, 2001, I wrote a check out to Hostage for the quoted price of $1050 (copy enclosed). Before my furnishings were unloaded from the van, however, Sam Scuzzo demanded an additional $1000 (copy of canceled check enclosed). When I protested, he informed me that my possessions would remain on the truck until he received the extra sum. I had no choice but to pay.

- I immediately called Ted Taint, Hostage's regional supervisor, explained this appalling problem, and demanded reimbursement of the additional $1000. Mr. Taint promised to investigate the matter and return my call no later than Tuesday, May 1. Not only was this a false promise, but also I have called him on six more occasions and he refuses to speak with me. Perhaps, he simply believes that because Hostage has been paid (for which I had no recourse), he can disregard my appeal for justice and fairness.

- When Mr. Scuzzo held my belongings captive, I even explained that I have cancer and every spare dime must go to pay out-of-pocket expenses. I iterated the same to Mr. Taint. Not only did this information fail to sway Mr. Scuzzo, perhaps because of the physical and emotional demands of the cancer, Mr. Taint also believes that I will utterly give up my claim. I can assure you this is not the case at all; in fact, because my physical condition has been exacerbated by this entire ordeal, I <u>must</u> see it through to completion.

I prevail upon you to immediately examine this outrageous matter and to correct the injustice to which I have been subjected.

Thank you, and I look forward to hearing from you within the next ten business days.

Sincerely,

Patty Possessions

Enclosures

cc: The Honorable Paul Summers
    Attorney General of Tennessee
    500 Charlotte Avenue
    Nashville, TN 36243

    Mark S. Williams, Director
    Division of Consumer Affairs
    Fifth Floor
    500 James Robertson Parkway
    Nashville, TN 37243

    Linda J. Morgan, Chairperson
    Surface Transportation Board
    1925 K Street, NW
    Washington, DC 20006

    Vincent Schimmoller, Deputy Executive Director
    Federal Highway Administration
    400 Seventh Street, SW
    Washington, DC 20590

It's such a tragedy that Patty's cancer took a turn for the worse in a very short while. Any resolution was just too late. (All the more reason to stay alert since too many businesses could give a rat's patootie about the health of their customers.)

While we're on the subject of furniture, a brief word of caution about those "rent-to-buy" furniture items. Even though you should be able to cancel payments to the store at anytime, if you do keep up your monthly fee, you're losing money up the wazoo. In fact, in most situations you will end up paying more over the rental company's generally-eighteen month payment schedule than if you paid by credit card – with interest. What's even worse, most stores aren't obligated to disclose specifics with regards to payment arrangements except with contracts that are difficult to read and you question the terms of that contract. Again, as always, use your eyeballs. The written word is a powerful tool, whether it's yours or theirs.

Timeshares

Ah, the palm trees wave as you loll on the pink Caribbean sands. Or perhaps the glistening ski slopes beckon from the deck of your chalet. Maybe a medieval castle in Europe, complete with ghost-sightings of ladies in flowing robes, catches your fancy. It doesn't really matter the place or the time of year; your home-away-from-home captures the most vivid imagination of a time-share owner.

So what exactly is a timeshare? "Owners" buy the right to occupy a furnished unit for a specific period of time. The week or more can be every year or every other year. The buyer pays not only the purchase price, but also a maintenance fee. The unit may be owned for a limited period of time or for even as much as a ninety-nine year lease. ("Hooray!" shout your heirs.)

Timeshare owners may also swap their weeks to other resorts. Most owners do tire of visiting the same old same old year after year; consequently, they arrange to swap their time at the home resort to vacation elsewhere. The trick, though, is to be sure that your own resort is good enough to warrant another vacationer's desire to stay at your place. For example, don't think that you'll be able to exchange your Bahamian beach for the Monte Carlo beaches, even if it isn't in peak season. On the other hand, many, many other destinations beckon, which can make a great reason to "own" a timeshare.

But hold up! While sales of these leased vacation spots are on the rise, caution must still prevail so we're not ripped off or, at the very least, find ourselves on the short end of the vacation stick. If you're seriously considering a timeshare purchase, then write the **Federal Trade Commission**, Public Reference Branch, Room 130, Sixth Street and Pennsylvania Avenue, NW, Washington, DC 20580. Ask for brochures on timeshares. If you decide to buy, then bear in mind the following:

- **Your time versus their time**. "We promise we'll only take two hours of your time and, even if you don't wish to buy, we'll give you a really nice gift." As much as I advocate good manners, you shouldn't be a pushover, either. Once that specified time is over, grab your prize and go – and you don't have to feel guilty about leaving. If you allow yourself to be browbeaten, not only might you stay with these folks for several hours, but you also might walk away with a timeshare you didn't, don't and never want.

- **Watch for scams**. "Come on in and view our video and we'll give you a new television" is one come-on. Another is a "free" trip to see the timeshare for yourself. Beware, though; these deals-and <u>steals</u> may be your downfall if you're not dealing with a reputable source or resort. Telemarketers and disreputable salesmen use brainwashing approaches like this all the time to reel you in like an unsuspecting fish. However, travel promoters get cheap — and I do mean *cheap* — timeshare units for which they receive enormous commissions when they sell to the public. States and even the federal government are cracking down on these fraudulent activities, but if you find yourself caught on the line with a large hook in your mouth, then complain, complain, complain. (And don't forget: if a deal sounds too good to be true, it usually is.)

But even though you've done your homework and you talk to a legitimate timeshare representative, there are still hints to remember.

- **Be alert**. Your decision to "buy" should be based first on how much the timeshare costs and, secondly, how often you'll use it. Some buyers think how easy it'll be to rent or to sell if they can't make the payments or want a little extra money in their pockets. Unless you've got a prime piece of resort real estate that lots of vacationers want, then ditch this idea immediately.

- **Ask questions**. What are the additional costs, such as yearly maintenance fees? This sum may be too high for you to comfortably handle. Additionally, ask how often the amount goes up. A couple of hundred dollars every one, two or three years will add up over the course of many years. Additionally, make sure that a "homeowners" association exists and, preferably, two to three of these people sit on the resort's Board of Directors. Each of the latter protects *you*.

- **Compare vacation travel costs**. If all you can afford is a yearly junket to Las Vegas (and you don't max out your credit card at the slot machines), then perhaps you're better off sticking with this vacation. On the other hand, you can swap out resorts, based on availability, and go anywhere in the world your little heart desires – *if* you have enough money for plane fares and miscellaneous expenses.

- **Get everything in writing**. I know you're sick of reading this advice, but it's just plain common sense. If the salesperson makes a promise verbally, such as a bonus week upon signing the contract, have the assurance as part of the contract. If you're purchasing a unit in a building that's under construction, then insist on a bank letter that guarantees that your funds are protected in escrow until the building is completed. It wouldn't hurt to zip over any written material to your family lawyer so he can check the contract before you sign. The eyeball may be money well spent.

- **Check your state's cooling-off period**. Most have a period of three to ten days. During this time you can cancel the contract if you decide you don't want, can't afford, won't use, and so forth.

The Internet is a fount of information on timeshare resorts and even resale prices of ones you might consider purchasing from current owners. The **Timeshare Users Group** (www.tug2.net) is composed of a volunteer group of owners who post reviews, host chats and discussion boards, and post classified ads for timeshare rentals and resales. Much of TUG's information is free, but you must pay a $15 membership fee to access reviews.

With all this being said, a timeshare can be the best purchase you ever make. As stated previously, most come with a ninety-nine year lease and you can leave it to your heirs when you die. And best of all, you have a chance to get away from all of life's worries, and to rest, relax, and rejuvenate. Alan Moss, Sales Executive at La Vista Resort in St. Maarten, Netherland Antilles, has something to say about happy resort-owners and how he responds to complaints.

"People come to St. Maarten and the rest of the Caribbean seeking relaxation and a bit of paradise, if only for a week or two. The last thing they need are troubles on the timeshare end. We want to know if something is wrong, and then we'll make every reasonable effort to correct the problem and to restore faith and tranquillity in the product.

Also, the only way to generate referrals is to create and maintain happy owners. Follow-up of problems and concerns is mandatory for any successful project."

It really doesn't matter with whom you deal when making decisions regarding any aspect of "Home Sweet Home." If you've done your schoolwork beforehand, then your complaints will be fewer.

Helpful Agencies and Services

The American Moving and Storage Association acts in disputes between its members and disgruntled customers. Contact AMSA at (703) 683-7410 or write to AMSA, Dispute Settlement Program, 1611 Duke Street, Alexandria, VA 22314. AMSA can also be accessed at www.moving.org.

Call your state or local **Better Business Bureau** to ascertain if complaints are on file against a contractor you're considering.

The Federal Reserve Board provides information about the Truth in Lending Act and the Equal Credit Opportunity Act. Write to the agency at Twentieth Street and Constitution Avenue, NW, Washington, DC 20551 or go online at www.bog.frb.fed.us.

To request brochures on timeshare sales, write the **Federal Trade Commission, Public Reference Branch**, Room 130, Sixth Street and Pennsylvania Avenue, NW, Washington, DC 20580.

Enclose a stamped, self-addressed envelope to the **National Association of Home Builders** at 1201 Fifteenth Street, NW, Washington, DC 20005-2800, Attn: Member Service Center. It will provide you with information on licensed contractors.

The Real Estate Settlement Procedures Act (RESPA) protects consumers from unethical practices by brokers, settlement companies and so forth. Write to RESPA at the Office of Fair Housing and Equal Opportunity, U.S. Department of Housing and Urban Development, 451 Seventh Street, SW, Washington, DC 20410 (www.hud.gov).

Call your State Licensing Board to verify a contractor's current license and to discover any outstanding judgments against him or her.

To check moving companies' credentials, contact the **Surface Transportation Board** at the Federal Highway Administration, 1925 K Street, NW, Washington, DC 20006 or call at (202) 366-0450. Also, be sure to check the *Tariff 400-M*, the interstate-move rate book.

The Timeshare Users Group (www.tug2.net) provides interested persons with information regarding timeshares.

Chapter 9
Service With a Smile

*"We have petitioned and our petitions have been disregarded;
We have entreated and our entreaties have been scorned. We
beg no more; we petition no longer, we now defy!"*
- William Jennings Bryan

For those of you who have read *Shocked, Appalled, and Dismayed!* or who have listened to my (I hope) words of wisdom in the media, you know how I feel about some aspects of the service industry and most all attitudes of customer service itself. So what, you may ask, *is* wrong with customer service these days? The term actually stood for something in years past, but now, in many instances, it's become an oxymoron (often with the stress on the last two syllables, I might add). I can remember a time when I walked into a store and employees converged from every point to assist me – so much in fact that I wished they'd all go away and let me look at the merchandise in peace. Little did I realize my wish would be literally granted and seemingly forever. Or I'd call to speak with a trouble-shooter and know I'd be helped. Now we hear the proverbial elevator music and, even assuming a real person eventually comes on the line, he or she often misinforms, promises to call back, or in a worse case scenario, refuses to help at all.

Who cares if you sit by the phone, endlessly dialing twenty-four menus and ninety-nine options? After all, it's *your* valuable time flushed down the toilet and *your* vile curses that'll make friends with the pitchforked, hoof-toed, and evil one upon your death. I assure everyone reading this that many folks on the other end of the phone could care less about the state of your moments (or hours) in time and they certainly don't give a rat's patootie about where you spend eternity!

In a kinder, gentler past, consumers could expect service with a smile. They knew they could expect a speedy resolution to a question or complaint. Not so these days. Whether because of company downsizing, employees not taking pride in their jobs, uninformed or overworked personnel, or those who are simply rude and uncaring, the consumer often ends up on the short end of the stick. And it doesn't matter, either, whether you deal with a large corporation or chain or your local jewelry store. There certainly are lots of folks who are fantastic with their customer service positions and who don't fit into this "oxy*moron*" category but, unfortunately, they often seem to be in the minority and again, the consumer is the loser. Retailers book over a staggering $2.5 <u>trillion</u> a year in sales. One would think they would show a more customer-friendly face to us, but they now average a less-than-satisfactory seventy-one out of one hundred percent ratio. So regardless of their attitude stemming from ill manners (a sad commentary on society) or a lack of respect for consumers (even worse), don't continue to be the underdog. Not only should you complain about these individuals with whom you unfortunately come in contact, but then take your business elsewhere. And make sure you tell the manager in person and the Head Honcho in writing that you're doing so and why.

Even though this chapter doesn't especially relate to restaurants (and mainly because the management usually tries immediately to make things right), I did want to point out the industry as a whole. What sets it apart from others? Why, in this age of high turnover, does restaurants' service often seem better than that found elsewhere?

The time is great for the food services industry. More people are dining out than ever before; plus, according to <u>Restaurants and Institutions Magazine</u>, sales were up 9.9% to $177.2 billion for most of the year 2000. (The figures aren't yet in for 2001.) Unfortunately, the number of available hourly employees dropped substantially, leaving restaurant operators scampering to find creative ways to tantalize prospective employees and then to maintain them. One of my favorite international restaurants, Tropicana, is one that tantalizes the mouth-watering and discriminating palate and is found on the beautiful island of St. Martin, FWI. The exquisite French cuisine is matched only by its service. In fact, one of the owners, Christophe, tells me of his daily talk with his employees.

"Superior service comes from many ways. You [the employee] *must first 'orbit' – look at the customers in the eye and smile. Our employees can't be too into themselves; they must be open and caring to customers.*

It doesn't matter whether you [the employee] *are feeling bad, angry, or tired. Every time we open the door, it's a new day."*

From fine dining to fast foods, the story remains the same. The salaries that McDonald's now pay their workers exceeds minimum wage; otherwise, the turnover rate would be much higher than it normally is in the fast-food industry. The company also has a flexible scheduling policy for younger workers so as not to interfere with their educational needs, including time for homework.

And that's what it all amounts to: employee loyalty. For example, management surveys tell us that, of the companies surveyed, 78% offer health and dental coverage, 91% give paid vacations, and 77% provide sick leave to part timers who work more than thirty hours a week. These are pretty darn good incentives to retain a loyal employee.

Let's take a look at Starbucks Coffee. It was the first private company to offer a comprehensive benefits package that included stock options to full and part-time employees in 1991. Furthermore, goodies such as grants, health, medical, dental, and vision benefits make Starbucks even better bait for hungry prospects. (Each Starbucks employee who works more than twenty hours a week receives full healthcare benefits after just ninety days at work. And to sweeten the pot, these same folks are invited to join the company's retirement plan after one year, in which Starbucks puts in roughly twenty-five cents for every contributing dollar.)

The stock plan is quite a nice one, too. An employee is eligible to participate in "Bean" stock under the following conditions:

1. He or she is employed by Starbucks as of April 1 and has been paid for at least 500 hours from April 1 through the end of the fiscal year.
2. The employee still works for the company when the grant package is distributed the following January and is in a position up through the director level.

The result of all these perks? An unbelievable 65% annual turnover rate, a number that falls far below industry numbers that range from anywhere from 150% to 400%. It's too bad that more food service and outside-industry companies, too, don't take a sip from Starbucks' cup (as opposed from taking a page from its book).

Aside from the mighty Starbucks, the exquisite Tropicana, the superb Angus Barn in Raleigh, North Carolina, or the delightful Village Wharf in Mt. Vernon, Virginia (the latter two with *fantabulous* customer service), you and I both know for a fact that abuse does continue to occur in the service industry. Do we take this mistreatment time and again or do we do something constructive about it? If you're a savvy consumer (I assume you are by this time if you've read *Shocked, Appalled, and Dismayed!* and you're currently devouring *Fight Back and Win!*) then fight, fight, fight for your rights!

Telephone Service

Is there a single, solitary soul out there who doesn't have at least one phone line in his or her home? I very much doubt it. Just like cars, telephones are indispensable items. Various phone companies try to get us to switch to their service by holding out carrots, such as a month's free service or even cash. Added to the confusion, as to which company is the best for our needs, we also have groups like dime-nickel-pennies-for-minutes coaxing us to use their long-distance service.

Deregulation has resulted in a myriad of complexity with regards to our phone bill, no matter which company gets our money. A simple one-page statement has grown into five or more, and fees besiege us. I know sometimes it's hard, but you've got to take time to carefully examine your statement and avoid falling into the trap of overpaying because you don't understand the charges.

- **Shop around to find the long-distance carrier that best meets your needs**. Even better, try to negotiate a better deal by threatening to switch to another carrier. To check out what you would pay under different plans, visit the **Telecommunications Research and Action Center** Web site at www.trac.org before making a final decision. A comparison service that offers rate quotes that are just the same as if you went to the long-distant companies directly is **Tele Worth** Call (888) 353-9678 or log on to www.teleworth.com. Another Web service for the same task is www.decide.com.
- **Extra options are costly**. Do you really need call-waiting or that paging option? Be sure you use what you pay for. If not, then drop the extras to save money.
- **Directory assistance doesn't "assist" your checkbook**. If you're too lazy to thumb through the phone book or you've misplaced Great Aunt Vampira's number in Transylvania, then use and abuse sources such as **http://www.four11.com** to save on Directory Assistance billings.
- **Caller ID may not be such a good idea**. If you don't want your phone number broadcast every time you make a call, perhaps you should call your local carrier to order Complete Blocking or Per Line Blocking. Years ago, before I learned better, I made parent calls from my home. It wasn't too long before they (and every kiddie in the entire school) were calling me at home, too. No thanks.

A worse case scenario is that many of us have become the victims of *cramming*. A modern-day scam, cramming results from charges for unwanted services, such as voice mail, 800, 888, or 900 numbers "crammed" into your phone bill. The fees are small and, therefore, often go unnoticed (especially with wading through pages and pages of billing). Keep your eagle eyes sharp to avoid being victimized. If you do note a discrepancy like this, then immediately call your local carrier, most of whom will remove the fraudulent charges. Also contact the company (the *crammer*) who charged you (the *crammee*) by calling its number usually found at the top of your bill. Another baddie is when one phone company "slams" another. One day you receive your monthly statement but you realize it isn't from Tweededee Telephone Company, the one that has serviced you for the last umpteen years; instead, the bill is from Tweede*dum* Telephone and you've been switched without your permission. Write to two federal agencies to lodge a righteous complaint: the **Federal Communications Commission (FCC)**, Common Carrier Bureau, Customer Complaints, Mail Stop Code 1600A2, Washington, DC 20554 and the **National Fraud Information Center**, P.O. Box 65868, Washington, DC 20035. Be sure to have your proverbial ducks in a row when documenting your complaint.

Another hint is to take three months worth of typical phone charges and note the total calls/minutes made out of state and in state, as well as the time of day when you normally make the most calls. Then contact carriers and give this information to their agents who can then match you with their companies' least inexpensive plans for which you qualify. And while your local phone service may be a monopoly, don't forget that you're not hog-tied to the same long-distance company; if you're not satisfied, then switch. Go online to www.decide.com to compare rates, too. Phone musical chairs may be a tad time-consuming, but you won't hear your checkbook complain.

Sprint FON is praised by its employees as the better of all the others in the industry. Not only do Sprint's workers have great perks, such as stock options and tuition reimbursement of up to $5,250, but also the goodies get even better. For expectant mothers, there's no longer a headache about not having the time off to take care of a newborn. Moms receive six weeks paid leave for natural births and eight weeks for C-sections. Also, a Dependent Day Care Reimbursement Account is available to all employees. And (hot dog!) a company gym to keep fit, if one desires. Even without Jamie Lee Curtis, happier employees make for happier customers.

A lot of busy folks now lease cellular phones. For some people they are a luxury yet these phones are a necessity for others. "Bethany Busy" fell into the latter category. Now before we get into her problem, let's have a few tips on do's and don'ts for mobile cell service.

- **Shop around**. This same advice is pertinent, whether "buying" home telephone phone service or that for a mobile model. Retailers have struck deals with a single service so there are limitations to their portfolio of phones and service plans. To discover bargains in your area, visit the website www.wirelessdimension.com.

- **Decide how much you'll use the cell phone before purchasing a plan**. If the phone is only for emergencies, then avoid the more costly plans with "free" airtime. On the other hand, if you call all your relatives on the weekend and make a lot of other calls as well during the week, you might want to consider a more expensive plan. Usually the higher the monthly charge, the more free minutes you get. If you plan to use the phone infrequently, however, you probably won't need anything but the most basic of models. Don't get talked into a combination pager, voice-mail, and so forth.

- **Consider "roaming" charges**. These allow you to call more cheaply within a specific region to charges that permit calls made and received across the country, for example. And again, the more extensive the roam, the higher the cost.

- **Know your billing increments**. Sometimes the supplier bills in thirty-second increments while others bill in increases of one minute or even more. The higher the increment, the less you'll save.

- **Be careful what you say once you've purchased and are using**. Contrary to belief, this isn't a "private line." You're actually transmitting a radio signal and, even though it's against the law, radio scanners can pick up on your calls. Be cautious if you're talking about sensitive information, particularly if you have an analog rather than a digital cell phone.

"Bethany Busy's" cell phone was basically an extension of her right hand and she used it constantly. She paid her enormous bills on time and always upgraded when the latest (and more expensive) model became available. Therefore, Betty expected any problems that arose to be handled swiftly by the company. Ha!

8754 Drudgery Drive
Racine, WI 55016
January 19, 2001

Carl Cell, President/CEO
Cellphones of America, Inc.
1097 Fifth Avenue, Suite 1505
New York, NY 10333

Dear Mr. Cell:

I am certain you will be as shocked and appalled as I when you learn of my recent problem with your company.

- **While in the process of moving in December 2000, I realized that my Cellphone charges had not been paid. I contacted customer service on December 8, 11, and 12 in an attempt to obtain a statement so that I could pay by credit card. On each occasion I spoke with Darlene Dummy who promised to respond to my queries; however, she failed to do so.**

- On December 14, my service was abruptly cut off and, I might add, during an important business call. I immediately contacted Ms. Dummy who seemed to have no recall of our earlier conversations and my efforts to pay this last bill. She was of no assistance whatsoever.
- I then spoke directly with the manager of customer service, Ralph Rude. When I explained the dilemma and reminded him of my past exemplary history with Cellphones, Inc., his response was, "That was then; this is now." Mr. Rude was even less helpful and, in my opinion, more unprofessional than Ms. Dummy.

If you review my records, you will discover that my charges amount to hundreds of dollars monthly and that these are paid in a timely manner. To be treated thus by your personnel after my years of loyalty to Cellphones, Inc. is outrageous and inexcusable. Even though I never received a statement of the charges in question, I paid the bill simply to rid myself of the aggravation (see enclosed copy of check #246).

While I am now using the services of another telephone company, I would wish to return to Cellphones, Inc. Assuming I receive an <u>immediate</u> response from you with an explanation of why this problem occurred as well as my subsequent treatment by Ms. Dummy and Mr. Rude, then I will once more become a loyal and expensive customer of Cellphones, Inc.
Thank you, and I look forward to hearing from you within the next ten business days.

Sincerely,

Bethany Busy

Enclosure

cc: Michael Powell, Chairman
Federal Communications Commission
1919 M Street, NW
Washington, DC 20554

Common Carrier Bureau
Federal Communications Commission
Consumer Protection Division
Mail Stop Code 1600A2
Washington, DC 20554

Maureen O. Helmer, Chairman
Public Service Commission
3 Empire State Plaza
New York, NY 12223

Margaret Quaid, Supervisor
Division of Trade and Consumer Protection
2811 Agriculture Drive
P.O. Box 8911
Madison, WI 53708

James Dehne, Consumer Fraud Investigator
Racine County Sheriff's Department
717 Wisconsin Avenue
Racine, WI 53403

To her delight, Bethany received not only the requested letter but also a credit of $200 for her next upgrade. Who says big business doesn't listen when it realizes profit loss is at stake?

Collection Agencies

"Hello, this is Carla Collection. If you don't pay your bill to Company XYZ, then we'll sue you for non-payment." Oh, those nasty calls from those nasty collection agencies. Sure, they may be only doing their job, but when we're deluged with letters and telephone calls, it often seems as if these people take a sadistic pleasure in harassing us.

The **Fair Debt Collection Practices Act** ensures that debt collectors and collection agencies are *not* allowed to:

- Harass you with repetitious, anonymous, or collect calls;
- Threaten violence, use abusive language, or intimidate you into believing your property can be snatched without appropriate court action;
- Lie and say they are someone other than who they actually are (for example, this person can't say he's a representative of a company's legal department);
- Call you before 8:00 A.M., at work, or after 9:00 P.M. at home;
- Misconstrue the amount of money you owe. Creditors can add late charges and penalties. If you don't agree to the bottom line, then dispute the charges and request a fuller accounting before you pay; and
- Mail you postcards, since doing so violates your protected right to privacy.

To safeguard against harassment, first tell these idiots not to bother you anymore. If they continue to do so, then report them to **The Federal Trade Commission's Bureau of Consumer Protection** at (202) 326-2222 or at its Web site address (http://www.ftc.gov). What to do next? Write a letter, of course.

The father of "Maurice Mourning" died, the funeral was over, and all charges had been paid. And if you've ever found yourself in Maurice's boat, then you know just how expensive a funeral can be. The poor man was not even allowed to grieve before he began to receive dunning notices for the funeral fees. Now remember, Maurice owed nothing, zip, nada. His sorrow quickly turned to anger against these intrusive agents and the corporation that owned the local funeral home.

9413 Saddened Street
Fairfax, VA 22222
June 2, 2001

Fred Fabrication, President
Funerals, USA Headquarters
1923 Wilson Boulevard, Suite 503
Washington, DC 20009

Dear Mr. Fabrication:

Unctuous Funeral Home and the We-Have-You Collection Agency has caused me an appalling amount of mental and emotional anxiety. To iterate the events of which I am sure you are aware:

- On April 9, 2000, my father, Melvin Mourning, passed away. Because he was a man of valor in death as well as in life, he previously arranged for and set funds aside for all funeral expenses with Unctuous Funeral Home in Fairfax, Virginia. This was a final gift he gave to his family so that we would not undergo the turmoil of paying bills during the midst of our sorrow. The total bill was $19,144.69, all of which was paid within thirty days of his death.
- On Wednesday evening, May 2, 2001, I was contacted via telephone by, in my opinion, the rudest, most abrasive individual with whom it has ever been my misfortune to speak. Ms. Abominable (if indeed this is her true identity) informed me that she was a collection agent calling on behalf of Funerals USA (Unctuous) and that I owed $4,000. I tried with no success to explain that not only had this amount been paid well over a year ago, but also that I had the canceled check as proof. She continued to harangue me, then called me a liar, and

threatened further action. At that point, I hung up the telephone.

- I immediately called Unctuous and spoke with Edward Entombment who promised to call me the following day with a resolution to the problem. He did not call; instead, Greta Greedy did so and stated that she had turned this "outstanding" account over to the We-Have- You Collection Agency because <u>your office claimed that my original check bounced</u>.

- I informed Ms. Greedy that not only was this not the case, but the check had been endorsed by the bank and cashed (see enclosed copy). She insisted I come to Unctuous with the canceled check, but I refused to do so. I further explained that I would fax the information to her, which I did on Thursday, May 10. Later that day, Ms. Greedy called me to assure me that a terrible error had occurred at the corporate office and that I owed no balance whatsoever.

- I demanded a paid in full receipt from both Unctuous and from We-Have-You for future reference; in addition, I also expressed my outrage and demanded an immediate written statement from the collection agency that this claim was a false one and that my credit rating would not be affected. Even though your response to my first letter included the paid in full statement form, I am not satisfied with your assurance that We-Have-You is unable to release the name of neither the individual nor a statement verifying that this account has been paid. The word of a company, which employs personnel such as the woman who contacted me, is not, in my opinion, to be trusted, and this is why I still expect a written verification from this agency. In addition, on Tuesday, May 29, I spoke with the Federal Trade Commission and was informed that because Funerals USA hired We-Have-You, your company has the authority to release its address and contact person to whom I can write.

226

This entire ordeal has been unconscionable. Not only did I never receive any delinquent notice from the local funeral home or from the corporate office, but also your collection agency has blatantly violated Federal law. The Federal Trade Commission states that debt collectors and collection agencies are not allowed by law to use abusive and threatening language. Therefore, We-Have-You and, thus, as its representative, Funerals USA has broken the law. How many others have been subjected unjustly to these harassing measures?

Based upon my lodging a complaint and the ensuing conversation with the FTC, I wish you to not only provide me with the address of We-Have-You but also to obtain a letter from your collection agency admitting its error and offering a full apology. I also expect that Ms. "Abominable" is officially reprimanded for her part in this matter.

Thank you, and I look forward to receiving the above information within ten (10) business days.

Sincerely,

Maurice Mourning

Enclosure

cc: The Honorable Donald Evans, Secretary
     United States Department of Commerce
     Fifteenth Street & Constitution Avenue, NW
     Washington, DC 20230

     Howard Beales, Director
     Office of Consumer Protection
     Federal Trade Commission

Pennsylvania Avenue & Sixth Street, NW
Washington, DC 20680

Consumer Response Center (Complaint # 458900)
Federal Trade Commission
Room 285
Pennsylvania Avenue & Sixth Street, NW
Washington, DC 20580

Carlton Courter, Project Manager
Office of Consumer Affairs
Washington Building, Suite 100
Richmond, VA 23219

Frank Seales, Jr., Chief
Office of Attorney General
900 East Main Street
Richmond, VA 23219

Cemetery Consumer Service Council
P.O. Box 2028
Reston, VA 20195-0028

Funeral Consumer Alliance
P.O. Box 10
Hinesburg, VT 05461

Because Maurice (via me) knew his rights under the law, this strongly-worded letter received an immediate answer. The Head Honcho did everything that Maurice demanded of him and, you can bet your bottom dollar that this national organization fired "We-Have-You" Collection Agency as well.

If, God forbid, you should find yourself in a similar situation, also call **FAMSA – Funeral Consumer Alliance** at (802) 482-3437. Not only does the organization prove helpful prior to the funeral of a loved one, but it also stands ready to assist with complaints about a funeral and the funeral home.

Retail

There's not a single one of us who doesn't shop in retail stores. Whether to buy clothing, electronics, jewelry or any other product, consumers pour out money like syrup on pancakes seven days a week. Unfortunately, however, sometimes the "syrup" is stickier than we anticipated and the need for a complaint letter rears its ugly head. Not to worry. You're now an expert at solving your problems through letter writing so off you go on the path to redemption once more.

Let's say your new vacuum cleaner went on the blink. One morning you're merrily cleaning your living room carpet when, all of a sudden, your newest purchase (and an expensive one at that) begins growling and groaning. Uncertain if it will explode right in front of you, sending bits and pieces of dirt, carpet, furniture, and even your body flying through the atmosphere, you take no chances, unplug the sucker, and march it right back to the store.

Hopefully, you'll encounter a salesperson with more than an ounce of courtesy and helpfulness who'll make things right. If, on the other hand, you approach a different type of person, please don't make the mistake "Freddy *Finger*" did when he lost his temper. (You'll gasp - and probably laugh - when you note his big, bad boo-boo when reading the following letter.) As I told Freddy when he called me, we had to address his own anger and its result before requesting a new vacuum. After all, we must be members of a polite society.

9864 Apologetic Avenue
Sioux Falls, SD 57104
August 9, 2001

Marvin Manners, Owner
Vacuum City, Inc.
780 Cleaning Circle
Sioux Falls, SD 57106

Dear Mr. Manners:

On July 31, 2001 I purchased model #556690 for $399, plus tax (copy of receipt enclosed). The first few days of use, the vacuum cleaner worked wonders; however, on August 7, during the course of cleaning my carpet, it began to make terrible noises. I immediately returned it to Vacuum City, and that was the beginning of the shocking incident that occurred.

- Upon entering the store I met your salesman, Paul Blowhard. When I explained to him what had just happened, his response was "So what? You bought it, you handle it." Needless to say, I was appalled and furious at his manner and, in my opinion, total lack of professionalism.
- Mr. Blowhard then turned his back on me and walked away. I am very ashamed to admit that I lost my temper and made an obscene gesture to his back, whereupon other customers began laughing. As Mr. Blowhard turned back to me and saw what I was doing, he began screaming at me. I can provide you with witnesses to this entire situation (including my own impolite behavior). At that point, I took my defective vacuum cleaner and left your store.

While I do admit allowing my temper to get the best of me, which resulted in flawed conduct on my part, this does not excuse the actions of Mr. Blowhard both before and after the incident. Nor does this situation detract from my original complaint concerning the poor-quality vacuum cleaner.

I trust you will immediately investigate this inexcusable matter. I expect a replacement of the vacuum and a written apology from Paul Blowhard. I have included my own to him as an attachment to this letter.

Thank you, and I look forward to hearing from you no later than August 23, 2001.

Sincerely,

Freddy Finger

Enclosure

I couldn't talk Freddy into carbon copying investigating agencies, but as it turned out they weren't necessary anyway. In less than the two-week limit with which Freddy/Ellen had concluded the letter, Mr. Mannerly called, Mr. Blowhard wrote his own letter of apology, and Freddy got a brand-new machine.

And speaking of carpets, maybe you're in the market for a new one. It doesn't matter if it's standard wall-to-wall or an expensive Oriental, your hard-earned money is at stake. Anytime you shop 'til you drop and make retail purchases, remember the salient points that are appropriate for *anything* you buy in the way of products and services that may result in a complaint letter:

- **Stay calm**. Just like "Freddy," temper tantrums get you nowhere — and make the rest of us consumers look bad.
- **Keep receipts**. It's the kiss of death to lose, toss, or otherwise have no proof of purchase. If you have no spare drawer, march right out and buy a three-ring binder, a large notebook, or something similar. It's amazing how many receipts and comments, and so forth you can tape into one of these babies, and they take up no room at all.
- **Document and organize**. Use that notebook, honey.
- **Use polite language**. "Freddy's" polite language (and especially his apologetic manner) probably did as much as his documentation to resolve his complaint.

- **Be concise**. Who wants to read Volumes I, II, and III of a complaint letter? Certainly not a busy executive. Keep the letter to a page-and-a-half unless it deals with a complicated issue.
- **Be clear that the company's profits are at stake**. No, I don't mean a lawsuit threat. An *implied* threat of profit loss is so much more effective, as in "All of my friends, family, and colleagues are equally appalled at this shoddy product." The implication, of course, is that if the complaint is not resolved, it's not only your business the company will lose.
- **Tell the Big Boss what you want**. Don't let this person guess your expectations. State whether you wish a refund, replacement, credit, or Big Boss's right hand. On the other hand, don't be a greedy hog, either. Just as we expect companies to be responsible for their products and services, so must consumers be responsible with respect to their own expectations.
- **Specify a deadline for answer**. If you don't do this, you may be waiting around for the next decade or two.
- **Close politely**. Always conclude with a thank you to the recipient.
- **Copy key people**. Even though Freddy chose to do otherwise and the letter itself did the trick, this doesn't occur as often as you might think. Your state attorney general, if you suspect fraud, and the Office of Consumer Protection, for instance, should always receive a copy. Not only do many of these folks come to your defense, Big Boss will probably have heart palpitations when he sees that list of cc's at the letter's conclusion.

Armstrong World Industries, Inc. looks for people who want to work with old-fashioned values, such as honesty and integrity. From parties to picnics, employees continue to be reminded that they're part of a family, instead of workers for a company. And believe-you-me, Armstrong's philosophy is that a satisfied customer is a repeat customer.

On Customer Satisfaction

Stephen E. Stockwell, Senior Vice President of Sales for the Worldwide Floor Products Operations Department of Armstrong World Industries, Inc.:

"We are building business excellence to meet the needs of our customers. Success is defined by excelling in customer satisfaction ratings and gaining new customers. We will do this by improving quality, enhancing services, and being best cost!"

O.K., back to the *Scene-of-the-Carpet Crime*. "Madeleine Mad" spent a great deal of money to re-carpet her home. She did all the right things, too, before purchasing: researched carpet manufacturers to find the best quality and price; discovered the local store that carried what she wanted; and carefully checked out the installer. What she didn't realize, as is the case with many of us, is that sometimes the best carpet in the world has defects that aren't obvious until after the fact. Madeleine encountered this problem soon after her new carpet was laid.

408 Dismayed Drive
Grand Rapids, MI 49555
February 7, 2001

Francis Faulty, President/CEO
Tainted Rugs Industries Inc.
Inferior Division
2000 Tainted Terrace, Suite 1454
Atlanta, GA 30304

Dear Mr. Faulty:

Because I have been unable to receive any resolution from an appalling problem with my Tainted Inferior

carpet, I am turning to you for your personal intervention. Less than one year ago, Besmirched Rug Company in Grand Rapids (receipt enclosed) installed this new wall-to-wall carpet, and this purchase along with the service of your representatives has been a disaster. The chronology of events follows:

- Only a few months elapsed before the carpet began to change colors as if something had been spilled upon it and stained the color. I stress, however, this was not the case. Thereafter, the pile in many places began to appear so flat and worn that visitors frequently remarked upon its defective appearance.
- On September 12, 2000, I contacted Vic Veep, Vice President of Besmirched Rugs. Even though he assured me someone would come immediately to view the problem, no one came until I called him again on September 19, whereupon Mr. Veep himself came to my home on September 23. After inspecting the carpet, he agreed that the carpet was flawed and he personally contacted Tainted.
- On October 9, 2001, Henry Handle, Territory Manager for Tainted Industries, Inferior Division, came to our home. He, too, agreed that something was wrong with the carpet; in fact, he suggested that when the company made an adjustment, we should consider a textured carpeting. He promised to send in his report and stated that we should hear from the company within ten days. Almost four months later, we are still waiting.
- On both November 11 and 18, I spoke with Mr. Veep and on the latter date he informed me that Tainted's response was that [they] "saw nothing wrong with the carpet" and that we would receive a written report. Again, we are still waiting. To make matters worse, upon his suggestion I attempted to contact Mr. Handle. He has yet to return my messages.

- On November 24, I called Tainted to obtain your name and then spoke with Ardis Accommodating in the Claims Department. She referred me to Stephanie Supervisor, and I informed her of my dissatisfaction with the carpet and Mr. Handle's lack of communication and, in my opinion, professional courtesy. Ms. Supervisor stated the problem sounded like "watermarking," and that this is "a mysterious condition which happens from time to time." She alerted *See-Your-Carpet* to check the carpet, and Harriet Horrified arrived to do so on December 3.

- Ms. Horrified's first words were memorable, to say the least: "You mean to say this carpet isn't even one year old?" She then examined everything, took notes, and stated we should receive a response within two weeks.

- On December 15, Mr. Veep called to report the findings that denoted no "deficiency in manufacturing and no structural defect exists" (See enclosed.) As I reminded him of my anger and frustration, Mr. Veep, Tainted's own executive, stated that he would be willing to be a witness if I should decide to contact my attorney and go forth with a legal resolution. This certainly speaks volumes and attests to the integrity of at least one of your company's representatives.

This entire fiasco is unconscionable. Not only is Besmirched service guaranteed for one year, the carpet itself is guaranteed for five years. With the exception of Mr. Veep, no one from Besmirched Rugs or from Tainted Industries has seen fit to even attempt to assist me, much less to resolve this travesty. There were other manufacturers from whom I could have originally purchased; however, the Tainted brand is one known for its quality and longevity. If this so-called "watermarking" was something of which I or any consumer should be aware, then Besmirched Rug Company should have been forthcoming enough to explain this prior to my purchase.

I anticipate your immediate and prompt investigation into this matter. I also expect that I will either be reimbursed the full amount of the carpet or that a new and sturdier version be placed in my home.

Thank you, and I look forward to hearing from you within the next ten business days.

Sincerely,

Madeleine Mad

Enclosures

cc: Vic Veep, Vice President
    Besmirched Rug Company, Inc.
    10782 Shoddy Street
    Grand Rapids, MI 49510

    Henry Handle, Territory Manager
    Tainted Industries, Inc.
    8903 Loathsome Lane
    Lansing, MI 48911

    Stephanie Supervisor, Territory Supervisor
    Tainted Industries, Inc.
    8903 Loathsome Lane
    Lansing, MI 48911

    Howard Beales, Director
    Office of Consumer Protection
    Federal Trade Commission

Pennsylvania Avenue and Sixth Street, NW
Washington, DC 20580

The Honorable Jennifer Granholm
Attorney General of Michigan
Office of Attorney General
P.O. Box 30212
525 West Ottawa
Lansing, MI 48909-0212

Frederick Hoffecker, Assistant in Charge
Consumer Protection Division
Office of the Attorney General
P.O. Box 20312
Lansing, MI 48909

Gail Raiman, Director
American Textile Manufacturers Institute
1130 Connecticut Avenue, NW, Suite 1200
Washington, DC 20006

Madeleine was no longer "Mad" after she received replacement carpet with no more evidence of watermarking or anything else wrong.

From your feet to your back. It stands to reason that if your carpet or floor is such that your feet hurt, which then more than likely leads to an achy back, then certainly you can count on lying down on a nice, firm mattress to cease your suffering. Not necessarily so as we see in the following letter.

1059 Back Boulevard
Louisville, KY 40233
April 11, 2001

Harry Hurt, President
Hurt-You Mattresses, Inc.

Ellen Phillips

6759 Paine Place, Suite 455
Melville, NY 11747

Dear Mr. Hurt:

I am appalled by a problem that has occurred with your products and with the attitude of certain members within your company's service department. I trust after perusing the enclosed documentation, you will agree that this matter warrants your immediate and personal attention.

- In March 1999, my wife and I purchased a king-size and two double Hurt-You beds from your Laydown store in Louisville, complete with box springs and frames. The total cost of this purchase was $2,603.31 (copy of receipt enclosed). Within six months, all three sets began to sag and proved to be far less than acceptable comfort and quality. Against our better judgment, we kept these products until they became simply unbearable in the spring of 2000.

- In June 2000, we stated our wish to <u>return</u> the beds; however, one of Laydown's service department staff, Richard, persuaded us to exchange the sets for "improved models" of Hurt-You as it was believed that the original mattresses might be defective. Again, the quality has proven to be deplorable.

- In February 2001, only eight months after the exchange, I wrote to your company (copy enclosed) and detailed the history of the problems resulting from the "improved" mattress sets. I requested a refund to once and for all to put an end to months of sleepless nights and agonizing backaches. One month later, I received a letter from Laydown's Furniture Service Department that has outraged me (copy enclosed). It seems that persons within the service department are "suspicious" about the

238

problem. I am infuriated that an inference was made as to the integrity of anyone within my family.

It is unconscionable that we have been subjected to such poor and, in my opinion, unprofessional treatment on the part of your representatives. I expect either a full refund for the entire amount of the original <u>guaranteed warranty</u> purchase price or an exchange of the Hurt-You for another brand, such as a Sealy, a Serta, or a Spring Air. I do not wish any further transaction with Hurt-You. I purchased this merchandise in good faith from Laydown, yet no one in that store wishes to assist us; thus, it is the responsibility of your company to resolve the matter. Obviously, if there is any difference in the <u>full</u> refund price and the cost of a different brand, we will deal equitably with you.

I am confident that you will investigate this matter thoroughly and promptly. You certainly will wish to maintain the reputation of your company in rectifying the situation in a fair and just manner.

Thank you, and I look forward to hearing from you within the next ten business days.

Sincerely,

Arthur Ache

Enclosures

cc: The Honorable Ben Chandler
    Attorney General of Kentucky
    State Capitol, Room 116
    Frankfort, KY 40601

James Shackelford, Acting Director
Consumer Protection Division
Office of the Attorney General
1024 Capital Center Drive
Frankfort, KY 40601

Robert Winlock, Administrator
Consumer Protection Division
Office of the Attorney General
9001 Shelbyville Road, #3
Louisville, KY 40222

Howard Beales, Director
Office of Consumer Protection
Federal Trade Commission
Pennsylvania Avenue and Sixth Street, NW
Washington, DC 20580

Arthur's and his wife's aches and pains disappeared with the new and free mattresses soon found on their beds.

While the following case isn't what most of us experience (thank the good Lord), it does go to prove how inadequate some companies are with record keeping and the like. Pretty frightening, too, is that this particular example deals with a large national chain that should have known better. They do now.

"Alicia Alive" called one day in an absolute fit of hysteria. Just recently, she discovered that the local department store in this chain had made a humongous mistake. They said she was *dead* — that's right, you heard me, dead! We quickly wrote this letter:

909 Breathing Street
Boise, ID 83722
January 25, 2001

Ima Idiot, CEO

Idiotic Corporate Office
98643 Ignoramus Avenue, Suite 498
Los Angeles, CA 95811

Dear Ms. Idiot:

An appalling situation recently occurred with the Idiotic store in Best Mall, Boise, Idaho and under such shocking circumstances that I wish you to personally and immediately investigate. The documentation is as follows:

- On December 20, 2000, I opened an Idiotic's charge account at the Better Mall store, also in Boise. Naturally, I had to show proof of identification in the form of my driver's license to receive a temporary card. I charged purchases twice that same evening in both of the aforementioned stores.
- On December 29, I waited in a very long register line in order to charge some linens; after ringing up my purchase, the clerk, Sally Suspicious, made a telephone call, informed me there was a problem with my account, and directed me to customer service.
- When I gave my temporary charge card to Deborah Doubtful in customer service, she called Los Angeles for a lengthy conversation. At one point, she requested my driver's license, which I gave to her. She verified that I was, indeed, the Alicia Alive on both the license and the charge card and then gave the telephone to me to confer with your corporate office. To my shock I was then informed that "someone" had called on December 15, stated that I had died on December 1, and closed the account.
- At that point in the conversation, I was asked to show my social security card (a flagrant disregard of federal law) to Ms. Doubtful to again verify that I was

who I claimed to be - this after having shown my photo identification earlier. The person with whom I was speaking on the telephone then reopened my account.

By that point I was so disturbed that I paid cash for the item and left the store. What is so horrific is that your personnel simply took the word of someone over the telephone with false information and <u>never even bothered to check store records</u>. If this had been done, someone with any wisdom whatsoever would have ascertained that the account was opened with a photo I.D. three weeks after the date of my supposed death. Not only should this discrepancy been questioned, but this "someone" should have been told to come in person with some identification to close my account.

To add further insult, at the register and the customer service desk this news of "something wrong with my account" and then the call regarding my death was within hearing of both friends and total strangers. To say that I was terribly humiliated is an understatement. My privacy and status as a customer and as a human being was publicly violated, notwithstanding, too, the legal ramification of being directed to show my social security card. Additionally, on January 18, 2001, a bill arrived at my home addressed to the Alicia Alive Estate.

I demand that all records with this erroneous information be purged (see all enclosed copies of verification) and that you send a letter of explanation and apology to me immediately.

Thank you, and I look forward to hearing from you within the next seven business days.

Sincerely,

Alicia I. Alive

Enclosures

cc: Bob Business, Idiotic Store Manager
   Best Mall
   8750 Store Street
   Boise, ID 83820

   Theodore Trade, Idiotic Store Manager
   Better Mall
   7776 Public Parkway
   Boise, ID 83827

   The Honorable Alan Lance
   Attorney General of Idaho
   Office of the Attorney General
   Statehouse
   Boise, ID 83720-1000

   Brett De Lang, Deputy Attorney General
   Office of the Attorney General
   Consumer Protection Unit
   650 West State Street
   Boise, ID 83720-0010

   The Honorable Donald Evans, Secretary
   United States Department of Commerce
   Fifteenth Street and Constitution Avenue, NW
   Washington, DC 20230

In short order, Alicia got everything she demanded (and there wasn't even a body for the undertaker to dig up).

Delivery fees are often pretty high when we make purchases and need trucks to post them to our homes. On the other hand, if our own vehicles have the capacity to do so and we're assured by the store that delivery via ourselves is safe, we save some bucks. Too bad we sometimes get the wrong advice from incompetent retailers, as evidenced by the following letter from "Daniel Distraught."

6563 Shakened Street
Tempe, AZ 84444
September 10, 2001

Richard Retailer, President
Flying Phoenix Department Store
6538 Ashes Avenue, Suite 199
Phoenix, AR 85077

Dear Mr. Retailer:

An appalling situation resulted from our September 3, 2001 purchase of a king-size headboard from your Tempe store at its Labor Day sales cost of $399.95 (copy of receipt enclosed). I trust you will immediately investigate the terrible experience that occurred because of inept advice from your personnel.

- **My wife and I wished to have the piece delivered on that date, but we were assured that this was an unnecessary expense - the headboard could be tied onto the top of our car and would be perfectly safe. With some reservations, we agreed to do so. Charleton Cord and Rob Rope both tied the piece down with twine. I commented that the twine looked rather insubstantial, but we were again assured of its safety and common use for this purpose.**
- **We had traveled no more than two miles on the busy interstate when the twine broke and the headboard flew off. It is amazing that the piece did not crash into another driver's windshield or that there was no**

accident as a result. After retrieving the headboard from a ditch approximately one-quarter mile back, I stood on the side of the road, maneuvered it back onto the top of our car and tied it down with <u>real</u> rope. It is an additional miracle that I was not injured myself during this process.

- We returned to Flying Phoenix and reported the incident to store manager, Ira Indifference. He informed us that the damage the piece sustained could be repaired and refused to even consider a replacement headboard as the one we purchased was on sale. It was obvious to us that he could care less about the poor quality of the twine, the mismanagement of Mr. Cord and Mr. Rope, or the horrific occurrence that was the result.

- Even though the salesman, Barry Bolster, was in complete agreement with our expectations, he was unable to change Mr. Indifference's mind. Therefore, we brought the headboard home with us where it now occupies a portion of our basement, unable to be used because of its condition.

We have been both loyal customers and charge card holders of Flying Phoenix for over ten years. It is both outrageous and unbelievable that this matter occurred in the first place and then that it was not immediately resolved. I expect a brand-new headboard delivered at no charge to my home within the next two weeks and an explanation from you within this same time period.

Thank you.

Sincerely,

Daniel Distraught

Ellen Phillips

Enclosures

cc: The Honorable Janet Napolitano
Attorney General of Arizona
Office of the Attorney General
1275 West Washington Street
Phoenix, AZ 85007

Sydney Davis, Chief Counsel
Consumer Protection Office
Office of the Attorney General
1275 West Washington Street
Phoenix, AZ 85007

The Honorable Elaine Chao, Secretary
United States Department of Labor
200 Constitution Avenue, NW
Washington, DC 20210

Mr. Distraught was one happy sleeper when he received the headboard of his <u>choice</u> instead of one that cost the same amount (probably because the company was so relieved they weren't facing a monstrous lawsuit).

What about those photo shops, the ones that develop your film or make copies of treasured videotapes? Are these services important enough to complain to? Absolutely. It doesn't matter if the film contains shots of your vacation or, even worse, the screwing up of videotaping dubbing that may mean the difference in a new job that will make you a pile of money. Take the case of a colleague who wanted to interview for a local television station. "Wesley Wishful" had performed a number of cable spots and felt that he had a good shot with one or more of the national affiliates. He took the master tape into his neighborhood photo business for the "professionals" there to make some copies. Wes' "wish" was *not* their command.

7509 Traumatized Trail
Alexandria, VA 22308

October 21, 2001

Christine Chicanery
Perilous Photo
1506 Careless Circle
Alexandria, VA 22320

Dear Ms. Chicanery:

I do not understand how such massive errors can continue to occur.

1. Last spring I brought in several tapes to be compiled into one (see copy of receipt). The compilation is the one that you had in your possession as of this week and is documented with my appearances on Crystal Cable Company.
2. I then brought this tape back to make seven (7) other copies in June, for which I paid $126. Unfortunately, upon receipt, I did not check these new tapes as I assumed they were correct ones made from the original compilation.
3. This week, I left the original master videotape with the names of the appearances on the box, three other tapes from the June order, and the most recent Crystal spot to be added on.
4. Jim was concerned that we needed to make all new tapes rather than adding on, and I agreed. On Thursday, I picked up the original, the July order, the three new tapes, and a separate one containing the newest Crystal segment only.
5. Thursday evening, in preparation to sending them to the Washington television affiliates, I checked one of the new ones. The tape went straight from the June 15 spot to the new add-on; therefore numbers 8-12 were missing entirely. I then checked a tape from the June order and that one as well was also missing

these features. At this point, I re-checked the original that you compiled last spring and it was correct.

6. In speaking with Constance on Friday, I think I know how this week's error occurred: the newest three tapes were copied from the <u>wrong</u> June tape instead of the original correct one made last spring. This, of course, does not address why the former tapes were in error. Unfortunately, I mailed one of these copies last week to the President of the ABC affiliate as an interview tape and had to e-mail him last evening when I discovered the error. Sending an incomplete copy did not place in me in a very professional light.

I also do not appreciate the lack of customer service and your tone the two times that I spoke with you on Friday. I have spent quite a bit of money with Perilous Photo within the last four months, including over $150 for the additional copies (see enclosed copies of receipts). In addition, I have experienced the aggravation of making both constant telephone calls and driving back and forth when dealing with several errors made by your personnel. In addition, you and your staff are supposed to be the experts in this field and, therefore, should realize if a thirty, sixty, or even a six-hour tape is insufficient when making new copies (if this was, indeed, the error, as you asserted). Constance was helpful, but Perilous had ample information to resolve this matter without your being so abrupt and without my having to come in yet again with this travesty.

When Erica gave me the "corrected" tapes this morning, these were <u>also</u> <u>incorrect</u>. The master was fine with the exception of some doctor whose segment appears after the most recent spot. Two of the others had horrible quality of this spot, and the fourth tape was completely wrong – the sequence was totally out of order and the aforementioned spot was again of terrible quality. I also checked one from June, which is in error, but Perilous has the other two copies so I was unable to check these as well. I then called Erica, who is very professional and helpful, and she told me to return the videotapes. So once more I will have to travel to Perilous, and once more I must make my excuses to the executives in Washington for the delay.

I look forward to receiving within the next ten days 1) the corrected three videotapes and 2) a credit on my charge card for the July transaction. (Please note that the July charge does not take into account the subsequent amount I spent on your poor service.)

Thank you.

Sincerely,

Wesley Wishful

Enclosures

cc: VF Johnson, Consumer Specialist
    Fairfax County Department of Consumer Affairs
    12000 Government Center Parkway
    Suite 433
    Fairfax, VA 22035

    Carlton Courter, Program Manager
    Office of Consumer Affairs
    Washington Building, Suite 100
    P.O. Box 1163
    Richmond, VA 23219

I wish I could say the letter did the trick, but neither it nor a subsequent one helped. As far as I'm concerned, a court of law should be the very last means possible to settle problems, but in this case, I suggested Small Claims Court to Wes. The last I heard, he was seriously considering my advice. (And I'm sure he'll win, too.)

So you've bought a product and didn't follow my advice about the scrapbook, notebook, and so forth for maintaining receipts and somewhere along the line the dog, the trash, or the toilet ate it. If you're like most of us, all too often the next day or week, that same item shouts *I'm on sale! Come get me!* or, even worse, the item proves to be a rotten one and you want your money back. You try but the salesperson doesn't listen because you've lost guess what. Before you sorrowfully trudge home, peek at the bar code on the tag – all products have them. What companies don't draw to our attention is that sometimes this tiny tag can tell the original cost of the item to which many stores entitle you. There are lots of tidbits out there to help us become more savvy shoppers (and returners). Look and listen.

Whether products or services, you have major rights under the **Fair Credit Reporting Act**. A federal government protection mechanism, it's designed to promote fairness, accuracy, and privacy of information in the files of every consumer-reporting agency (which, honest to God, can be a great source, *if* it doesn't screw up or a problem doesn't occur with identity theft - the worse monster in your nightmares). I referenced these CRAs, such as Trans Union, a number of times as they pertain to different sections; the FTC tells us how the regulations relate to the gathering and selling of information – correct and incorrect. A more elaborate detailing of what the Act encompasses may be found on the FTC's Web site (www.ftc.gov), but here are a few eye-openers to tease your interest (and your credit rating).

- **CRAs must tell you if any information in your files has been used against you**. The next time you're denied credit for any reason, the denying party must give you the name, address, and phone number of the CRA that provided the report. Don't be bullied by these giants, either. They are frequently in error.
- **You can dispute inaccurate information**. When you request it, the CRA *must* provide all file

information and a list of every party that has recently requested it. Once you spy an error, the agency must investigate the items. It must provide you with a written report of the investigation and a written resolution (or the reason for none). Any items in dispute and then settled can be requested to be sent to any company that recently asked for the report. While inaccurate information must be corrected or deleted, sometimes it's your word against theirs (or your creditors), which is another reason for *always* saving documentation as proof. Another problem is that CRAs can't be forced to remove info from your file unless it's outdated or can't be verified.

- **Violators may have to pay you damages**. If you've maintained great records and can't get anywhere with CRAs or a user, you can sue them in state or federal court (in which case, you'll *really* get a red tag zapped on your file for future reference. Just kidding...). There is much more information about CRAs and the Fair Credit Reporting Act that consumers need to know, so do check out the FTC's site.

As you might imagine, I buy *lots* of office products. One company that gobbles up a large percentage of my money is Staples and is also one that invites customer satisfaction and employee bliss. Vesting that begins after only one year is just the beginning of Staples' commitment to its employees. It continues on with a $1500 tuition reimbursement and up to 100% of salary for childbirth reimbursements. Another attractive feature is flexible work arrangements, which I think probably is the wave of the future for smart companies. Additionally, Staples offers other perks, including child and eldercare referrals, family sick days off, dependent and medical care spending accounts, and what has come to be known as "casual dress days." Staples is a good example of a company that not only knows how to ensure success, but also beats out a number of its competitors because of its philosophy.

So regarding customer service in general, just remember, customers should *never* let an in-store or out salesperson or customer service representative treat you with anything other than the utmost respect. You work hard for your money, as the old tune goes, and it's your <u>right</u> to expect the best for what you pay. If you've been wronged, remember your (and all the rest of our) purchasing power is what makes up the paychecks for these insensitive smucks, and if you let them and their actions go unchallenged, then matters never improve. The consumer revolution that I advocate is at hand. Become your own champion and also work miracles for every other consumer. Stand up and be counted: write a complaint letter!

Helpful Agencies and Services

The Fair Credit Reporting Act helps to protect consumers from false or misleading information found in the files of credit reporting agencies. Check it out at www.ftc.gov.

The Fair Debt Collection Practices Act protects consumers from harassment by debt collectors and collection agencies as does the Federal Trade Commission's Bureau of Consumer Protection. Call the Bureau at (202) 326-2222 or lodge your complaint at www.ftc.gov

For complaints about telephone service, including cramming and slamming, write the **Federal Communications Commission,** Common Carrier Bureau, Customer Complaints, Mail Stop Code 1600A2, Washington, DC 20554.

The FAMSA –Funeral Consumer Alliance assists with a wealth of consumer rights information both prior to the funeral and afterwards, if there's a complaint. Contact FAMSA at P.O. Box 10, Hinesburg, VT 05461, (802) 482-3437, www.funerals.org

The National Fraud Information Center assists with telephone cramming and slamming charges. Write to P.O. Box 65868, Washington, DC 20035 or go online to www.fraud.org.

Find out what you may pay for different long-distance carrier charges by contacting the **Telecommunications Research and Action Center** at its Website (www.trac.org).

TeleWorth (www.teleworth.com or (888) 353-9678) helps find the best long-distance rates in your area, as does www.decide.com.

Ellen Phillips

www.four11.com will assist consumers with savings on Directory Assistance billings.

www.wireless dimension.com will give you comparisons for wireless phone plans in your area.

Chapter 10
The Weary Traveler

"When you get to the end of your rope – tie a knot in it and hang on."
- Eleanor Roosevelt

Once upon a time in the distant past, a tired but happy mother, Imogene Industry, birthed quadruplets. She and her husband, Ira, had tried for years to make their little family a threesome. And when the big change occurred with four babies rather than just one, the proud parents just <u>knew</u> that these children would one day make a major impact upon the lives of everyone that they encountered. Little did Mom and Pop realize just <u>what</u> kind of impression awaited the public.

Because this was a Southern family and many Southerners have double names, the newborns were promptly christened Annie Automobile, Andrew Airlines (Andy for short), Thomas Train, and Shelly Ship. As these precious kiddies grew older, everyone wanted to be the children's friends. All swore that Annie, Andy, Thomas, and Shelly were the greatest accomplishments since the invention of the mint julep. When the children reached adolescence, however, they weren't as precious. The typical problems with teenagers erupted, and the quads gleefully entered this stage and had a bunch of fun. For example, Annie often refused to go anywhere and just wanted to stay stuck in the house. Andy would overload himself with things to do and then pitch a tantrum if he thought he had to stay on schedule. Shelly, who was the eldest, ate so much that her weight ballooned, while Thomas, on the other hand, just loved to crash in front of the television.

The children grew to adulthood and the older they became, the less responsible and enjoyable they seemed for those around them. Bad habits often grow worse as we age, and the quads were no exception. They each had a trust fund left to them by Imogene and Ira, and they were quick to form their own companies. (Did I mention they were also greedy little suckers from the get go?) *Andy became CEO of a huge industry that carried millions and millions of people each year through the skies. Annie's company manufactured transportation vehicles, without which few could get to where they needed to go. Thomas's business provided bullet-shaped locomotives that sped through the day and night carrying people and equipment (and sometimes even Andy's products). And dear Shelly who grew larger and larger founded an enterprise of great boats that, oddly enough, even resembled her in size.*

*As the quads' businesses (and their bank accounts) grew, they became greedier and greedier. Even though the masses depended upon them, each year Annie, Andy, Shelly, and Thomas became less and less caring about their customers' needs and concerns. Sometimes a lone complaint letter would flitter through the corporate mail slots bewailing the lack of poor service and quality but was usually ignored, until one day (gasp!) something unbelievable happened. These customers all united under one name: **Consumer** and they raised the flag of rebellion. "REVOLUTION" became their battle cry and an enormous letter-writing campaign their plan of action. Finally, besieged night and day on all sides, the "Terrible Travels" as they were known on Wall Street began to crumble. Faced with the deaths of so many postal carriers who delivered so many letters from unhappy, frustrated, and angry customers, the TTs decided to take a long, hard look at their policies with regards to service and quality. Humbled by what they saw, they gathered together as a family and made a lasting decision that would change the lives of billions of people forever.*

"My airlines will no longer overbook, lose luggage, or delay flights," exclaimed Andy.

"My automobiles will all pass a new eagle-eyed quality control before they leave the factories," cried Annie.

"My trains will become safer to ride and more customer-friendly," burst out Thomas.

"And my ships will get no bigger, and I'll hire more sensitive personnel," promised Shelly.

256

And so the four became more responsive and responsible; they provided generous surrender terms to the Consumer Revolution, which promised an end to the letter-writing war. And so it came to be that everyone was satisfied, and the world became a much cheerier, happier, and safer one in which to live and do business.

***Consume**r never gave up watching, though. Watching ... and waiting.*

Let's face it, even though I'm not one of the Brothers Grimm the message is still loud and clear. If we're stuck in an airport, we complain. If our train crashes (and we're still alive), we complain. If our car sucks raw eggs, we complain. If our cruise ship has a nasty roulette dealer or the service stinks otherwise, we complain. Since many of these excursions are booked for pleasure, our dream vacation may turn into a nightmare unless we take precautions.

First of all, consider the need for trip cancellation insurance. If you become ill or the cruise line goes defunct, and so forth, you're normally stuck with the-out-of-pocket-no-place-to-go blues. The insurance covers nonrefundable fares and deposits if you're unable to go. The insurance is not cheap, though, so it's best to buy only for more expensive vacations. Don't let the agent talk you into a plan that also covers an airline fare since you normally pay somewhere around a $75-100 rebooking penalty. (The insurance may be much more, so use caution and check with the airline about its penalty beforehand.)

Car rental add-ons and insurance can be other bug-a-boos if we're not careful. Whether it's a charge to use its airport shuttle or a fuel surcharge, make sure you know up front what's going on with a rental agency before you rent and certainly before you drive off. Be sure, too, that you read the fine print before signing and pay with a major credit card. (If you don't, then you haven't been following my protective advice very closely.) Some rental companies, and particularly those found outside the U.S., may pressure you to buy their own temporary insurance, and you could find yourself having done so if you

257

don't carefully read the fine print on the contract. The best way to avoid any confusion is to check with both your credit card company and with your own automobile insurance agent to see that you're covered with each or both (and I can't imagine you wouldn't be).

The third nightmarish insurance problem that might occur is if you haven't bought travel health insurance and then, unfortunately, find it necessary indeed. Several years ago, one of my clients went to a <u>very</u> exclusive American-owned resort in the Caribbean. They never dreamed that if something happened, they wouldn't be protected. One day after the couple's arrival, he leaned against and fell through the glass patio door, which turned out to be a faulty one. Not only was there no doctor on the premises of this fashionable resort, the local hospital also wouldn't admit Mr. Pain without cash on the barrel. So it's a good idea to check with your regular insurance company or with a specialty company to buy a rider that pays for emergency care or even the removal of your poor old sick or injured body back to the US of A.

But let's take each of the traveling possibilities one by one with a couple of different slants thrown in for good measure.

Airlines

None of us will ever forget the horrific events of September 11, 2001, when we couldn't tear ourselves away from the news of the atrocities happening in New York City and Washington, DC. Frankly, a great number of us still can't bear to place a foot on an airplane and, of those who do fly, we don't do so without prayer and vigilance. As we "travel" further into this chapter, I'll discuss and reinforce the new federal rules that we currently and will forever face when we go by plane. However, in the meantime, let's don't forget that the airlines gave us heaps of problems long before the terrorist attacks, and we also must stay on alert against further abuse from these corporate giants. So watch out, consumers, and continue to stand up for your rights.

Good ole "Andy" had a heyday with this industry before he ate his piece of humble pie. Too bad my fairy tale isn't true life as airline travelers all over the globe are fit to be tied these days. I have certainly had my fair share of *Appalling Airlines* experiences, but one sticks out in my mind as truly the most appalling from hell.

A couple of years ago, my husband and I decided on a restful and stress-free vacation. Our trip to the Caribbean promised a vision of a no hassle week, complete with sleeping late, lazy sunbathing on the beach, and my reading some juicy romance novels. Author John Steinbeck's observation regarding "The best laid plans of mice and men..." was never more evident than what <u>really</u> occurred.

Everything initially went as planned until we actually landed in Freeport. As we waited by the luggage carousel (and waited and waited and waited), we realized that while we had reached our destination, our clothes and other paraphernalia had not. By now it was early evening, we were exhausted, and it was *very* hot. Southerners are familiar with the expression "Horses sweat, men perspire, and ladies glow." I wasn't glowing nor perspiring – I was **sweating** and not just because of the temperature. I was also in a red-hot rage. And to add further insult to injury, no more planes were arriving that day from this particular airline. When the representative tried calling Miami, no one responded so he advised us to return the following morning for the first flight that would surely carry our bags. We left the airport for our resort (and, boy, what a misnomer that title turned out to be), still sweating in the broiling August sun.

Even though a cold shower helped momentarily, the relief was short-lived as we put our damp and soiled clothing back on. Matters worsened in our useless attempts to find a store still open in order to purchase a change of clothing. By this time, I definitely wasn't imagining the stares and flared nostrils of disapproval (i.e. smelly disgust) from passersby.

The next morning, we met the anticipated plane. No luggage. Now I was really sure a conspiracy was afoot to guarantee my stress level never abated, especially after *six* more trips to the airport and *six* more planes arrived without our belongings. The airline representative did what he could by continuously calling Miami, leaving messages that were never returned, and when he did speak with a human (and I use that term very loosely), he only received a bad attitude. In fact, the woman in charge of baggage claims in Miami insisted our luggage wasn't there and even hung up on our guy.

Finally, late that afternoon, just minutes before the final plane of the day left for the island from hell, I grabbed the phone and gave the Miami baggage manager an earful. Take heed, dear readers, this was <u>not</u> the same calm and detached tones that I always advise you take nor the ones I normally use. Usually, with the signal to a single brain cell, I instantly recall names of Head Honchos. And though I'm ashamed to admit it, I was so beside myself I even decided a little threat was in order. (Big rule: never, never threaten.) I concluded the conversation with the furious statement, "If both of my bags do not arrive on this last flight, I will immediately call Mr. [CEO] and let's see how long you keep your job, shall we?" Obviously, she wasn't prepared for a vengeful madwoman to spout off the name of her biggest Boss Man so, therefore, on the very next flight, floating merrily along the carousel in front of our red-rimmed eyes and smelly bodies, we spotted our suitcases. Attached to each was a sticker that read: **Phillips. Priority Rush**.

After we returned to the States, I transformed myself from the Bitch Who Ate Baggage Managers to my (whew!) professional poison persona. You better believe I wrote some heavy-duty complaint letters, all of which resulted in a new suitcase to replace the one that, with my luck, was missing a wheel, as well as two travel vouchers. This resolution furthered defined my experience that those in the airline industry really are among the very best to act responsively and responsibly to consumer complaints (even when their actions are totally blameworthy in the first place). While airline complaints are racing fast on the heels of the #1 automobile villains, still all corporations should take a page from the airlines' book. Unfortunately, when reading the philosophy of Donald J. Carty, Chairman and CEO of American Airlines, it seems significant that this was the only airline company that responded to my request for a quote (and American certainly has its own lion's share of complaints, particularly with the recent catastrophes).

> *"We're making a concerted effort to run American Airlines to the equal benefit of our employees, customers and shareholders – on the simple theory that happy and satisfied employees deliver exceptional customer service, which creates satisfied return customers, which generates superior returns for our shareholders. The only way we can truly satisfy our customers is to get from them the kind of honest and constructive feedback that helps everyone do a better job when the next opportunity arises. To continuously improve, we need both compliments and complaints so we understand why we either hit the mark or miss it a mile."*

Yet there are still issues the industry should solve to make air travel more convenient and enjoyable for consumers. For example, while they make us check into the airport one to two hours early, airlines force their customer to wait at the departure gate because they've overbooked. Another source of irritation and a tardy departure (and I swear I've heard this one personally) results from the *hour* it takes for a plane to taxi from a hangar to the departure gate. And the list just grows longer and longer. Because luggage compartments are at such a premium, airlines make us check as much as possible, yet it takes an eon for our bags to roll around the carousel (assuming they didn't end up in Timbuktu instead). And what about the promise of "dinner" on a long flight that, instead, turns out to be a hard roll topped with a tiny bit of cheese? Why can't we get an entire can of soft drink instead of one, measly, plastic cup? Surely a $450 fare (or more) entitles us to seventy-five cent can of Coke.

Chapter 5 in *Shocked, Appalled, and Dismayed!* presented tips and secrets to ensure more flyers knew their rights under the law (many of which the airlines keep under close guard). Unfortunately, lots of advisors, including yours truly, have made some errors with regards to airline rules and regulations. I certainly can't speak for anyone else's sources, but my current informant at DOT's legal department, Tim Kelley, says he's delighted to help to correct all the misinformation floating around, even among televised travel experts. Here's my best effort without going into a lot of legalese (and approved by Mr. Kelley).

Rule 240 of which I wrote in *Shocked, Appalled, and Dismayed!* and which many others tout is actually only a tiny portion of the airlines' Contracts of Carriage left over from the days of government regulation. Sometimes the language is still familiar, such as the "Subject to the terms and conditions… yada, yada, yada" that we see printed on our tickets. These days, though, this particular regulation pertains to the individual airlines and the rules they differentiate for their own passengers, rather than a DOT regulation. For example, US Airways does not allow for a free phone call when there's a flight delay of any length; on the other hand, Continental provides a free three-minute phone call if your delay exceeds two hours. The best way to prepare yourself for an upcoming flight is to log on to your airline's Web site and see all the specifics yourself in the event you should experience delays (and if you don't think there's a strong likelihood of this happening, I'd like to sell you that bridge in Brooklyn!).

So what, if anything, can we expect from the Feds with regards to airline regulations to help John and Jane Q. Public? Well, for starters, "Oversales, Part 250, Code of Federal Regulations" addresses the problem of overbooking and oversold flights for all airlines using aircraft with more than sixty seats. So what if the airline overbooked by 150 percent, maybe you fell and broke your ankle right outside the terminal, and you frantically hobble to check in a scarce five seconds later than the required one hour before boarding. Because they did overbook (and you're now just a nanosecond tardy because your foot now flaps in the wind), they might try to justify having sold your ticket to someone else or involuntarily bumping you off the oversold flight. Folks, sit up and take notice. If you visit the **U.S. Department of Transportation** at its Website (http://www.dot.gov/airconsumer/flyrights/htm), you can order the booklet **"Fly-Rights: A Consumer Guide to Air Travel."** Among other rights, the booklet will tell you that if you are involuntarily bumped from a flight that departs without you because of overbooking and the next plane you're booked on arrives between one and two hours later than your original arrival time, the carrier must pay you the lesser of $200 or the cost of your one way fare. Even better, the sum rises to $400 or double the fare cost if you're delayed for more than two hours (four hours internationally). You may also order "Fly-Rights" by mail by sending $1.75 to the **Consumer Information Center**, Pueblo, CO 81009 or by calling (202) 366-1111.

Secondly, the government mandates that each large and medium-size airline must possess its Contract of Carriage and

Rule 240 on hand for our eyeball inspections. This means that when we walk up to any counter where tickets are sold and request to see that particular airline's Rule 240, it better be there. In fact, certain airlines have found themselves paying out heavy-duty fines because they were in violation of this order and consumers reported the infringement to DOT. Hey, it's not the fault of the consumer if the airlines don't think we're savvy enough to demand our rights or if their own personnel aren't adequately trained enough to answer questions or to know where the Contract of Carriage is located. Before you kick up your heels, however, and sashshay on down the concourse planning on flying out in first class because that's all that's available on the next flight out and your airline has this policy in its Rule 240, don't forget a *Force Majeure* event does not fall within the same category as schedule irregularities.

A Force Majeure is any situation beyond an airline's control. Such circumstances include weather problems (and, yes, they love to use a snowstorm in Chicago to talk delays with a flight between San Francisco and San Diego), acts of God, riots, acts of civil disobedience, and so forth. Included recently is language that specifies labor-related disputes involving or affecting the airline's service. Now, why an attendants' strike isn't deemed the fault of the airline, I'll never know. It's just one more way those in the industry can push the screws and blame someone or something else for the lack of its own responsibility.

But there are certainly other hints that savvy consumers need to know as well.

- **Try not to travel during peak times**. Don't try for early morning between 7:00 and 10:00 a.m. or rush hour, from 4:00 to 7:00 p.m. This is when business traveling is at its height. If there's no choice, however, then take some precautions. Book an even earlier flight if available since it's less likely to be delayed and also may be less expensive.
- **Avoid airline hubs, if possible**. You can shave a lot of time off your journey if you don't fly through hub cities.

Even if this isn't an option, try to get a direct flight so you don't have to change planes.

- **Don't dally around**. If you're required to check in at the gate during a set time limit before a hopeful departure time, boarding pass or not, don't waste time looking in the news stand or buying that last cup of coffee at McDonalds. Many airlines will cancel your reservation if you haven't checked in or boarded according to their specifications, especially if it's a full flight.
- **Demand a food voucher**. Speaking of coffee, if your ticket states breakfast, lunch or dinner, and all you receive is the aforementioned hard roll "meal," then tell the attendant or even the captain if necessary that you want either a food voucher for the next airport or money off your next flight. Guess which one they'll give you?
- **Know your rights**. Just as described in *SA&D*, flyers have rights under federal law. Lots of advisors, including yours truly and even one certain travel expert I encountered while we were both featured on a famous television program last summer, have made some inadvertent errors with regards to airline rules and regulations. I trust Mr. Kelly, though, and obviously the US Department of Transportation does, too.

If there's a problem you can't seem to solve with these bozos, then after you've cced DOT with your official complaint letter, lodge an online complaint at (www.dot.gov/ost/ogc/subject/consumer/aviation/publications/te lljudge.html). In many instances, the federal agency may contact the airline on your behalf –just like in a letter. Another good contact to complain to is the **Aviation Consumer Action Project** at P.O. Box 19029, 589 Fourteenth Street, NW, Suite 1265, Washington, DC 20036. You can visit this organization online at www.acap1971.org/acap.html. And don't forget, even if your flight is delayed for only an hour and even if it doesn't specifically fall within an airline's Contract of Carriage, some will often give you a voucher, usually worth about $10 for lunch or dinner, or a seat on another airline, or place you on a flight to a nearby city. Ask customer service to list you as a "distressed passenger." <u>Now</u> do you see why I always advocate knowing your rights before you jump from the frying pan into the fare – I mean fire?

- **Be vigilant about inferior service**. I don't care whether you paid that $450 fare or an el cheapo $99 roundtrip special (actually, I haven't seen one of those in a longgggg while). No matter how trivial, you're entitled to certain amenities when you travel by air. For instance, the little, white pillows and those thin blankets are supposed to be on hand for every passenger, especially on long flights. If they run out, it's not your fault. If there's no magician's hat handy, then you better believe I'll demand compensation for my next ride with Appalling Airlines. I'm not adverse to causing a small scene if need be, too, although I'm much more cautious these days knowing that passengers and crew are jumpy and that armed marshals may be my seatmates. My sister calls me a *PLB* ("Pushy Little Broad") and I can think of a time or two I've ended up in first class just to shut me up. Assert yourself. Expect what you pay for and don't ever take less.
- **Check on using one airline's discount coupon on another carrier**. If you receive a voucher or one of those mailings that periodically arrive announcing a special fare and you can't use this airline for a particular flight, then hang on to it. Some airlines will honor a competitor's coupon if it flies to your destination.

The new federal and airline regulations that confront us as a result of September 11, 2001 are very much a reality. So if you know what's good for you and you really think security will allow you to trek down the jetway, then hotwire these rules into your brain.

- **Leave home earlier**. The government suggests that you arrive at the airport at least two hours early for a domestic flight and three hours for international flights.
- **Don't pack anything that may be construed as a weapon**. Even fingernail scissors or a tiny penknife will be confiscated and you won't get back your items. Worse, though, is that you run the risk of arrest. In fact, pack as lightly as you can. The less you have, the more quickly you'll move through security.
- **Choose paper tickets**. Airports have been in such a case of chaos since September 11 that, frankly, you're not demonstrating good judgment if you choose electronic tickets (E-tickets). Paper tickets ensure a faster security check; moreover, if you should have to change airlines upon arrival, a paper ticket is accepted more readily by another airline.
- **Carry proper identification**. Photo IDs can include a valid driver's license or a passport. If you have no photo ID, then you must have two other forms, including one that's government-issued. Some knowledgeable folks even urge that you take your passport *and* license when traveling overseas.
- **Keep airline contact information on hand**. If a difficulty arises, then you can rebook much faster by calling the airline or your travel agent rather than waiting in another long line.
- **Be polite**. Airline personnel and passengers are mighty skittish. I know I tend to make my displeasure known, but even *I* watch my mouth. Even an innocent remark can be (and has been) perceived as a threat, and, if this does occur, then you and that large Guardsman or Air Marshal will become **really** good buddies. Trust me!

The bipartisan "Airline Passenger Fairness Act" became a battle as a direct result of flyer rage. Unfortunately for us consumers, Congress decided to believe the airlines' promises that it would straighten up and fly right, so to speak; instead, we now have a "Customer First" guideline, as sanctioned by the industry. Too bad, the former regulation still lags far behind in terms of passage. Even though the people in command of all the different airlines pledged to be more friendly, such as in telling customers when flights are delayed, canceled or oversold, and to fully disclose their policies and rules, the plans for doing so remain somewhat vague. The carriers even go so far as to pledge that passengers can receive a refund on a nonrefundable ticket, provided the reservation is canceled within twenty-four hours of making it.

If we are to believe the industry, they assure us that they've behaved better with respect to (that old oxymoron) customer service. For instance, if you call to complain about lost luggage, the airlines *say* that their representatives will immediately search out and deliver the bags and the airline will ask the Transportation Department to double the maximum compensation for lost baggage to $2,500. More ludicrous examples (and I swear I'm not making these up) include Continental's promise to "attempt to locate a missing bag for three months" and Northwest's assurance that, when a flight is delayed or canceled, it "will apologize every fifteen minutes." So, you betcha, all isn't well in Sky Land. Senator Ron Wyden (D-Oregon) who, along with Senator John McCain (R-Arizona), championed the original Airline Passenger's Bill of Rights, believes that the plans are unenforceable. Too, one of Mr. Wyden's amendments that would have specifically defined the failure to disclose an overbooked flight, for example, as an unfair trade practice was watered down substantially.

In early 2001, DOT's Inspector General did find that the airlines somewhat improved customer service for the year 2000; unfortunately, the study also emphasized that the corporate big shots and their underlings refused to address flight delays and cancellations, which still remain monstrous passenger frustrations. Even though experts believe that passengers will never be truly served by the airlines until more airports and runways are built, Senator Wyden reminds the public that "No matter how much concrete you pour, or how many air-traffic computers you connect, things aren't going to change much unless this industry is required to respect the public's right to know." (*The Wall Street Journal* February 13, 2001.) All of this simply means we must continue to be vigilant in our Consumer Revolution and to remind the airline industry that we will *not* forfeit the battle or the war.

Senator Wyden stated, "Air rage stems from shoddy service." And Congressman John Dingell tells us "Airline attitudes and their service problems are intimately tied up with the declining level of airline competition." (Add this "declining level" to all of the proposed airline mergers and I'm very much afraid that we really will be the losers.) The only advantage we have currently – and I'm embarrassed to call it such because of the horrific circumstances – is that September 11 made a huge impact on air travelers. Even now, most airlines are only up to approximately a 70% filled flight. I don't know whether it's because of such a financial burden the airlines now carry or that its service personnel is just more likely to personalize their customers, but consumers note a different attitude, one that is kinder and more helpful. I surely hope that this way of thinking continues, even when planes return to full capacity.

So you're at the airport well ahead of the airline's scheduled time. You've checked in and are now waiting for Appalling to pull its 747 up to the gate. The agent begins to call seat rows, everyone either waits patiently for his or her turn, or the general stampede begins. You've got your regulated-sized carry on luggage in hand. You step up, hold your ticket out and then hear "Oh, I'm sorry, sir. You'll have to check one of your two bags." (Remember these days, a lady's <u>purse</u> sometimes constitutes a piece of luggage.) What to do, what to do?

Tony Jeary isn't an ordinary, run-of-the-mill passenger. While most of us fly to "regular" business meetings or to visit the folks back home, he jets around the world on a regular basis. In fact, he's one of those CEO's you so often hear me refer to, even though of the nicest variety. While Tony's corporate position vastly differs from most of ours, the complaints are similar.

3199 Passenger Parkway
Sweetwater, TX 68002

Ellen Phillips

May 28, 2000

Andrew Airline, President/CEO
Tyrant Airlines, Inc.
1000 Appalling Avenue, Suite 571
Houston, TX 66660

Dear Mr. Airline:

This past Thursday, May 21, I encountered a problem with your personnel in the Detroit airport at which time, in my opinion, an egregious and embarrassing judgment was made. As passengers proceeded to board for the Dallas-bound flight 331, scheduled to depart at 6:40 P.M., as a Titanium Mileage member I was the very first person in line (copy of boarding pass enclosed). Imagine my shock when the gate agent informed me that I could not bring my two carry-on bags on board; so then did the supervisor for Tyrant whom I requested.

The regulations, printed in the current issue of the *Tyrant Times* and which I have attached, state: "Combined free baggage allowances are: three pieces checked and no carry-ons, two pieces checked and one carry-on, one piece checked and two carry-ons, or no pieces checked and three carry-ons provided such pieces fit in an approved storage space." I must stress that this was the reason I was the first passenger to board, as surely this would ensure there would be space for my two bags. I then contacted the 1-800 Titanium operator who confirmed my prerogative to carry on two bags, but still the supervisor insisted on only one bag.

This incident was not the first frustration I encountered with Tyrant during my business trip; earlier, two equally appalling situations transpired. I upgraded to First Class on Sunday, May 17 (100 hours prior to my flight), but the agent mistakenly logged me with another one-way trip and connected the two flights onto my Titanium number. Not only did this cancel my First Class reservation without my request, it also canceled the flight itself. I was booked in seat 5F as I most often am.

I find this entire fiasco reprehensible. If you check my Titanium records, you will see that I fly with your airline approximately every three days and travel many thousands of miles each year. It is my understanding that it is a part of Tyrant's training to treat its passengers differently, based upon the number of miles flown per year and, thus, their frequent flyer status. While I do not wish to sound elitist, as the CEO of an international consulting firm and one who spends an enormous amount of money with Tyrant Airlines, I <u>do</u> expect a certain amount of reciprocity. I am very cognizant that in any business a judgment call has to be made from time to time, such as in this instance. However, I am clearly disappointed and feel the judgment was made in error, based upon the facts that were openly and peacefully discussed between the supervisor and me. I also use the exact same luggage around the world on all flights and on all airlines, and this is the first occasion where I could not transport two carry-on items as the very first person to board. The impression I received on May 21 certainly did not indicate any general measure of customer loyalty and absolutely none to a Titanium Mileage member.

It is my hope that you do not condone or accept conditions such as these; therefore, I trust that I will receive two round-trip tickets for my inconvenience,

Ellen Phillips

and I also expect a call at 1-800-999-8888 within the next ten business days.

Thank you.

Sincerely,

Tony Jeary

Titanium Member # U55520

Enclosure

cc: Allan Administrator, General Manager
Tyrant Airlines, Inc.
Detroit Metro Airport
Wayne County
Detroit, MI 48242

Eula Executive, Managing Director
Consumer Relations
Tyrant Airlines, Inc.
1000 Appalling Avenue, Suite 571
Houston, TX 66660

I choose not to think that our old friend, "Andy," compensated Mr. Jeary solely because of his important status, but whatever the reason the tickets soon *flew* to their destination.

One way you can avoid a hassle at the gate if a flight attendant or gate agent insists you check a bag is to demand a gate-to-gate check. This way your luggage is waiting for you when you arrive instead of whirling round and round the Merry-Go-Round. If they refuse or act nasty, then inform them (which you shouldn't have to do) that baby strollers and car seats are checked like this all the time.

Unfortunately, airlines differ in their rules. Too, many times when flyers call ahead to check they're often given the wrong information, which leads to angry fur "flying" at the gate. If you're a First or Business class, or an elite-level passenger, you may not be forced to comply with the regs altogether. For the remainder of us peons, however, the best thing to do is sneak in line with the elite group so we can get an overhead bin. I'm truly not kidding; just make sure your slinking venture is with the regulated-*size* bags. If, however, you have no choice in the matter and absolutely must check that second bag, and if you've carried both to the gate as a savvy consumer will do, then your bag is the last to be checked. This way it'll most often appear first on the carousel. A source of additional information for airline customers is the American Travel Association. This advocacy group represents its consumer membership with all phases of air travel and a lot of perks thrown in for good measure. Catch its website at http://www.1800airsafe.com or call toll-free to (1-800) 858-4233 to enroll in its program.

A totally different airline scenario concerns a woman who experienced problems of a special nature. Her complaint had nothing to do with luggage or being first in line. She just wanted to get to her departure gate that was way off at another concourse.

Even though we don't necessarily shout it to the skies, many of us suffer from chronic back pain. Unless you can snag a pillow or bring your own relief device onboard, you may find yourself in the throes of acute pain upon arrival. However, there are some tips for traveling with back pain, quoted from Dr. Harris McIlwauin's book <u>Winning With Back Pain</u>, as well as from my own experiences as one who endures daily pain from spinal osteoarthritis and especially when I travel.

1. All airlines are federally mandated to provide gate assistance to disabled passengers or those who cannot physically walk from gate to gate. DOT publishes a booklet entitled "New Horizons," which offers travel information such as the latter. And don't think you're taking space from someone who is worse off than you; the airlines should have plenty of wheelchairs (and/or electric carts) to go

Ellen Phillips

around. I always request a wheelchair and woe to the airline that doesn't try its very best to accommodate me!

2. Nonstop flights are better than changing planes. If you're changing from one flight to another (or, worse, from one concourse to another), your journey means more standing, walking, and carrying bags. This equals more pain for you. Not the most pleasant vacation you've ever had, huh?

3. As a matter of fact, if you are on vacation, be careful with your sightseeing. Paris or even New York can't be so touristy" that you try to do too much too fast and suffer later from these activities.

4. Make certain to carry all prescription medication when traveling. If you've ever had a bag to arrive late (is there anyone who hasn't?) after you realize you've packed your pills in checked luggage, you know for sure the definition of the word "frantic."

So do you need gate assistance? If the answer is yes, it doesn't matter if the problem is a bad back or if you're a senior citizen who can't walk that far and that fast. Upon prior request you're entitled to a wheel chair at the airport to get you where you're going. If you're denied this service for whatever reason, then complain, complain, complain.

8903 Rankled Road
Apartment 1
Portland, OR 96588
January 11, 2001

Lewis Lulu, President/CEO
Atrocious Air Lines
Incompetent International Airport
Chicago, IL 60609

Dear Mr. Lulu:

An appalling situation recently transpired when I traveled with Atrocious from Portland National Airport to Chicago (copies of boarding passes enclosed). I trust after reading the following documentation you will promptly and thoroughly investigate this matter.

- I departed Portland on Monday morning, December 28 on flight 333. As always, when I fly with Atrocious I request a wheelchair to assist me. Not only do I suffer from a spinal problem, but also I fractured my coccyx three months ago and both conditions necessitate a wheelchair when traveling. Usually, Atrocious' service is at least acceptable, but on this occasion it was nothing shy of egregious.
- When I arrived in Chicago, there was no assistance available. Along with approximately ten other people, including two very elderly ladies, we waited at the gate for twenty minutes after the agent transmitted calls in an attempt to obtain assistance. None was forthcoming and each of us had a flight due to depart from another concourse within a short time.
- Finally, we were told to walk several gates where we would go downstairs to catch a bus. Here we waited another ten minutes - again with calls being made to the driver. Once I reached the B concourse, I was assured that a wheelchair was waiting for me upstairs. It was not. By this time, my plane was due to depart and I had to <u>run</u> eight gates. Additionally, I had even stopped at a gate upstairs and requested assistance but was informed by the agent at the desk, "You don't need a wheelchair. It's only a few gates." Just because a passenger does not <u>appear</u> to need help is no reason for such a patronizing and sarcastic attitude.

Not only was I <u>not supposed to walk,</u> my medical condition was further exacerbated by my race down the terminal. At least with the plane being late as usual, I was not left at the terminal. To add insult to injury, as I was boarding and asked the attendant to help me place my small rolling bag above my seat, I was told to do it myself, as she "didn't feel well." I then informed her that I was unable to do so and this was her job to help me, which she finally did.

I might say that my return trip was more pleasant and events more smooth; however, there is no excuse for what I endured initially in Chicago. I used to fly Atrocious exclusively, but after similar incidents regularly occurred, I chose to instead fly another airline to Springfield and have someone to meet me to drive to my final destination. However, the past few months I have returned to Atrocious for these visits home. The incident about which I am writing is a perfect example of what I endured in the past and what caused me to choose another airline. In my opinion, Atrocious' service was substandard and some of its personnel extremely rude and unprofessional. I regret I had no time and was subsequently in such pain that I did not procure the names of your agent and the flight attendant.

I expect you to investigate this shocking matter immediately. I think it only fair that I receive a free round-trip ticket for future travel from Portland to Chicago.

Thank you, and I look forward to hearing from you within the next ten business days.

Sincerely,

Tesa Tailbone

Enclosures

cc: **The Honorable Hardy Myers**
     Attorney General of Oregon
     Office of the Attorney General
     Justice Building
     1162 Court Street, NE
     Salem, OR 97310

   Peter Sheperd, Attorney in Charge
   Department of Justice
   1162 Court Street, NE
   Salem, OR 97310

   The Honorable Norman Mineta, Secretary
   United States Department of Transportation
   400 Seventh Street, SW
   Washington, DC 20590

   The Honorable Kenneth Meade, Inspector General
   United States Department of Transportation
   JA-Twenty-seventh Street, SW
   Washington, DC 20590

Mrs. "Tailbone" quickly received a letter of apology and a $200 travel voucher. Even though this wasn't the round-trip ticket she wanted, she was satisfied with the result.

One last few tidbits on air travel. As with every other situation, we need to guard against airport scams. Common sense rules are best, but here are three specifics to remember.

1. Men need to be extra careful when using the restroom. Thieves hang around and seek out some unsuspecting guy who leaves his bags behind him as he "does his business" at the urinal. Quicker than you can sing, "Snatch and Run," the thief has done it. Don't set your ring or watch on the ledge above the sink, either. Tuck them in your pocket and place your carry-on between your legs as you wash up.

2. Think your wallet is protected inside a fanny pack? Think again. A snippety snip slices the waistband and, before you know it, the crook is gone and you're left holding the bag (so to speak).
3. Computers, carry-ons, cell phones, and purses are all tempting for a thief to grab as they come through on the x-ray belt. One popular scam is for one person to detain you before you go through and the other person grabs your belongings and go about his or her merry way. The best way to avoid this trap is to empty your pockets of anything metal that may set off the alarm. Then, be certain that you're the first one through the checkpoint immediately after placing your things on the belt.

Before I leave dear Andy Airline and his comrades-in-arms, can we be assured that there's at least one airline (other than Southwest of which I wrote in *Shocked, Appalled, and Dismayed!*) that stands apart from the others in a positive manner? Well, it appears that Continental definitely takes the prize, at least in the eyes of its employees, as evidenced by Forbes' "100 Best Places to Work." While former President Greg Brenneman decided against sending me information from a personal perspective, it's still important to know that not only has the company turned itself around from older, less prosperous days on the verge of bankruptcy, but also this transition is related directly to the dramatic improvement of employee satisfaction and morale.

The perks for Continental employees are varied. For example, the airline offers a nice profit sharing package and flying to any of its destinations for any member of the family for only $10 each way. (And to go a step further, employees receive two first class vacation passes twice a year at no charge.) Combine these with "fun" activities that promote collegiality, such as company picnics and holiday parties, and you've got a successful program. And certainly, when employees are happy, they'll do a better job at making consumers happy, as well. With this in mind, we can even forgive Continental's ridiculous statement that it'll try "to locate a missing bag for three months."

Automobiles

As far as I'm concerned, this industry is the absolute <u>worse</u> on the face of the earth. Out of all the applicable letters I've written on behalf on furious clients who've experienced defective vehicles, been involved in accidents because of the defects, been ignored or treated with rudeness by personnel (and the gripes go on and on and on), the auto "profession" takes the cake. One would think that the three or more ton death traps that transport millions a day would be safer and those who deal with the buyer would be more responsive. Nope. Rarely ever.

One of the most recognized names in automobile advocacy (as well as the presidential candidate who "gored" Vice President Gore in the 2000 presidential election) is Ralph Nader. Mr. Nader founded the **Center for Auto Safety (CAS)** in 1970 and has proven over the years that consumers usually cannot trust the word of manufacturers and dealers when they advertise their products or when they swing their deals to us – in many instances their easy marks. CAS has poked and prodded into the industry's secrets and the discoveries are both shocking and frightening. Without naming names, here's just a sampling of what's occurred over the years.

It used to be that reputable or otherwise used car dealers could sell a wrecked and re-built car and swear it was in perfect condition. That changed, but now these smarmies want Congress to pass a law legalizing the sale of rebuilt wrecks and to take away the consumer's right to sue when they buy the undisclosed wrecked autos. One major manufacturer deliberately withheld information in numerous safety investigations in order to avoid recalls that would cost it a pretty penny. Another big name lobbied Congress to block a safety recall of its minivans for defective tailgate latches that popped open in moderate crashes and killed a number of innocent children. And we can certainly review the tale of Jennifer Hamilton's Lemon that almost killed her son, even after she got continued reassurances from both the manufacturer and the dealer that the car was "perfectly safe."

Such a callous disregard for peoples' lives is more and more evident these days. The automobile lobby is enormous and has more money than we can imagine in its attempts to buy its way out of corporate responsibility. And every time we purchase an overpriced vehicle, pay for lemon repairs, and bear the burden of accident costs (remember the Ford Explorer and Firestone tires?), the top executives get richer and richer off of our bad luck. What can we do with our *Consumer Revolution*? Write and write some more – not just complaint letters after the fact, but letters to protect us before more atrocities happen. The Center for Auto Safety offers the following advice:

- **Discover how your legislators vote**. If they support anti-consumer laws such as allowing rebuilt wrecks, toss 'em out of office as quickly as possible.
- **Demand standards**. For example, federal regulators must issue standards that prevent children from suffocating in trunks. All vehicles should be equipped with releases *inside* trunks. In 1984 a federal official denied a petition for such and today he works for the American Automobile Manufacturers Association. What did I say about low-life lobbyists?
- **Learn to use the Internet**. Not only can you find information about risks, you can find better values.
- **Complain if you're ripped off**. Wow, Mr. Nader and the CAS must have heard of *Ellen*. Support CAS and other national consumer groups as well as those that are local.
- **Fight back**. Not only should you write complaint letters, it's also a necessity to buy a better car, to save money, and to join with other consumers in the revolution to protect society both with financial and safety issues.

Ellen Phillips

One of the best publications around is **Car Book**, by Jack Gillis. For a nominal fee ($35) to join the ranks of CAS's membership roster, you'll receive this giant book that tells everything you need to know about safety features, warranties, crash tests, complaint ratings, insurance savings, dealer showroom strategies, and getting the best price for your money. In addition, there's an abundance of info about airbags, car maintenance costs, lemon laws, leasing, and so forth. Also included in the $35 is a subscription to CAS's quarterly newsletter "Lemon Times." Contact the **Center for Auto Safety**, 1825 Connecticut Avenue, NW, Suite 330, Washington, DC 20009-5706 with your request. The CAS even helps consumers with legal assistance for repair problems so be sure and request the names of attorneys who specialize in your area as well. For a shorter list of local lemon law lawyers, check the organization's website at http://www.autosafety.org.

While all states have some kind of Lemon Law statute, they vary greatly from state to state. However, each has similar laws with which we should begin our search for justice. A period of coverage is established, usually one year or the written warranty period, whichever one is shorter. Some form of arbitration may be necessary. But most important of all is the definition of a lemon: for example, it constitutes a new car, truck, or van that has been returned to the dealer or shop at least four times for the same repair (some states mandate less times than this) or is out of service for a total of thirty days calendar during the covered period, among other factors. One word of caution, though. Some manufacturers buy back a lemon, and it will be re-sold in a used car lot to any sucker who happens along. *Always* contact any previous owners to make sure this vehicle hasn't been the subject of lemon abuse (with you as its victim). A really great source of information is **Carfax** (http://www.carfax.com). Whip onto this site if you're buying a used car, selling your own, or simply to check up on the one you currently own. Carfax provides so much information that after we receive the facts, we'll wonder why we ever thought we might have any expertise ourselves. It's always better to be safe than sorry, especially when dealing with *this* particular industry.

Another way to become an informed used-car buyer is to check out its Blue Book value. If you don't have access to a computer, then trek on over to your local public library; otherwise, go online. www.kbb.com is the site for the **Kelly Blue Book**. It's a free price guide that prospective purchasers can utilize to determine the value of a used car. Negotiations should be a breeze after that.

I wish I could say the letters I write for infuriated car owners get the results that Mrs. Hamilton received; unfortunately, my level of success drops dramatically with auto issues (in large part because of those fat cats at the top, I guess). But I do try and try again and caution the owners to do the same.

9802 Screwed Street
Little Rock, AK 70223
March 13, 2001

Annie Automobile, President/CEO
Unconcerned Motor Corporation
P.O. Box 875
1906 Rash Road
San Francisco, CA 00214-0875

Dear Ms. Automobile:

I have exhausted all resources within my limited means to attain satisfaction regarding a situation that occurred with my Unconcerned Wreck (VIN # UDONTCAREC776402), and I trust you will assist me in this appalling matter. A brief chronology of events follows:

- **On January 10, 2000, my Wreck would not start and had to be towed to a trusted auto repair center.**

Trustworthy Tire and Auto conducted an engine analysis, performed a complete tune-up and oil change, replaced the distributor cap, spark plugs, air filter, pcv valve, wiper blades, and serviced the fuel injection system. The total cost was $475.19 (see enclosed). The primary cause of the problem was a "burnt out" ignition rotor, which normally costs only $10.00. However, for my particular model, it was necessary to purchase not only an ignition rotor but also a distributor cap priced at $25.00. The final cost to me was $533.72 with an additional cost of $59.00 for labor.

- At the time of the repair my warranty had just barely expired at 36,439 miles. Already shaken from a costly nightmare, I was horrified when the attending mechanic and store manager, Rick Reliance, told me that he had never before encountered a situation like this. He further stated that the design of my automobile was "terrible" and a "failed design" and that something of this nature should not have occurred at 36,439 miles, especially with having the Wreck regularly serviced.

- On April 1, 2000, I wrote to Nick Noncompliance (letter enclosed) in an attempt to negotiate a resolution. I received no response.

- I further made attempts at communication to corporate headquarters in order to request reimbursement. Sometimes I was informed my letters had been received; yet at other times I had to again mail a letter or fax it.

- On July 18, 2000, I called Unconcerned and requested an answer to my appeal for reimbursement. I spoke with Barry Barracuda and was told my request was being reviewed. I listened in disbelief as he stated, "a review of independent repairs is dependent on who answers the telephone and that Unconcerned [was] still following up."

- On August 8, 2000, I once more called and spoke to Tillie Trifle who told me that Della Dillydally was my case manager and she was reviewing my files. Again, I was ignored.
- On September 3, 2000, I spoke to Herb Henchman and was told that any assistance to me was denied. I requested a written decision, but Mr. Henchman informed me that his office did not have the ability to do this correspondence; however, he stated he would place my request in the computer. He then suggested I send another letter to the corporate office, which I did on September 8 (copy enclosed). I requested a written explanation for the denial decision and the appeal procedures. Six months later, I am still waiting.

The manner in which I have been treated by Unconcerned is unconscionable. Even though I am just one consumer in a nation of millions, I still believe in treating people fairly and having that same fairness reciprocated. Because I as well as many of my friends and family have been a loyal customer of your company, I am certain that you will investigate promptly and thoroughly. I cannot believe that you have knowledge of or condone this type of what I believe to be unprofessional and discourteous behavior on the part of the employees of your corporation.

Thank you and I look forward to hearing from you within the next two weeks.

Sincerely,

Ellie Exasperated

Enclosures

cc: Nick Noncompliance, Regional Customer Service
Unconcerned Motor Corporation
196 Clandestine Court, Suite 400
Hot Springs, AR 76777

Herb Henchman, Customer Service Supervisor
Unconcerned Motor Corporation
P.O. Box 875
1906 Rash Road
San Francisco, CA 00214-0875

Della Dillydally, Corporate Service Director
Unconcerned Motor Corporation
P.O. Box 875
1906 Rash Road
San Francisco, CA 00214-0875

Larry Lout, Division Manager
Unconcerned Motor Corporation
Southwestern Region
90321 Flimflam Parkway, Suite 434
Little Rock, AR 72234

Freddy Flunky, Service Manager
Demented Drivers Auto Group
8525 Sucker Street
Little Rock, AR 70223

The Honorable Mark Pryor
Attorney General of Arkansas
Office of the Attorney General
200 Tower Building
Fourth and 323 Center Streets
Little Rock, AR 72201

Shelia McDonald, Director
Consumer Protection Division
Office of the Attorney General

200 Catlett Prien
323 Center Street
Little Rock, AR 72201

Clarence Ditlow, Executive Director
Center for Auto Safety
20001 S Street, NW, Suite 410
Washington, DC 20009

Citizen Action
1730 Rhode Island Avenue, NW
Washington, DC 20036

Ellie and I wrote time and again, but nothing was resolved. Even the agencies that investigated got the door slammed in their faces. Against my better wishes, she finally got so tired of all the run-arounds that she gave up the ghost. And of course when she did, so did the agencies. Lesson: Never give up. Persevere 'til the end.

While Ellie's campaign proved to be fruitless, other claims have been auspicious. Take the illustration of Danny Wilson. Mr. Wilson leased a top-of-the-line automobile, and within only a few miles of driving his new pride and joy, experienced a terrible problem. His efforts to rectify the issue came to naught so I gave it the old college try on his behalf.

1131 South Seethe Street
Athens, GA 32222
March 21, 2001

William Weaselly, CEO
Inferior Automobiles Company, Inc.
1789 Badboy Boulevard
Columbus, OH 43256

Dear Mr. Weaselly:

A shocking problem recently occurred with my newly-leased 1999 Deviant XXYK. From my initial purchase date to the incidents that followed, I encountered, in my opinion, unscrupulous Inferior practices, and I am confident that you will personally investigate this travesty both thoroughly and immediately on my behalf.

- On February 8, 2001, I leased the automobile (VIN # BH4HAHAHA880186) from Inferior and More in Athens, Georgia. The terms of your lease are based upon an M.S.R.P. of $88,725. The odometer reading at the time of purchase was nineteen (19) miles.
- On February 26 while driving only fifty miles per hour, the engine in this brand-new automobile suddenly stalled. This resulted in a grave safety issue for both my passenger and for me as well as for motorists surrounding me. The disabled power steering and the power braking system made the car extremely difficult to control. I was finally able to bring it to the side of the busy street and attempted to start it again. The first several attempts were unsuccessful, but then I was able to start the car and drove to my father's home, approximately one mile away. I realized the car still had a serious problem because the engine refused to run while idling so I called the 1-800 number in the owner's manual as well as the dealer in Athens. A tow truck was dispersed and towed the Deviant to the Big Boy dealership in Birmingham, Alabama, which was approximately fifty miles from the pickup point. Because I did not receive the title until February 22, I had not had the opportunity to even register the car. Additionally, although it had been driven only a few hundred miles when this incident occurred, I still made the February payment.
- I met with Ricky Reliable, the service manager at Big Boy, before and after his technician inspected the

vehicle and checked the computer system, fuel pump, and fuses. Then, after examining the engine's oil level and finding it a quart low, Mr. Reliable determined that this scenario was most unusual for such an expensive a car with only 713 miles. As Mr. Reliable prides himself on his professional honesty, he gave me the names of persons to contact within the Inferior Corporation.

- I began numerous attempts to contact your corporate headquarters with no success. A number of calls made between March 1 and March 8 were completely ignored. I did speak with Customer Service Manager, Suzanne Sassy, on March 2 who informed me that she would investigate the matter and would speak with the repairing dealer. On March 5, Ms. Sassy telephoned and informed me that the technicians believed the problem was identified: a cylinder inside the engine was without the proper compression and the valves were bent. She then stated there were two possible reasons for this, one being a problem with the car leaving the factory and the other "driver error" while downshifting. The Inferior technician believed the latter to be the case, with which assessment I vehemently disagreed. I reminded her that my passenger would vouch for this inaccurate assessment. I then contacted the dealer myself for confirmation of this technical assessment.

- Because of the seriousness of this situation, I then requested of Ms. Sassy that I receive an identical new Deviant in exchange for this defective one, but she informed me that headquarters had decided not to replace but to repair my car. She did indicate, however, that the company would be willing to extend some other financial adjustment as a result of the car being out of service, even though I reiterated that replacing the car is the only fair and just resolution. I also informed Ms. Sassy that upon leasing, it was my intent to purchase the car at the lease's end and that the residual value would be significantly overstated as a result of this defect and the subsequent repairs. In fact, once an engine is taken apart, a car's value decreases considerably.

- On March 8, Mr. Reliable ordered "*some* parts" (even though ostensibly there were not "some" problems as previously decided by Deviant technicians.) This indicates to me there could be <u>many</u> problems, rather than just what Inferior initially decided to be the case.
- I again spoke with Mr. Reliable on March 15. In his words, the problem was "The camshaft ceased in the cylinder head" and "Because it made hard contact, we are going to change everything on that side of the engine. This was not driver error; it was nothing of that type, something went wrong and we don't know why it went wrong." He then went to on to note, "This is a brand new engine and should not have a failure like this." With this information from Mr. Reliable, I then attempted to reach Bill Booby, District Technical Representative, at 4:30 P.M. but met with no success.

When I consulted my attorney regarding this matter, he advised me that Inferior was acting in a most unethical manner. I work in a managerial position with ConfidenceFaith, certainly a much larger company than Inferior Corporation. We realize the importance of customer satisfaction in the integrity of all of our products. When a problem occurs, as is sometimes the case, ConfidenceFaith instantly acts to resolve the situation. Certainly when the food tampering incident of several years ago transpired, the loss of profit and the potential and permanent damage to our company was enormous. However, we took the necessary steps to solve the problem, even losing many millions of dollars in the process, and now our sales are higher than any other comparable product on the market. We stood behind our professional reputation, consumers believed in our efforts and our word, and billions of people now <u>know</u> that ConfidenceFaith and all of its subsidiaries are honest and reciprocate loyalty with loyalty. Inferior should do no less, particularly in the instance where one of its impaired products has slipped past its quality control department (which, even though Ms. Sassy denies, has been verified by Mr. Reliable).

When my Deviant was being loaded onto the flatbed trailer on February 26, the twenty-plus people who watched did not notice that it was an exorbitantly priced automobile; all they saw was a new and defective "Inferior." At what cost is your corporation's reputation in terms of sales and dissatisfied current and potential consumers, whether it is a $12,000 Budget or one of your top-of-the-line models? I can assure you that all of my friends as well as my colleagues with whom I have spoken about this egregious matter are in total agreement with me: Inferior should and must replace the Deviant.

Thank you, and I look forward to hearing from you within the next ten business days.

Sincerely,

Danny L. Wilson

Enclosures

cc: AUTOCAP
    Deviant Division
    Inferior Automobiles Company, Inc.
    1789 Badboy Boulevard
    Columbus, OH 43256

Suzanne Sassy, Manager
Customer Service
Inferior Automobiles Company, Inc.
1789 Badboy Boulevard
Columbus, OH 43256

Ferd Fartenagle, Owner
Inferior and More of Athens
22235 Atlanta Parkway
Athens, GA 30600

Randy Ringleader, Sales Manager
Inferior and More of Athens
22235 Atlanta Parkway
Athens, GA 30600

Rick Davis, Service Manager
Big Boy Sales, Inc.
1687 Vestavia Highway
Birmingham, AL 35222

The Honorable Donald Evans, Secretary
United States Department of Commerce
Fifteenth Street and Constitution Avenue, NW
Washington, DC 20230
ATTN: Office of Consumer Affairs

Howard Beales, Director
Office of Consumer Protection
Federal Trade Commission
Pennsylvania Avenue and Sixth Street, NW
Washington, DC 20580

The Honorable Thurbert E. Baker
Attorney General of Georgia
Office of the Attorney General
40 Capitol Square, SW

Atlanta, GA 30334-1300

Barry Reid, Administrator
Governor's Office of Consumer Affairs
2 Martin Luther King, Jr. Drive, SE
Suite 356
Atlanta, GA 30334

The Honorable Bill Pryor
Attorney General of Alabama
Office of the Attorney General
11 South Union Street
Montgomery, AL 36130

Dennis Wright, Chief Director
Consumer Affairs Section
Office of the Attorney General
11 South Union Street
Montgomery, AL 36130

The Honorable Betty D. Montgomery
Attorney General of Ohio
Office of the Attorney General
30 East Broad Street
Columbus, OH 43266

Robert Shelton, Executive Director
National Highway Traffic Safety Administration
400 Seventh Street, SW
Washington, DC 20590

Clarence Ditlow, Executive Director
Center for Auto Safety
20001 S Street, NW, Suite 410
Washington, DC 20009

The Honorable Norman Mineta, Secretary
United States Department of Transportation

400 Seventh Street, SW
Washington, DC 20590

Federal Highway Administration
Southern Resource Center
61 Forsyth Street, SW, Suite 17T26
Atlanta, GA 30303-3104

Automotive Consumer Action Program
8400 Westpark Drive
McLean, VA 22102

Cleo Manuel, Executive Vice President
Consumer Federation of America
1424 Sixteenth Street, NW, Suite 604
Washington, DC 20036

Public Citizen, Inc.
1600 Twentieth Street, NW
Washington, DC 20009

The "deviants" in this case responded immediately with a nice deal. Mr. Wilson was offered the following: $2100 for three months lease payments, full maintenance for the life of the lease, and the installation of a keyless entry and a CD player. He thought this was a fair compensation, assuming his Deviant ran the way it should. When these promises on the part of the manufacturer proved false, however, <u>and</u> when within a matter of weeks this costly auto malfunctioned again, we burned off another letter. This time we met with bunches of success. The manufacturer bought the car back and canceled Mr. Wilson's lease. The check he received fully refunded all the expenses he had incurred as well as a small bonus for the *deviant* "troubles" he had with his automobile. Hooray for the persevering consumer.

On Dealing With Customers

Too bad each automobile manufacturer doesn't adhere to the philosophy of Michael Dale, former President of Jaguar Cars North America, Inc.:

"We have made sure the basics of our business plan are absolutely sound and they have been bought into by the whole company. Everyone understands the central objective, which is customer loyalty."

Be really careful about other unscrupulous tactics, too, when buying a "new" automobile. Some dealers and salespeople have no shame when a potential commission wanders into the showroom. After you've read the ads for a wonderful sale, remember the newspaper prints the information as it's given to them, and neither the paper nor you realize the shadier side of what's *really* on sale.

- **Rental cars sold as new**. These cars may have been driven thousands of miles. Be sure to check the odometer and make sure it hasn't been rolled back. The best advice is to take the car to a trustworthy independent mechanic and if the dealership balks at this suggestion, then move on down the road to one that will.

- **Demo cars advertised as new ones**. This is a perfectly legal practice in many states. Investigate the law in your area and also follow the preceding tip about checking the odometer.

- **Be wary of free offers**. Whether it's a sunroof, a CD player or so forth, you can bet your bottom dollar (which is what they want you to do) it ain't free! Somewhere, somehow, they're packing the deal with the sum of your so-called freebie. Get the promises in writing.

- **Stop by the service department early in the morning**. Ask car owners if they've had to repeatedly bring their cars in for repairs. Also find out if the technicians usually find something else wrong. While you certainly would want to know that your power steering is fixing to run amuck, if comments like "Your shocks must be replaced today," this may be a red flag that "today" may be <u>most</u> times the car is brought in for service.

- **Question the service department before you buy**. Check technicians' training and how they're compensated (again, if it's by the "shocks today," piecemeal work, your nose should smell a week-old fish). Find out if any work is ever subcontracted. If so, hit the road. Ask if these folks are willing to pay you for your time if the repair isn't repaired and you have to return the car; additionally, demand a deduction in cost for each day the car isn't ready per promise. As always, get everything in writing.

- **Take a road test**. You wouldn't dream of buying a new car without doing this, and you'd better do the same after any repairs have been made to your car. Better yet, take the technician or mechanic along for the ride and don't pay a dime unless you're sure the problem is fixed to your satisfaction.

- **Pay for repairs with your credit card**. Just as with other purchases, you can dispute a bill and obtain resolution with your credit card company.

Is there a single solitary soul who doesn't wish to get the right vehicle for the right price? Not unless you've got more money than sense. The best way to begin is to visit <u>www.edmunds.com</u> to find out the manufacturer's retail price, the dealer invoice, the holdback (subtract the amount from the invoice), and any dealer incentives, also subtracted from the invoice price. This total will give you the dealer's real cost (and you won't be subjected to his woeful tales of "I won't make a penny on this deal"). Another great tip to get a great car is to send out the following letter to different car dealers. The effect should start a bidding war and you'll walk away with your dream car and at the very lowest price.

Dear [Dealer]:

I am immediately prepared to purchase a [model] with the equipment listed below. (List what you want.)

I have already received quotes from other [brand] and competitive-make dealers and just today realized that, although you are an authorized [brand] dealer, I had not requested your quote.

I intend to service the vehicle at the dealership where I buy and would be happy to recommend that dealership to family, friends, and colleagues.

Please provide me with a quote of a complete price for the vehicle I have described. If we come to an agreement, I will bring certified funds in the exact amount of your quote. Make certain that your quote includes all fees, taxes, and costs. I will not accept substitutes, nor will I pay for upgrades or additions.

If you have additional warranties or cosmetic treatments that you recommend, please quote those items separately. I will respond to those recommendations individually.

Please mail me your quote within the next five days. I will conclude this transaction shortly thereafter.

Sincerely,

[Your name]

Even within the confines of a stress-related economy and massive employee lay-offs, DaimlerChrysler remains one of the best-known automobile manufacturers for consumer innovations and for employee support. For example, the company is on the cutting edge of ideas, such as environmentally friendly cars running on alternative fuels or those vehicles with standard Internet connections. And in the same breath, on August 1, 2000, DaimlerChrysler began to offer full medical, dental, and prescription drug benefits for same-sex partners who are on both hourly and salaried wages. Carrying the good news even further, the corporation runs more to manpower than the other manufacturers; of course, to be successful demands that hiring practices incorporate people who work well without much supervision. Additionally, these employees are trained to take on as much responsibility as they can handle. What a great concept and one that goes right back to my customer service premise that the more responsibility a representative is given, the fewer customer complaints we'll see.

DaimlerChrysler is also one of the most diverse corporations around. A wide array of cultures and creeds first originated with Chrysler, but with the merge, the company is currently in the forefront. We see diversity across gender lines as well. Plus, to make a great work environment an even better one and to ensure a happy employee base, the company has one of the lowest employee turnover rates. Such a stable environment exists in large part because its work force is paid *very* well and the benefits far outdistance most other businesses.

Okay, consumers, you've won the bidding war, bought the car of your dreams and then, for whatever reason, *Ole Faithful* needs a repair. In addition to the above tips, there are an awful lot of repair-scams making lots of money off of your ignorance. Some of the best scam artists take your checkbook and run by claiming they must do the following:

- **Tear down the transmission**. If your car has a shifting problem, beware of this ploy. Once the transmission is down, then you'll be informed it needs a total re-building at, usually, a cost of $500 to several thousands of dollars. A shifting problem generally occurs because of less costly matters, such as small metal shavings in the transmission fluid, which is normal.

- **Replace the brakes**. This procedure entails replacing the calipers, rotor pistons, and wheel cylinders and will cost you in excess of $500.
- **Repair the steering**. After your car is lifted up, Mr. Trustworthy will wiggle a wheel (naturally causing it to wobble) and tell you that new ball joints are necessary. He'll even appeal to your panic when he informs you your wheel might actually <u>fall off</u>! The only thing likely to really fall off, however, is the balance in your checkbook where you've paid this scammer.

Be careful with "as-is" sales, too. You get what you pay for and an "as-is" usually doesn't get you a whole lot. Basically, what this type of sale means is that you're buying a vehicle with all its flaws and faults and with no warranty of merchantability. If, on the other hand, you discover that your car, truck, or van had been stolen, was in a wreck, its odometer had been rolled back, and so forth (in other words, you discover the dealer is a smarmy liar!), you can go after the dealer. Fraud is fraud is fraud. You can save yourself a lot of grief, though, by having the vehicle fully inspected by a dependable, independent mechanic and then negotiating a price that takes into consideration what you'll have to pay for repairs.

So you've been ripped off by a repair shop (like millions of others). Maybe you took Old Faithful in for a tire alignment but then received a call from the mechanic insisting that the transmission needed a complete overhaul and he was *sure* you'd be delighted that he performed the job for only $999.99. When you strenuously object, you discover that if you don't pay the bill, you don't get the car. If you have other means of transportation, complain first. If not, then you may just have to fork over this despicable person's money (who, unfortunately, happens to be the owner of the repair shop) and then lodge a written complaint, just like "Victor Vehicle."

118 Filched Street
Providence, RI 02905

June 13, 2001

The Honorable Sheldon Whitehouse
Attorney General of Rhode Island
Office of the Attorney General
150 South Main Street
Providence, RI 02903

Dear General Whitehouse:

I have exhausted all resources within my limited means to attain satisfaction regarding a, what I believe to be, a fraudulent situation that occurred with Harry Hoax at Flimflam Service Shop in Providence. I trust you will assist me in this appalling matter. A brief chronology of events follows:

- On April 10, 2001, while driving on the highway, it became apparent that the tires on my Nettlesome Sentry desperately needed alignment. Because I am new to the area and did not know a trusted auto repair shop, I took my car to Flimflam. Mr. Hoax informed me that this minor problem would be fixed within twenty-four hours at a cost of $69.99.
- The following day, I received a call from Mr. Hoax who told me that my transmission was in such poor condition that he felt it necessary to perform a complete overhaul. You can imagine my shock after I refused this service only to be informed that the overhaul, one I did <u>not</u> authorize, had been already completed. The cost to me was $999.99 (copy of statement enclosed)
- I immediately returned to Flimflam to voice my objections in person and to dispute this charge. Mr. Hoax stated that if he did not receive payment, I would not receive my Sentry. I had no choice but to pay him.

This entire situation is reprehensible. Even though I am just one consumer in the state, I still believe in trustworthy businesses and having that same trust reciprocated. Further, if Mr. Hoax treated me to this type of activity, I am certain that others have suffered as well from his ruses. As Attorney General, you should be aware of practices such as this in order to defend defrauded and innocent citizens.

Thank you and I look forward to hearing from you within the next two weeks.

Sincerely,

Victor Vehicle

Enclosures

cc: Ani Haroian, Director
    Consumer Protection Unit
    Department of the Attorney General
    150 South Main Street
    Providence, RI 02903

    Clarence Ditlow, Executive Director
    Center for Auto Safety
    2001 S Street, NW, Suite 410
    Washington, DC 20009

    Automotive Consumer Action Program
    8400 Westpark Drive
    McLean, VA 22102

    The Honorable Donald Evans, Secretary
    United States Department of Commerce
    Fourteenth Street and Constitution Avenue, NW

Washington, DC 20230
Office of Consumer Protection
United States Department of Commerce
Room 5718
Fourteenth Street and Constitution Avenue, NW
Washington, DC 20230

Harry the Flimflam Man cut a check rather quickly for the full amount after he received a stern directive from the agencies, and Victor became much wiser in future transactions.

Always, always get a second or a third opinion before any major work is performed on your vehicle. Again, be a *savvy* consumer.

Keeping in Touch with Customers

Top executives do listen to consumers in order to maintain their customer base, as evidenced by the following quote from Keith A. Morgan, Chief Executive Officer of AAMCO Transmissions, Inc.

"After 20 million customers over 36 years, we put special emphasis on those who contact AAMCO with a complaint or a concern. We've found that it is these customers who, although they may start out less than satisfied, wind up being our biggest supporters – and, our most prolific referral sources."

And we hear from Karen Beard, President of the North America Division of Alamo Rent-A-Car, Inc., who also offers a promise that

"The culture of Alamo Rent-A-Car revolves around the concept that customers' needs come first. Our customer for life philosophy is part of the fabric of our company. Repeat rentals occur only when the customer has been treated properly and feels that he or she is valued. Alamo Rent-A-Car is dedicated to the premise that it's better to build a customer for a lifetime than it is to sell to a customer one time."

Trains
   "This Train's Bound for Glory, This Train" is a grand gospel song, but sometimes we wonder if "glory" might not be easier to reach and with fewer headaches. While trains are much less expensive than a plane ride and can be much more convenient than driving your car, it doesn't necessarily hold true that this means of transportation will be hassle-free. We hear horror stories of de-railings, plunging into rivers, drug-sodden conductors, and so forth, even though these are in the tiny minority. Most trains, whether commuter, subway, or nationals, are perfectly safe. It's the little things that usually get our goats and make for a complaint letter.
   Take the dilemma of "Ruth Rider." She found herself (as did the other passengers with whom she traveled) embroiled in lose-lose situation with a rude and unprofessional café attendant. The letter she mailed previously was a real no-no in that she ranted and raved and used defamatory statements about this person. Just to give you a peek into the mind of someone who doesn't follow the first principal of *Calm Down* as well as subsequent admonitions, then read on.

9857 Pissed Parkway
Powell, OH 43069
April 24, 2001

Customer Service
Office of Consumer Relations
TRAINS Inc.
P.O. Box 3490
New York, NY 21290

To Whom It May Concern:

On April 19, 2001, I was a passenger aboard the New York to New Haven train, #10, where I encountered your café attendant, Bob Belligerent. This man was the rudest, most insolent and hostile person it has ever

been my misfortune to meet. He cares nothing for the comfort of TRAIN passengers, or for the truth itself, which I later discovered by dialing your 800-telephone number.

After two stops, the train became totally full, with standing room only. Mr. Belligerent had taken up four seats with his personal belongings; even after the conductor announced for this type of seat to be cleared so that passengers could be seated, he refused to do so, even at the request of the passengers themselves. At each stop, he closed his station for five minutes, and at the Boston stop, he closed for thirty minutes; each time he stated it was his prerogative to do so. I later found this to be a complete lie.

In the past, I have used TRAINS many times for travel and have been satisfied; however, due to this experience, I can assure you that I will consider alternate means of transportation for the future. I don't intend to again place myself in the position of being condescended to by such an extremely ill-mannered representative of TRAINS.

I expect to hear from you soon concerning this matter.

Sincerely yours,

Ruth Rider

I really expected that "Ruth" had also been served a summons by the local sheriff to answer to a libel lawsuit. Insofar as she didn't receive a response to her letter at all, she was lucky indeed. The letter I then wrote for her was a tad more subtle than hers.

9857 Pissed Parkway
Powell, OK 74122
May 31, 2001

Thomas T. Train
TRAINS Inc.
1764 Avenue of the Americas
Suite 990
New York, NY 21207-0990

Dear Mr. Train:

An outrageous situation occurred on TRAIN #10's New York to New Haven route on April 19, 2001. I am certain you do not condone rude behavior on the part of your representatives and will wish to investigate this matter promptly and thoroughly.

• The train became completely filled after two stops; in fact, passengers were even standing because of the lack of seating. The café attendant, Bob Belligerent, had previously spread his possessions across four seats, seats that were needed by paying customers of TRAINS. The passengers requested that he move his belongings as did the conductor, but Mr. Belligerent refused the requests and became verbally abusive to all.
• In addition, your employee closed his station for five minutes at each and every stop and, even worse, closed for thirty minutes at the Boston stop. Again, when people complained of this inconvenience, Mr. Belligerent became even more discourteous. Upon reaching New Haven, I called TRAINS' 800-telephone number and discovered that Mr. Belligerent's actions were totally against company policy.

I have enjoyed TRAINS transportation many times in the past and have been quite satisfied with the service. However, if it is your current practice to hire persons of Mr.

Belligerent's caliber to represent your organization, I will seek other means of transportation for the future. I do not wish to again place myself in the position of having to deal with, in my opinion, such an abrasive and unprofessional individual.

I know you are as appalled as are others to whom I've told this terrible story; therefore, I expect a refund of the cost of my ticket in the amount of $198 (copy of receipt enclosed).

Thank you, and I look forward to hearing from you no later than June 18, 2001.

Sincerely,

Ruth Rider

Enclosure

cc: Jane Wheeler, Director
Consumer Protection Division
Office of the Attorney General
440 South Houston, Suite 505
Oklahoma City, OK 74127-8913

S. Mark Lindsey, Deputy Administrator
Federal Railroad Administration
United States Department of Transportation
400 Seventh Street, SW
Washington, DC 20590

Hiram J. Walker, Administrator
Federal Transit Administration
400 Seventh Street, SW
Washington, DC 20590

United States Tour Operators Association
342 Madison Avenue, Suite 1522
New York, NY 10173

This time results happened, and Ruth received the cost of her train ticket and a profuse apology from the company.

Even though encountering a Mr. Belligerent hopefully doesn't happen too frequently and certainly just doesn't occur on train travel, follow this advice before you buy that rail pass.

- **Be flexible**. Just as with airlines, if you can find the best bargains with the least restrictive travel times, you'll come out ahead.
- **Be sure of special deals**. If it's advertised that a ticket and a hotel stay are part of the same package, then check to see if each is less expensive when sold separately. Check Internet sites for lowest-cost tours, hotels, etc. Two of the best are **Expedia** (http:www.expedia.com) and **Preview Travel** (http://www.previewtravel.com).
- **Carefully review policies**. What if you must change your plans? Check all the restrictions that may apply.
- **Pull out your credit card**. As I always advise, pay with plastic in order to protect yourself if a complaint later becomes necessary.

In conclusion, it's too bad that others within the travel industry don't take a page from Amtrak's book, a monumental decision announced in July 2000. Big Boss George Warrington announced a *real* customer service policy, whereby if for any reason a passenger is dissatisfied, that person either receives a voucher for free travel equal in value to the ticket price paid by the passenger on the complaint route – no questions asked! Even better, these "Service Guarantee Certificates" can be used with other discounts, such as those for senior citizens. Of course this doesn't mean you don't verbally and later in writing let Mr. Warrington know the problem and also extend a great, big thanks for the new customer service policy. (Amtrak is developing checks and balance measures so that dishonest riders can't take advantage of the situation.) Can you even begin to imagine the loyalty that a policy like this will invoke in the public?

Ships and Boats

Do you ever wonder when aboard that fabulous cruise ship if your ears might catch the strains of "Nearer my God to Thee"? Well, maybe today's cruise lines are in much better shape than the *Titanic*, but that doesn't mean problems don't occur with increasing frequency aboard these Big Girls. Complaints vary from poor service onboard to not being forewarned about port-of-call purchases. And while we're stuffing ourselves with sixteen meals a day, and lying in the sun, and sipping margaritas, we have no idea whatsoever that the experience can quickly turn nightmarish more quickly than we can call a steward to refill our drink. While there's no sure-fire way to avoid events turning ugly, there are a few ways you can protect yourself before heading up the gangplank (as opposed to *walking* it).

- **Be sure the cruise you book is the right one for you**. If you loathe and despise little kiddies running around and disturbing your relaxation, then be sure you're not on a "family" cruise. The **Cruise Ship Center** site at http://www.safari.net/ (SWA symbol)marketc/CruiseShipPage.html provides worlds of information, including current deals from cruise lines and brokers.
- **Book the best accommodations with the best amenities your purse can handle**. Instead of tossing your cookies within the confines of a six by eight room with one double bed for you and hubbie, opt for a porthole or two. Even better is if you can afford a stateroom with a balcony (where you can throw up *outside* the cabin). Check out **Moment's Notice** (http://www.moments-notice.com), a discount travel club. For a $25 annual fee, you can come up on some great discounts for not only cruises but also for their accommodations. Call Moment's Notice at (718) 837-1657.

- **Be prepared to tip liberally**. While the hired help is usually great on these excursions, it certainly doesn't hurt to palm a fiver or two in order to get better service than some other stingier passengers.
- **Be perfectly clear on ship-to-shore excursions**. If the ship is cruising around the Caribbean and promises five stops at exciting ports where you can shop 'til you drop, make sure it's locations you want. If you're expecting the exotic French St. Martin, for example, and the reality is the backwoods of Freeport, you won't be a happy customer.
- **Get everything in writing**. Again, I cannot advise this enough. While unforeseen dilemmas may arise, at least the basics of the cruise will be covered. It also wouldn't hurt to contact the **U.S. Tour Operators Association**, 342 Madison Avenue, Suite 1522, New York, NY 10173 (212) 599-6599. These folks can tell you if your tour operator is a member and, as an added bonus, will send you free brochures.

George and Sharon Callaghan were cruise-proficient after having been passengers on a number of these types of vacations. Unfortunately, an unexpected problem developed with their last one. An innocent turn of events resulted in the verbal abuse of Mr. Callaghan by one of the ship's "friendly" crew, and he did not lie down like a dog and die, either. He (and I) took action.

4720 Abused Avenue
Alexandria, VA 22314
March 31, 2001

Shelly Ship, President
Neptune Cruise Lines
4590 Mermaid Parkway
Ft. Lauderdale, Fl 42333

Dear Ms. Ship:

An egregious problem occurred with my most recent cruise (February 1-7, 2001) with Neptune on the *Singing Siren*. While Rita Recompense ultimately contacted me on February 19 with Neptune's suggestion of "compensation," when compared to the appalling and despicable manner in which I was treated while aboard the *Siren*, I am not satisfied whatsoever. Therefore, I ask you to personally investigate this matter promptly and thoroughly.

- On February 5 I was in the casino playing at the Craps table and just as I had raised my hand to throw the die, the dealer, Henri Hellion, yelled out, "Don't throw them against the table that way!" I must stress here that I was playing in the identical manner in which I had done so each evening of the cruise with <u>no one asking me to do otherwise</u> (including this same dealer at whose table I previously had been playing). Of course, his comment caught me by surprise and I crapped out. This, however, is not the complaint as I lost only approximately $50 and had earlier won much more. What upset me was that Mr. Hellion refused to answer my questions concerning his not informing me of my "mistake" earlier in the evening and the subsequent treatment I received from the casino manager, Meg Malign.

- I spoke with Ms. Malign immediately following the incident, and she acted in a very rude and abrasive manner, as can be testified to by several of my party who were standing nearby. Because her attitude and remarks angered me so, I simply walked away. Later, I again approached Ms. Malign and requested that she speak with the dealers with whom I had played during the week - Diane, Alexander, and Zephine - to understand the type of patron I was. She stated she had done so and they all had informed her I had continually been asked to change the manner in which I played the dice but ignored their instructions. I knew this to be an untruth and I told her thus, but her response was, "If anyone is lying, it's you." I then demanded she and I meet with those dealers so that I would know for myself if they had stated this to Ms. Malign. She denied my request, again in an extremely hostile manner.

- I immediately spoke with each of the dealers personally, one by one, with the exception of Zephine who was not available; all assured me they had not told Ms. Malign what she stated they had done so; in fact, they also assured me that I was a very pleasant customer.

- On February 6 I reported the incident to Bobbi Banker, Chief Purser. Ms. Banker introduced me to Miles Manage, the hotel manager who took notes and gave me the 1-800-U-CRUISE number. Both Ms. Banker and Mr. Manage were professional and most apologetic.

- Upon my return home on February 8 I called Ida Ignore at the above number and related the incident. She asked me to wait for a letter concerning this situation. After receiving no response by September 11 I again called customer relations; the agent checked the computer and guaranteed I would hear soon. (I did receive the enclosed copy of a form letter from Ms. Ignore on February 23, dated February 15, 2001.)

- On February 25 I called the Casino Department (305-689-0000, Extension 6) and spoke with Rita Recompense who promised to contact the casino personnel and then return my call. That same day, she called to inform me she had placed a message with that department and would contact me again as soon as possible. By March 4 and after receiving no call from Ms. Recompense, I contacted her at 10:55 a.m. She apologized for not calling and stated she would check further. After <u>still</u> receiving no word from her after leaving messages on her voice mail on March 10 and 15, I then spoke with Franz Fruitloops on March 18. Ms. Recompense then left a message on my answering machine, which I returned on February 19 at (800) 936-

4440, Extension 828, and she indicated that Neptune would resolve the problem internally. I explained this was not a satisfactory solution and reminded her of Neptune's ad, "[We] guarantee a great time." Certainly, this was not the case for my wife or for me as I had been humiliated in front of a large number of people, insulted and degraded by Ms. Malign, and then seemingly ignored by corporate officials. I told Ms. Recompense that I believed Carnival should compensate me with a free cruise for my wife and me and that Ms. Malign should pay for it. I was then informed that supervisors were advised that I was polite, professional, and that Ms. Recompense did not believe me to be lying about any of the incidences that took place aboard ship.

- On March 29, 2001, I received a letter from Ms. Recompense with Neptune's "resolution" (copy enclosed). While corporate headquarters may believe that a 10% discount for future travel is satisfactory compensation for the outrageous and offensive manner in which I was treated, I certainly do not.

This cruise aboard the *Singing Siren* was one of several Neptune cruises my wife and I have previously enjoyed and, in addition, we have spent many thousands of dollars with your line. Furthermore, it has been on <u>my specific recommendation</u> that family and friends have also booked with your cruise line. Unfortunately, this most recent experience has annihilated any desire for all of us to book any of your ships in the future. Additionally, as a successful business owner myself and one who understands the concept of guaranteed customer satisfaction and, thus, loyalty, I find it reprehensible that Neptune feels little allegiance to its own customers. Therefore, I again expect a free cruise for my wife and for me as well as an official letter of reprimand to Meg Malign.

Thank you, and I look forward to hearing from you no later than April 16, 2001.

Sincerely,

George Callaghan

Enclosures

cc: Robert Whitley, President
U.S. Tour Operators Association
342 Madison Avenue, Suite 1522
New York, NY 10173
Vicki Freed, Chairman
Cruise Line International Association
500 Fifth Avenue, Suite 1407
New York, NY 10110

The Honorable Mark L. Earley
Attorney General, Commonwealth of Virginia
Office of the Attorney General
900 East Main Street
Richmond, VA 23219

Frank Seales, Jr., Chief
Antitrust and Consumer Litigation Section
Office of the Attorney General
900 East Main Street
Richmond, VA 23219

Carlton Courter, Commissioner
Office of Consumer Affairs
Department of Consumer Services
P.O. Box 1163
Richmond, VA 23219

Carolyn A. Quetsch, Director
Fairfax County Department of Consumer Affairs
12000 Government Center Parkway, Suite 433
Fairfax, VA 22035

VF Johnson, Consumer Specialist
Fairfax County Department of Consumer Affairs
12000 Government Center Parkway
Fairfax, VA 22035

American Society of Travel Agents, Inc.
Consumer Affairs
1101 King Street, Suite 200
Alexandria, VA 22314

Meg Malign, Casino Manager
Singing Siren
c/o Neptune Corporation
4590 Mermaid Parkway
Ft. Lauderdale, FL 42333

Bobbi Banker, Chief Purser
Singing Siren
c/o Neptune Cruise Lines
4590 Mermaid Parkway
Ft. Lauderdale, FL 42333

Miles Manage, Hotel Manager
Singing Siren
c/o Neptune Cruise Lines
4590 Mermaid Parkway
Ft. Lauderdale, FL 42333

Ida Ignore, Special Advisor
Office of the President
Neptune Cruise Lines
4590 Mermaid Parkway

Ft. Lauderdale, FL 42333

Rita Recompense, Special Advisor
Office of the President
Neptune Cruise Lines
4590 Mermaid Parkway
Ft. Lauderdale, FL 42333

Even though his specific expectations were denied, Mr. Callaghan was offered an additional discount on his next cruise and an upgrade amenities package.

Unfortunately, while we may complain to the **Federal Maritime Commission's Office of Informal Inquiries and Complaints**, the FMC is pretty much like the Better Business Bureau; neither organization has any legal clout. The FMC can write the cruise line on behalf of the complainant, but it certainly doesn't have a lot of luck, according to Joseph Farrell, FMC's director. In fact, the FMC doesn't even keep count of complaints against particular cruise lines, and compensation is usually at the sole discretion of the cruise line itself (unless the courts become involved). Your best sources of viewing comments by past passengers before you book your vacation are **CruiseOpinion** (http://www.cruiseopinion.com) and **Cruise.com** (http://www.cruise.com).

While Mr. Callaghan's documentation was superb, there are other methods by which you can legitimize your complaints.

- **Voice concerns immediately**. Just as Mr. C did, complain as soon as the incident occurs. Take it a step further, though, and encourage other passengers to complain as well.
- **Document everything**. Don't just write it down, either. Use that expensive camera or video recorder to prove your case. These may come in handy a lot more than a photo of that beautiful woman you sneaked while walking along the nude beach.
- **Consider a lawsuit**. If all else fails, small claims court is certainly an option. Just be sure you read the

315

cruise contract carefully for lawsuit deadlines; once that date has passed, you're dead meat.

Let's say your "ship" complaint lies with something a wee bit smaller. Rather than cruising around an ocean, you roam around a river or a lake taking in the beauties of nature and maybe catching a fish or two for supper. Just as you're heading for shore – *BLIP* – your motor shuts down and you're stuck with night fast approaching. As you frantically attempt to repair the problem, you curse a blue stream recalling that the motor is a fairly new one and there's no way on God's green earth it should have zonked out. "Joe Jaunt" was so infuriated (after he finally reached safety), he was determined to express his displeasure with the whole debacle.

6700 Aggravation Avenue
Franklin, TN 38844
August 24, 2001

R. D. Riverbend, President
Lakeshore Marine, Inc.
P.O. Box 1939
Edensburg, PA 15931

Dear Mr. Riverbend:

An appalling situation has recently occurred with my RIVERBEND-CRUISER motor, model # CRAP3466I/O, serial # DOODOO56768H97. I trust you will investigate this matter to my satisfaction both promptly and thoroughly.

- **On August 28, 2000, I purchased the Wanderer's Cruiser from Pleasure Marine in Nashville, Tennessee, at a cost of $20,998.52 (copy of receipt** enclosed). It was delivered on August 23, almost one year ago to the day.

- On Saturday, August 5, 2001, while driving the Wanderer, I noticed the battery showing a discharge on my instrument panel. When I stopped the boat to check the alternator, I immediately noted that the screws on the cap had somehow worked themselves loose and fallen off into the water along with the top of the coil. It was impossible to replace the cap as it was severely rusted.

- To add insult to injury, I had to wait for two hours by the shoreline until someone drove by to assist me in hauling the boat from the water. It must be stressed that this time and energy expended would not have been necessary had the screws not been defective.

- Upon taking time from work, thereby forfeiting a day's wages, to take the boat to Nashville to the dealer, I was shocked to learn his diagnosis. Mr. Trusty at The Boat Shop carefully examined the alternator cap and assured me the problem was because the screws had never been locked tightly enough and, therefore, had worked themselves loose. A copy of Mr. Trusty's statement is enclosed.

This situation is inexcusable. Your product could have caused a serious accident on the Tennessee River and endangered the lives of other boaters. In addition, I have been a boat owner for almost thirty years, and to realize that something of this nature has obviously slipped past your quality control department further exacerbates my frustration and anger. Therefore, I expect an immediate reimbursement of the cost of the rebuilt alternator in the amount of $204.68 (copy of invoice enclosed).

Thank you, and I look forward to hearing from you within ten business days.

Sincerely,

Joe Jaunt

Enclosures

cc: The Honorable Paul G. Summer
   Attorney General of Tennessee
   Office of the Attorney General
   500 Charlotte Avenue
   Nashville, TN 37243

   Mark S. Williams, Director
   Division of Consumer Affairs
   Fifth Floor
   500 James Robertson Parkway
   Nashville, TN 37243-0600

   Boating Safety Hotline
   United States Department of Transportation
   400 Seventh Street, SW
   Washington, DC 20590

   Boat Owners Association of the United States
   Consumer Protection Bureau
   880 South Pickett Street
   Alexandria, VA 22304

Joe was delighted to receive the full amount within a very short period of time.

So have a great vacation, whether by plane, train, car, or boat. But remember that by being a knowledgeable traveler, your trip will be a much happier one to file away in your scrapbook of memories.

Helpful Agencies and Services

The **American Travel Association** represents its membership with air travel issues. Call the organization at (800) 858-4233 to enroll or visit its website at www.1800airsafe.com.

The U.S. Department of Transportation's **Arrival/Departure Rule** and **Rule 250** can save you big bucks.

Lodge an airline complaint with the **Aviation Consumer Action Project** at www.acap1971.org/acap.html or write to P.O. Box 19029, Washington, DC 20036.

Car Book may be obtained by contacting the Center for Auto Safety, 2001 S Street, NW, Suite 410, Washington, DC 20009-1160. For information about local lemon law attorneys, log on to www.autosafety.org.

Carfax collects information from numerous sources to provide the most comprehensive vehicle history information available. Visit its website at www.carfax.com.

Check out **Cruise.com** (www.cruise.com) and **CruiseOpinion** (www.cruiseopinion.com) to see what previous passengers thought of their cruise experience.

The **Cruise Ship Center** (www.safari.net(SWA SYMBOL)marketc/CruiseShipPage.html) provides current deals from cruise lines and brokers.

Visit www.edmunds.com for a complete list of money-savers when shopping for a new vehicle.

Expedia (http://www.expedia.com) and **Preview Travel** (www.previewtravel.com) are two great Internet sites to find lowest-cost tours, hotels, etc.

"Fly-Rights," a brochure that details many of your air travel rights under the U.S. Department of Transportation, may be obtained by writing the Consumer Information Center, Pueblo, CO 81009 or via the Internet at www.dot.gov/airconsumer/flyrights/htm.

The **Kelley Blue Book** can be accessed at www.kbb.com and is a free price guide for used car values.

Moment's Notice is a fee-based discount travel club. Contact the club at (718) 837-1657 or check online at www.moments-notice.com.

ThePlan is a good source with help for auto issues, including insurance. Write to 145-23 61 Road, Queens, NY 11367-1203 or call (800) The Plan. Access its website at www.theplan.com.

Contact the **U.S. Tour Operators Association** at (212) 599-6599 to find out if your tour operator is a member.

Chapter 11

Common Sense for Seniors

"Perseverance is not a long race; it is many short races one after another."
- Walter Elliot

As a baby boomer myself (and a past-fifty-official card-carrying member of AARP), I have tremendous respect for our senior citizens. These are the folks who survived the Great Depression, fought for our country to win World War II, became female troops at home serving as breadwinners for their families, and all of them re-built a nation that enjoys prosperity. Yet with all the well-deserved commendations and more, these same people now face more problems than many of us can ever imagine.

Whether it be ill health and relying on a dwindling savings to being victimized by unscrupulous individuals or companies by virtue of their age, seniors must be reminded that they still have the power to invoke change, as do their families who may be caretakers. From problems with social security benefits to tax information, our elders deserve the best because often they are the best, and so it's urgent that they, too, learn the power of the pen.

The former Executive Director of The American Association of Retired Persons, Horace B. Deets, offers some words of wisdom and advice.

"AARP's 1999 survey of Consumer Behavior demonstrates that consumers are wary and dissatisfied. Three quarters of consumers report having had a bad buying experience in the past year and, if that's not bad enough, nearly one in six report having been a victim of a major consumer fraud or swindle at some point.

Consumers are at a distinct disadvantage. They are vulnerable to the whims of unscrupulous businesses and the complexity of their rapidly changing offerings, their inexplicable terms and the deceptively fine print.

Sadly, only about a third of consumers are completely satisfied with the action taken as a result of their complaint. Very few take the next step of complaining to a consumer agency or an Attorney General. Consumer complaints are a powerful tool to incite action on the part of regulators, law enforcement, and policy makers. Consumers need to take their complaints a step further – to provide the evidence that the proper authorities need to investigate, prosecute, or regulate."

So what happens when older Americans encounter problems? If they are lucky enough to still have the ability to care for themselves, often they can fight (and win) their own battles. Take the case of "Anna Appeal" who found herself in a dilemma with Social Security. While not quite within the technical "senior" category of sixty-five years, still she had worked hard her entire life, reared and supported children by herself, and then found herself disabled. Anna had no pension plan and very little in the way of financial support; she desperately needed the assistance she sought from the government. After three thwarted attempts, she came to me for a personal petition. She had only one more chance.

January 26, 1999

This statement is an earnest plea to the Social Security Administration concerning my fourth and final appeal to reconsider its denial of my claim for benefits. I have always been very proud to be an American who was able to work and not have to depend upon the government for my expenses, as, unfortunately, so many others do in this great country. I have worked throughout my lifetime and even after my disabilities began in 1988, I continued to work, though on a more limited basis ... [The bulk of this letter addressed the denial and the evidence for which she had to refute each one]

This is my last hope and my last opportunity to come before you today. Let me iterate that I have been a hard-working American for all of my life. I have never shirked my public duty. I have always loved this country and obeyed its laws. I have given it many years of faithful service and it is time that this loyalty is reciprocated. I cannot understand why there are so many people obtaining Social Security benefits who are physically able to work but simply, for whatever reason, their word is accepted that they cannot. Yet mine, which is validated throughout, is denied. . .What does it say when those who are in dire need cannot get the assistance which rightfully should be forthcoming to us? I beg of you to reconsider all of the facts so that I may be allowed to live out my life with some dignity and honor, knowing that my country has cared for me, just as I have always cared for it.

In an ecstatic letter I received almost two years later, "Anna" told me her quest was finally a successful reality. Our credo of *never give up* finally got her the desired results, and if you don't believe that one person can affect change with the slowly-turning wheels of government bureaucracy, then Anna reminds us to think again. There are many government officials and agencies that come to our defense when we sharpen our writing skills. By the way, if you're experiencing discrimination relating to a disability, then contact Ralph F. Boyd, Jr., Assistant Attorney General for Civil Rights, **The Civil Rights Division** at the **U.S. Justice Department** at (202) 514-2151. If it's a discriminatory problem with housing, then give a holler to the **U.S. Department of Housing and Urban Development's Office of Fair Housing and Equal Opportunity**. These folks will get on the stick for you when you call them at (1-800) 669-9777.

323

When dealing with issues of fraudulent activities, one of the most helpful organizations is the **National Fraud Information Center** at P.O. Box 65868, Washington, DC 20035. And let's not forget the powerful **U.S. Justice Department,** which loves to take this particular fraud tiger by the tail. Contact Attorney General John Ashcroft's office at Justice by calling (202) 514-2001 or by writing to him at 950 Pennsylvania Avenue, NW, Washington, DC 20530. With respect to Medicare complaints or fraud, call the **U.S. Department of Health and Human Services** at (202) 690-7000 to lodge your complaint and, of course, follow up with a letter.

There are so many scams and conscienceless individuals who just lie in wait to prey on the unsuspecting elderly. Whether it be a member of the cleaning service that steals a bit of silver or jewelry on each visit to telephone hoaxers who talk a trusting senior out of money to a non-existent philanthropic organization, all too often our aging population becomes more financially infirm because of these practices. Let's take the mail, for example.

Mail Fraud

Many of our seniors live alone and on fixed incomes; therefore, shopping by mail is very convenient. Too many times they become the victim of mail-order swindles or some crook steals their benefits check. If this happens to you or to someone you know, then help is in sight. Contact the local Postmaster for an investigation and follow the call up with a letter to **Chief Postal Inspector, Kenneth Weaver**, U.S. Postal Service, 475 L'Enfant Plaza, SW, Washington, DC 20260. Most communities also offer a **Carrier Alert Program**, where your mail carrier watches mailboxes for an accumulation of mail that might denote help is needed. Carriers also will bring your mail to your door if the mailbox is located a distance from your home. The U. S. Postal Services also has a great little booklet entitled ***A Consumer's Guide to Postal Crime Prevention***. Contact your local branch, call (202) 268-4293, or e-mail to http://www.usps.gov to receive your copy.

One elderly lady received a letter asking for money for a child-relief organization. Unfortunately, she didn't notice that there was no stamp attached when she emptied her mailbox that memorable morning. The "appeal" asked her to send $2600 over a couple of months' period to a post office box address. As it happens, this dear lady suffered from advancing stages of dementia, although her family wasn't too worried as of yet. (They very soon had cause to be.)

Envisioning all the children who were promised benefits from her generous contributions, Mrs. Senior dutifully mailed her check every few weeks with her own children none the wiser. As her dementia became quite evident to those around her, her kids took over her accounts and so forth, only to discover Mrs. Senior's checking account in shambles.

Determined not to let these creeps get away with such a monstrous deed, the following letter resulted.

1744 Aghast Avenue
Springfield, IL 62702
July 17, 2001

Kenneth Weaver, Chief Postal Inspector
United States Postal Service
475 L'Enfant Plaza, SW
Washington, DC 20260

Dear Inspector Weaver:

I have recently discovered a shocking situation concerning my eighty-six-year-old mother, Mrs. Samatha Senior, who fell prey to a scam artist. This person has defrauded my mother by mail of over $2600, and I turn to you for your personal intervention.

• The man first appeared by letter in the guise of a member of a philanthropic organization that, when mailed funds to a post office box, would contribute to the needs of poverty-stricken children. Naturally, my kind mother wished to donate. We knew she was forgetful but had no idea that she suffered from advanced stages of dementia; otherwise, we would have paid closer attention to her financial matters. It was only after she was diagnosed by a physician this past week and my sister and I began paying her bills that we noted three large withdrawals - on June 24, July 2 and 9.
• Each check was made out to a Henry Hoax with a note on the stubs that the checks were mailed to P.O. Box 111, Glen Carbon, IL 62000. Of course, we

immediately contacted the postmaster at that branch office, Denis Disturbed, who while investigating has recommended that we write directly to you.

Our mother lives on a fixed income and $2600 is an enormous amount of money at her age and income. Even though the sum never may be recovered, if we could be assured that this terrible person does not defraud another elderly citizen, our minds would be at rest.

Any assistance that your office can provide is greatly appreciated, and I look forward to hearing from you by July 30, 2001.

Thank you.

Sincerely,

Stewart Son

cc: Denis Disturbed, Postmaster
    United States Post Office Community Branch
    6788 Letter Lane
    Greenville, SC 89022

    National Fraud Information Center
    P.O. Box 65868
    Washington, DC 20035

    The Honorable John Ashcroft
    Attorney General of the United States
    United States Department of Justice
    950 Pennsylvania Avenue, NW
    Washington, DC 20210

Ellen Phillips

The Honorable Jim Ryan
Attorney General of Illinois
Office of the Attorney General
100 West Randolph Street
Chicago, IL 62706

Another very prevailing scam (even if the organizations tout themselves as legitimate) is the magazine sweepstakes that also arrive in the mail. Rather than visions of sugarplums dancing in their heads, visions of great, big bucks are magnified in the brains of millions of Americans. The elderly are, unfortunately, most often the target of these wolves in sheep's clothing.

On March 3, 1999, a *Dateline NBC* expose revealed some interesting information about what many law enforcement officials believed to be fraudulent activities on the parts of the magazine sweepstakes companies. Accusing the operatives of "misleading and deceptive practices" and "seductive come-ons, especially to the elderly," many state attorneys general and members of Congress cracked down and investigated, making sure that some of these operatives won't be pulling into your driveway anytime in the next couple of millenniums.

When you receive these mailings, don't ever believe you must buy <u>anything</u> in order to enter the contest and purchase does *not* ensure a better chance of winning. Use those eyeballs (I realize I frequently admonish with the "eyeballs" advice, but it is always your first line of defense) to ignore illegal messages like the following:

- **You're a guaranteed winner of a certain amount.** The only thing you're "guaranteed" is to lose your life's savings when you order magazines and accompanying products thinking you'll win money.
- **You stand a better chance of winning if you order our products**. Excuse me, but the only "winner" is the company that laughs all the way to the bank with *your* money in hand.
- **The time you'll be home to meet your money face to face and directions to your house**. Don't fall for

this one, either. Believe you me, that van most likely won't appear and you'll need a letter like the following example:

1908 Casualty Court
Carson City, NV 89986
May 29, 2001

The Honorable Frankie Sue Del Papa
Attorney General of Nevada
Office of the Attorney General
Old Supreme Court Building
198 South Carson
Carson City, NV 89710

Dear General Del Papa:

I have recently fallen prey to what I believe to be an appalling and illegal sweepstakes activity. In my opinion, Swindling Sweepstakes has defrauded me by mail of $275, and I turn to you for your personal intervention.

- When I first received the sweepstakes notice, it emphatically stated that I would receive $100,000 simply by sending in my entry blank (copy of notice and entry blank enclosed). The inference, however, was that by purchasing magazines, my chances of a larger amount would be even better. On April 10, I mailed a check in the amount of $150 to Swindling (copy enclosed).
- Two weeks later on April 21, I received a second notice that assured me of additional prize money if I ordered more of Swindling's products (copy enclosed). I did so, this time in the amount of $225.

- **The president of Swindling ostensibly wrote the third letter I received (copy enclosed). Mr. Scam promised that my prize checks were immediately forthcoming from the first two orders, and I would claim another check if I placed a third order.**
- **By this time, I realized that I had most probably been duped. I wrote to Swindling (copy enclosed) and demanded a refund of the sum I had previously paid. I also explained to Mr. Scam that I believed his company was an illegitimate one and that I would write to the consumer protection agency in my state if my letter were ignored. I received no response. Since I believe this matter to be one of mail fraud, I then contacted the postmaster at my branch office, Harold Helpful, who is investigating; however, Mr. Helpful recommended that I write directly to you.**

I live on a fixed income and $275 constitutes a large portion of my monthly allotment. Even though this amount may be never recovered, if I could be assured that this organization does not defraud other elderly citizens, my fears would be somewhat alleviated.

Any assistance that your office can provide is greatly appreciated, and I look forward to hearing from you by June 14, 2001.

Thank you.

Sincerely,

Stanley Sucker

Enclosures

cc: National Fraud Information Center

P.O. Box 65868
Washington, DC 20035

The Honorable John Ashcroft
Attorney General of the United States
United States Department of Justice
950 Pennsylvania Avenue, NW
Washington, DC 20210

Robert Mueller, Director
Federal Bureau of Investigation
935 Pennsylvania Avenue, NW
Washington, DC 20535

Office of Consumer Protection
United States Department of Commerce
Room 5718
Fourteenth Street and Constitution Avenue, NW
Washington, DC 20230

Kenneth Weaver, Chief Postal Inspector
United States Postal Service
475 L'Enfant Plaza, SW
Washington, DC 20260

The Honorable Harry Reid
United States Senate
SH-528
Second and C Streets. NE
Washington, DC 20510

The Honorable John Ensign
United States Senate
SR-269
First and C Streets, NE
Washington, DC 20510

The Honorable James A. Gibbons

Ellen Phillips

United States House of Representatives
100 CHOB
First Street and Independence Avenue, SE
Washington, DC 20515

Patricia Morse Jarman
Commissioner of Consumer Affairs
Department of Business and Industry
1850 East Sahara, Suite 101
Reno, NV 89104

Even though the sweepstakes letters do make an announcement that no purchase is necessary to win, it's often in small print, and the original notice as well as every other one they mail to you makes victims believe they will win the magazine "lottery" if they buy. Luckily, in December 1999, President Clinton signed into law the **Deceptive Mail Prevention and Enforcement Act.** Among other pertinent points, this law establishes standards for mailings, skill contests, and facsimile checks. It also restricts government look-alike documents and allows persons to have their names and addresses removed from sweepstakes mailing lists. So what's the message here? Even the big folks up on the White Hill are determined that the rest of us (and especially the elderly) will no longer become a casualty in this particular war.

Taxes
The U.S. Senate's Special Committee on Aging, chaired by a real champion of senior citizens, Senator Chuck Grassley, helps older Americans in many other situations. Taxes — that spine-chilling quagmire – is only one.

Because of Senator Grassley's awareness of and concerns with overpayment pitfalls, in February 1998 he directed the Aging Committee to publish a pamphlet designed to help seniors with filing their tax returns. The senator wanted a widespread avenue of information for those on a fixed income and who need to save on medical deductions. The upshot of his committee charge is the brochure "**Protecting Older**

Americans Against Overpayment of Income Taxes," which can be ordered by calling (202) 224-5364 or by mailing a postcard to the Senate Special Committee on Aging, G31 Dirksen Senate Building, Washington, DC 20510. Be sure to write your name, address, and the publication's title on the postcard. Also included in this pamphlet is a list of programs and other publications through the IRS to help assist seniors with their tax returns. Additionally, you can contact your local IRS Taxpayer Education Tax Administration Coordinator or the AARP for more details. Senator Grassley reminds us, "While every American should pay his or her fair share in taxes, no one should pay one penny more."

There are a number of bills – some very similar – truly stagnating in Congress that would enormously assist with our aging population's taxpayer relief. One is the **Senior Citizens Equity Act** that would remove seniors' financial burden by allowing them to earn even more without losing their Social Security benefits. The **Social Security Benefits Tax Relief Act** would amend the IRS Code of 1986 to repeal the 1993 increase in income tax on Social Security benefits, to repeal the earning limitations, and to repeal the estate and gift taxes. Of similar language to the Senior Citizens Equity Act and one that equally lags and lags in Congress is the proposed **Social Security Earnings Limit Repeal Act of 2001**. This Act would remove the limitation on the amount of outside income a person may receive while being paid Social Security benefits. Many bills have been proposed regarding Medicare benefits, Medicare extension of prescription drugs, access to health insurance, and so forth, and all proposals demand a barrage of letters. After all, as I mentioned earlier, our elderly are the backbone of this nation and *the* greatest lobby around. (And we Baby Boomers will enter that category sooner than later; we have enormous impact on voters, as well.) One bill to assist our senior citizens that finally passed is the **Freedom to Work Act of 2000**. A great resource for the folks it's aimed at, it eliminates the penalty that close to a million seniors currently paid, because they worked after they were sixty-five. Just remember, if there's ever a problem with your pension, contact one of the following agencies: **The Pension and Welfare Benefits Administration** at the U.S. Department of Labor (202) 219-8776; or **The Pension Benefits Guaranty Corporation** at (1-800) 400-7242.

Many other difficulties face a lot of older Americans and their families. While often it's tough going, these folks on whom the past sixty or so years have been built are tough themselves. But what are some of the other problems that face them, sometimes on a daily basis?

Prescription Drugs:

Even if you're fortunate enough to afford private insurance, drug bills are out of sight for everyone and, most especially, for seniors on limited incomes. My own mother's pharmacy bills often exceeded $1000 a month – far more than half of the sum she takes in. For a long while, my family found itself running around this particular briar patch just like Brer Rabbit. Then one day while researching for ways to circumnavigate the briars, I discovered **Patient Assistance Programs**. These programs are offered and solely funded by participating drug manufacturers and make available certain medications to needy patients – <u>free</u>. While all companies don't offer all prescription drugs, there's still enough of them around to extricate the elderly from the briar patch.

Eligibility varies among the manufacturers but is usually based on financial need. Sometimes patients themselves or family members can request the required paperwork; sometimes, the physician must do so. By the way, not all doctors participate in the program since it means they must take the time to dispense the medication rather than your getting it from the corner drugstore. If this happens with you and if you can do so without jeopardizing your health, find another physician willing to help you with your avalanche of bills.

Senator Grassley, again riding his white steed, will send you a letter for your physician or health care provider outlining the procedure. Just call that toll-free number I mentioned previously. A complete list of drug manufacturers, their telephone numbers, and the medications they currently offer in their patient assist programs can be found as part of a wonderful book, ***Free Stuff for Seniors***, by Matthew Lesko (FC&A Publishing, 103 Clover Green, Peachtree City, GA 30269, ISBN # 1-890957-07-0).

The American Association of Retired Persons (AARP), the massive organization that serves the needs of millions and millions of retired and elderly, is a tremendous font of information and assistance. Check out their Web page at **www.aarp.org** to receive all types of detailed advice. One item that I found particularly interesting is the section on Social Security's **Supplemental Security Income (SSI)**. AARP tells us that if individuals or couples meet certain guidelines, they can qualify for this federal program.

- Cash and savings mustn't exceed $2000 for one person or $3000 for two people.
- Monthly income can't be over $514 for one person and $761 for two people.
- The amount of SSI depends on the monthly income. The maximum monthly benefit is $494 for one person or $741 for two.

To find out if you're eligible, call the Social Security Administration at (800) 772-1213 and, to sweeten the pot, you can also apply over the phone. AARP also collaborated with the federal government to set up www.seniors.gov. This site, also brimming over with helpful information, ranges from comparing Medicare options to providing updates on health, employment, and volunteer activities.

Nursing Homes versus Staying in the Family Home:
So many of our seniors can no longer live by or take care of themselves, and sometimes it seems as if all independence is taken away from them by simple virtue of this fact. Certainly, when this happens, the care of parents – physically, emotionally, and financially – usually falls on one or more of their children, which further exacerbates an already-hapless situation. If, for some reason, family members are unwilling or

unable to take this responsibility, does this always mean a nursing home when the senior isn't totally incapacitated? No, not when we can turn to the **Eldercare Locator**, a section of the U.S. Department of Health and Human Services.

This service is a national directory that's designed to help locate local support resources. Whether your need is an immediate one or you and your family are just planning for the long term, call the Eldercare Locator at (800) 677-1116, Monday through Friday, 9:00 a.m. to 11:00 p.m. Eastern Standard Time. The folks at this number are trained to assist with and have access to an extensive list of information and referral services that lend support to seniors, such as meals, transportation, home repair, and a wealth of other benefits.

Not only does the Eldercare Locator support these options, but it also includes a program called **Operation Match**. Operation Match helps to match people looking for an affordable place to live with other folks who have space within their homes and need someone to assist with housing expenses. An additional advantage is having a person around for daily company so the Eldercare Locator really is a wonderful resource. It puts you in touch with local and state agencies that not only allow you to find help to stay in your own home or to be a member of someone else's, but, as an extra plus, it also gives your caretakers a much-deserved rest. Internet surfers can also point their browser to Eldercare online at **www.elderweb.com** to receive lots more info. This site has over four thousand reviewed links concerning health, financing, housing, and other aging issues. While your fingers are doing the walking, look up **www.seniors-site.com** as well. This website is for both seniors and caregivers and offers everything from personal E-mail advice to publications and special offers.

It's such a shame that we sometimes have no choice but to place our elderly loved ones in nursing homes. If we (and especially they) are fortunate enough, the facility is reputable and clean with caring and compassionate employees. It seems, however, that this type is in the minority these days.

We're deluged with nursing homes expose's in which dreadful and frightening abuses occur to innocents unable to fend for themselves. Whether the problem is what is known as Medicaid "dumping," where nursing homes literally throw out indigent elderly like dirty dishwater to attendants allowing residents to drown in their own bodily wastes, we must all join the battle for nursing home reform. The Senate's Special Committee on Aging reveals that more than one-quarter of the country's over 17,000 nursing homes causes residents actual harm or places them at risk of serious injury or even death! Even when abuses are investigated and, in many cases, where homes are repeat offenders, sanctions for failure to comply with the sanctions were often either delayed or ignored in the not-so-distant past.

The Health Care Financing Administration (now known as **The Centers for Medicare and Medicaid Services**) announced tougher regulations that became law in March 1999. If a complaint is lodged that a resident is in danger, state agencies must investigate within ten days; states can now fine nursing homes up to $10,000 for each serious violation it uncovers without allowing a grace period to correct the problem.

Prior to that March regulation, if Medicaid paid a resident's care and a nursing home ceased its participation in the government program, the resident could be transferred or evicted to make room for private-pay patients. Of course, this meant that the nursing home made more money. The new law places a big red *STOP* on this practice. Now Medicaid patients can't be forced to leave, and private-pay folks who enter these particular homes must be informed up front that when their assets are gone, they may have to leave when their Medicaid is activated.

Even if we don't actually know anyone who lives in a nursing home, as taxpayers we're still being suckered since our money goes to pay the bills for Medicaid. And God forbid that you find your parent, spouse, or other relative in a mess, but if so, then a letter such as the one that follows, is *imperative*.

811 Daughter Drive
Racine, WI 86100

November 2, 2000

William Wicked, President
Mammoth Management Corporation
5610 Covert Corner, Suite 666
Newbury, OH 44044

Dear Mr. Wicked:

A horrific state of affairs has transpired with my mother, Lucy Luckless, who is a patient at Painview Nursing Home in Racine. This situation is extremely urgent, and you must be made cognizant so that you can immediately and personally rectify the appalling problems.

- When it became apparent in July that my siblings and I were unable to continue caring for our mother, we placed her in Painview. Prior to this point, we spoke with the administrator, Helen Heinous, who assured us that our mother would receive compassionate and loving care. The complete opposite has proven to be the case.
- Generally, one of us visited Mother at least four to five times a week, and the staff came to expect these scheduled evening visits. However, beginning on September 27, after noting Mother's recent weight loss, I made an unexpected visit for the evening meal. As I stood undetected in the doorway, I was aghast at the scene in front of my eyes: Nurse Terri Torment took a spoonful of potatoes, brought it to my mother's mouth, then snatched it away and said, "You've been a bad girl again. I told you not to wet the bed so you won't have any dinner again." I, of course, immediately ordered Nurse Torture to leave the room, soothed my mother, and fed her. When I reported the incident to Ms.

Heinous, she assured me this was an isolated incident and that Nurse Torture would be reprimanded.

• My two sisters and I began to make unscheduled visits to Painview at all hours of the day and evening. We were upset on several more occasions (September 30, October 2, October 6, October 10, and October 15) to find our mother in a soiled condition of many hours' duration. Additionally, on October 24, when changing Mother into a fresh gown (which should have been done by a nurse earlier that evening), I was horrified to discover bruises on Mother's upper arms in the shape of handprints. I brought Ms. Heinous into the room to show her this evidence of deliberate abuse. Imagine my disbelief when your administrator alleged that my eighty-six year old parent who weights less than one hundred pounds made the marks on herself. At that point, I removed my mother from Painview and brought her to live in my home. I also wrote Ms. Heinous a formal letter of complaint in which I documented the various offenses (copy enclosed).

It is intolerable that these problems occurred in the first place; however, after being brought to the attention of Painview's administration on many occasions and all crises were subsequently ignored, the situation is nothing shy of monstrous. As you can see, I am copying federal regulators concerning these circumstances, but I certainly trust you will initiate your own prompt investigation.

I expect a response from you by no later than November 17, 2000.

Thank you.

Sincerely,

339

Ruth Reliable

Enclosure

cc: The Honorable Donna Shalala, Secretary
United States Department of Heath and Human
Services
200 Independence Avenue, SW
Washington, DC 20201

The Honorable June Gibbs Brown, Inspector
General
United States Department of Health and Human
Services
200 Independence Avenue, SW
Washington, DC 20201

The Honorable Alexis Herman, Secretary
United States Department of Labor
200 Constitution Avenue, NW
Washington, DC 20210

Nancy-Ann De Parle, Director
Medicare Fraud Division
Health Care Financing Administration
200 Independence Avenue, SW
Washington, DC 20201

Nursing Home Ombudsman
Board on Aging and Long Term Care
214 North Hamilton Street
Madison, WI 53703

The Honorable James Doyle
Attorney General of Wisconsin
Office of the Attorney General
State Capitol, Suite 114 East

P.O. Box 7857
Madison, WI 53707-7857

Even if a nursing home isn't in the picture, frequently people of my generation must provide care for their elderly parents. This we do out of love and appreciation for all the years they tended to us. But it's still a difficult task. Perhaps we live far away or our mother or father is suffering from senility or physical problems that require daily attention. Elizabeth Ketz-Robinson found herself in a similar situation but with a slightly different twist. Trying to provide the best of care for her now-deceased elderly mother, she found herself embroiled in legalities over which she seemed to have no control. The problem first began when fraudulent organizations began to harass her mother, and this elderly lady believed their promises. Think back to the advice about rip-off artists; unfortunately, all too often, their targets are senior citizens who either don't know how or who are mentally unable to follow through in order to protect themselves. Sometimes contacting the **National Association of Area Agencies on the Aging** may help. This group may be reached at 112 Sixteenth Street, NW, Suite 100, Washington, DC 20036 or at (202) 296-8130. (Also, to identify all federal and state assistance programs, logon to www.benefitscheckup.org for the specific program, "Benefits-CheckUp.") Unfortunately, Ms. Ketz-Robinson's problem had accelerated far beyond the assistance this agency could provide. The personal petition to the court as part of her lawyer's brief came as a result of a scam misadventure and the care that my client subsequently provided for her mother.

As the Court is aware, this Guardianship and Conservatorship originated in March 1993. My mother, eighty-eight year old [name], was living alone in her home in Washington, DC. As her senility and dementia of which we had seen some evidence gradually increased and became more pronounced, she began to fall prey to unscrupulous telephone sweepstakes solicitors and was writing checks for many thousands

of dollars. Luckily, she did not have enough money in her bank account to cover these costs. At that time when the full extent of her senility and pervasion of innocence became evident to me, I applied for the above.

Enclosed with my petition are <u>strong</u> testaments from physicians verifying that my husband and I provide the highest level of care, love and companionship for my mother. All of my mother's personal and financial needs are being provided, and she will continue to live at my home for the remainder of her life, if at all possible.

My wish to terminate the Guardianship and Conservatorship is based upon the following: [She lists her reasons and all necessary information]

I understand that the Courts have a duty to oversee those persons who are unable to take care of themselves in a Guardianship and Conservatorship situation. It is my hope and prayer that my mother will live her remaining years with our family in at least the health which she maintains today. I am sure that she is aware of and is troubled by the stress and turmoil to which I feel continually subjected to administering her estate under the Guardianship and Conservatorship procedures. If my mother is to remain living with her only daughter and family and to remain as healthy as she is able to be at this point in time, it is imperative that I be released from the demands of the Court from the Guardianship and Conservatorship by the termination of both. Enclosed are pertinent articles that address the dedicated care needed by persons like my mother and the impact of this care on the caregivers.

I love my mother deeply, and I will care for her faithfully and lovingly until the day she dies. All accounts strongly attest to this fact. At no time in the life that remains to her would I ever be anything other than the loving, concerned, and caring daughter that I have always been. However, if this Conservatorship, which burdens me, is removed, I would have more quality time and energy for all of my family, my mother's well-being, and my career.

Thank you.

Sincerely,

Elizabeth Ketz-Robinson

And so it was accomplished. Ms. Ketz-Robinson's mom lived out the remainder of her life, happy and surrounded by loving family.

Another example of negligent or denied care sometimes falls within the realm of state agencies, such as home health programs. Because so many Boomers do try to keep their parents in their own homes, if mother or father is ill and needs help with daily living, they depend on these facilities. "Sigmond Son" was assured that his invalid mother was receiving assistance with bathing, bed linens, etc. on a three-times a week basis. He was livid when he discovered this wasn't the case at all. He tried the verbal approach with the supervisor who was defensive, to say the least. His next and successful attempt resulted from a letter.

> **9089 First Street**
> **Lincoln, NE 68555**
> **May 21, 2001**

Clark Condemnable, Supervisor
Home Health Hotspot

Ellen Phillips

7895 Negligent Avenue
Suite 333
Lincoln, NE 68551

Dear Mr. Condemnable:

I am truly shocked that you do not appear to even wish to understand the problem concerning my mother, Debi Dependent. In fact, when we spoke one week ago, you were abrupt and, in my opinion, outright hostile.

As I explained, my mother's thrice-weekly visits have decreased to two and sometimes once a week. This is completely unacceptable. I also informed you that my father is unable to bathe my mother nor can he change her bed linens. Therefore, if the scheduled aide does not arrive and unless my sister can come and perform these chores herself, then my mother remains unbathed and her linens remain soiled.

I demand that these home visits be immediately placed back on the schedule and that you <u>personally</u> oversee the procedure. I am mailing a copy of this directive to my mother's physician. I will also send a copy to all regulatory agencies that have jurisdiction over your facility if the problem is not promptly resolved.
["Sigmond" didn't wish to cc anyone else at this point.]

Thank you, and I expect a return reply by May 28, 2001.

Sincerely,

Sigmond Son

(402) 416-9998

cc: David Doctor, M.D.
Lincoln Specialists Physicians, Inc.
764 Painless Parkway
Lincoln, NE 68554

Mr. Condemnable got on the stick *very* quickly, and no further ccs were necessary. I suggested to "Mr. Son" that he also contact the **Seniors-Site** at www.seniors-site.com that could afford some caregiver assistance by e-mail, publications, special offers, and so forth. And in the event that your loved one is suffering from the dreaded Alzheimer's or has other mental health problems, contact www.alz.org and www.mentalhealth.net, respectively.

What if you or your elderly relative isn't at the nursing home point quite yet. Perhaps an assisted living facility is a viable option. Let me reiterate one of my columns that first appeared on www.besthalf.com. After our father died, my brother, sister, and I needed a full-time caretaker to attend to our mother. While we found a wonderful lady who quickly became part of our family, between "regular" bills and Mother's monstrous medical bills, we came to the bitter realization after a year that our sweet sitter-chief-cook-and-bottle-washer was simply no longer affordable. In fact, by studying and then pooling every nickel and dime in our mother's financial pot (actually, in our own pots), we discovered that Mother could move to an assisted living facility for five years or stay in her own home with the caretaker for one more year and then be forced to move to a nursing home (a situation she always has dreaded).

So in September 2000, after my sister who lived a couple of hundred miles away, had researched one facility which she and I subsequently visited, I flew home. We packed Mother's belongings that would fit into her "apartment" – in actuality, just a medium-size room with a bathroom – and said goodbye to her home of almost sixty years. It only took two days at the assisted living facility before we determined that certain members of the staff at this place had lied to us and that our mother would not be receiving the care for which we were promised. Furthermore, these places are **not** cheap and on top of the monthly fee, we were paying almost $300 more a month for special services she <u>wasn't</u> receiving, such as assistance to and from her apartment, daily cleaning of her bathroom, and so forth. To add insult to injury, Mother lost over ten pounds in the first two months, which she could ill afford, because of the repulsive food that was served by the supposedly grand "chef." (Believe me, the proverbial school cafeteria food was far tastier than what he dished up!)

My poor sister faced the brunt in attempting to solve the outrageous and reprehensible issues that were going on at *Hellstone* (the name is changed to protect the guilty!). From a thousand miles away, I dripped my own special brand of expertise – poison pen letters (and calls) by the dozens. Even when I visited every six weeks, I found myself sneaking around, taking notes, and facing-off with the managers. My poor mother was afraid she would be intentionally mistreated because of my sister's and my actions, particularly when the corporate office finally enacted an investigation that resulted in a number of firings, from the top down. By the time the new manager arrived, Mother was ready to move elsewhere – and fast. Considering the fact that Hellstone was only her third "home" in her entire 79 years, moving again in less than five months was a huge step for her, especially in her fragile condition.

This time, my sibling and I <u>both</u> thoroughly investigated, asked the right questions, and, upon receipt of answers, let the new folks at Atria Assisted Living Community (specifically, the Atria Weatherly Springs in Huntsville, Alabama)) know that they would be held accountable if any shenanigans or mistreatment occurred. I even did something that I would normally never do: I gave the executive director a copy of my book and a list of the national media that has featured me. Not-so-subtle threat? You bet! And as I write this article today, my mother resides in a much more caring, compassionate environment. Many of the caregivers even have become her very favorite people. It may not be the home she was forced to leave behind, but when the homemade fried chicken meal is brought out by the dining room server, followed by homemade lemon meringue pie, Mother no longer gripes about losing weight – she digs right in!

While I'm sure that there are many great assisted living facilities around these United States, quite frankly the Atria national network more than meets the need of what people wish and need in order to provision for their older family members. After speaking with the folks at Atria's corporate (or, as it's known, the Support Center) office, I came away with even more of a warm, fuzzy feeling. Atria has what's known as a "Strategic Principle: 'the commitment to doing whatever it takes – every day – to enhance the lives and to exceed the expectations of our residents, their families, and our team members.'" This principle revolves around two concepts: enhancing lives and exceeding expectations. An example of the latter is when Atria hired former White House chef Henry Haller. Not only does Chef Haller provide his own delicious cuisine, but also he is amenable to recipes for varied parts of the country where residents enjoy homespun dishes. (Remember that Southern –style fried chicken?) With respect to the concept of enhancing lives, Atria recently published the book, <u>Lessons for Our Lifetime</u>, in which the wisdom and life stories from so many residents can be shared and enjoyed by everyone. These life stories remind me of a former and vivid part of my own life. As a professional storyteller, my area of expertise is that of family tales. I think it absolutely urgent that our older family members share with the younger members the exciting and not-so-exciting details of the seniors' earlier days. To this end, I tell stories when I visit my mother, and a number of the residents have really entered into the fun with their own fascinating family tales. (Hey, maybe <u>Lessons for Our Lifetime</u> originated with the gentle folks at Atria as we sat around our story circle.)

A large number of promises and expectations encompass Atria's Strategic Principle, and among these are the ones that certainly contribute to daily warm fuzzies to team (staff) members and to residents' families.

- Atria's database and tracking system ensure that these folks can and do contact immediately those families who call the Support Center. (And by "immediately," I mean within *one* business day!) Whether by email, postal address, or a call, the response is Johnny-on-the-spot.

And to make us feel even more that our concerns are valued, the <u>president</u> reads each letter that arrives and answers them personally. Wow, speaking of Head Honcho…

- One of Atria's major management tools is to conduct bi-yearly a Customer Satisfaction Survey with each resident or family member, with the purpose of discovering what's good or needs improvement areas, including food service and housekeeping to those less tangible attributes, such as caregiver knowledge and compassion.
- Team members (staff and management) are provided with the means to develop their career paths, if they choose. Atria offers a variety of mentoring programs, continuing education credits in some disciplines, and tuition reimbursement.
- Because the wealth is spread around so, Executive Directors (Hi, Miss Laurie) are allowed the freedom to make decisions based upon customer concerns; certainly, they are assisted and backed up by the national network. I've found that when the local directors are given enough autonomy, the communities are run much more effectively.

President and COO Werner Neuteufel has this to say: "*At Atria, we strive to anticipate our residents' needs. It is our job to discover how each of our residents is unique and then to find ways to enhance their lives. We want to serve our residents in such a way that they are eager to share their experiences with others. Nothing we do as a company is more important.*"

But could we have a choice when mother's money runs out in a few years? Is a nursing home the absolute only other option available? At the worse, I would rather be told upfront that this is the case so we plan for that event. Unfortunately, some assisted living homes aren't as honest as they should be as to what will occur on down the line. *The Washington Post* (February 20, 2001) tells us that many family members are informed that the facility can obtain relief, such as from Medicare, when the senior outlasts his or her savings. However, when that day arrives, imagine how terrible to watch when Mr. and Mrs. Elderly are bounced out on their respective heads. My own mother hopes and prays to die in her new residence, rather than be wrenched up and sent to a nursing home – the place of her worse nightmare. [Note: As of this final editing, my mother has suffered a life-threatening stroke and has been placed from the hospital to the rehab section of a nursing home. We pray she does not become aware of her surroundings.]

Some management companies promise much more than they can deliver, financially as well as practically (like Hellstone did). On the other hand, some companies use contracts that hide extra costs (and how many people read every word of a contract's *very* fine print?). Still other applicants, especially those who are desperate for a decent home for their elderly and often delicate relative, find themselves paying extra fees for services they think should be automatically included, such as assistance with bathing and so forth, with savings perhaps allocated for other emergencies. And the list goes on and on and on.

Are we looking at an industry that, through government deregulation, has turned into an enemy, much as managed care as a whole? Those days are gone by the wayside where a hospital stay would make one well rather than make us sicker and poorer. And speaking of fine print, what a sad commentary on society when companies consciously victimize our country's elderly – those who gave much of their lives and the lives of their loved ones to make America free and then to make it the strongest and wealthiest nation on the face of the earth – just to further line their corporate pocketbooks!

The prevalent albeit oft-times false portrait of assisted care homes as opposed to nursing homes is that the former are for the wealthy and the latter house the poor. This is simply not the case. Indeed, assisted living became a real growth industry in 1993, developed for those who needed extra care or attention but weren't yet ready for a nursing home. My mother is far from rich and, were it not for my siblings and me, she wouldn't even have close to the years of assisted care living that I previously discussed. Yet, if there are no savings for just such an eventuality and one doesn't have several nice diamonds or some such tucked away, assisted living does seem to cater to a more affluent clientele. Even the persons who appear to have more money than some of their fellow residents face the same scenario: money runs out; nursing home and Medicaid steps in. (There are so few Medicare, Medicaid, or state-run benefit programs with regards to assisted living that we may as well call them non-existent. Although the Joint Commission on Accreditation of Healthcare Organizations issued new regulations last year, mandating several seriously needed changes in the nursing home industry, horror stories still abound, especially with those in smaller locales.) However, based upon my research, if the need for a nursing home arises and a Manor Care Nursing Home is close to you or yours, then I strongly advise taking a look.

Employees at Manor Care, Inc. seem delighted that lots of internal promotions go on; furthermore, even though the pay may be low at first and the work is pretty rigorous, the potential to earn substantial salaries in a very speedy fashion must be taken into account. Additionally, to ensure employee comfort and loyalty (which translates into satisfied residents and their families), Manor Care personnel are afforded such bennies as tuition reimbursement and stock options. I'd be surprised to see any evidence of the stereotypical fiends lurking around at any of these organizations.

Then how can families learn to recognize inaccurate or just plain false information? One of the most pathetic excuses for a marketing manager (and obviously a close relative of the one with the same title at the first facility our mother lived in) is the person who <u>knows</u> the exact amount of funds an elderly applicant possesses or that the family can pay and **still** lies about fees and services. Along this same line is the equally-mean falsehood of "Oh, no, our fees never rise. Why this is one of our proudest accomplishments," knowing all the while that costs will definitely rise by $250 a month, beginning in six months. Worse, though, is the marketeer's knowledge that the prospective resident or the family can't scratch up another $250 monthly fee. This is one of those times, that no matter what's stated in the contract, you **insist** that promises like this be placed in writing and signed by the facility's "promiser." (We didn't do this with our first arrangement, because the marketing director had been one of my sister's favorite students several years earlier. We should have investigated just how much commission she makes off of each naïve candidate before we signed on the dotted line – "favorite" or not.)

Make sure when discussing fees (and procuring written assurances) that there's an understanding of just what the basic and any extra fee provides. For instance, don't assume that the family member will be provided with three squares a day and later on discover that the contract covers only two meals and the third costs $2.25 per day. Yes, I know this sounds like a paltry sum, but multiply $2.25 by 365 days and the cost of that third meal rises to $821.25 a year. This almost-thousand dollar charge most certainly can be used for other necessities, such as dental bills or medications. Watch out for, what you may presuppose to be, other rudimentary services – laundry, for example. No, this cost isn't a portion of the basic rate and, yes, if you believe the old adage that "cleanliness is next to godliness," then you better plan on spending between $50-$100 more a month. And the *Post* article cautions prospective residents and their families about what the industry calls "reevaluation." Every few months the resident's needs are again evaluated. While this is perfectly logical to determine his or her unique needs from both a physical and a mental perspective, fees can rise faster than a pig races to slop. Frankly, I get mighty suspicious when I hear of circumstances in which a senior is charged an extra $35-$50 per month just to have a caretaker knock on the latter's door every hour or two to make sure the person isn't lying in the floor, unable to reach the call button. Speaking of **basic** services…

So how long can we expect a family member (or each of us, for that matter) to remain in an assisted living facility? Statistics prove that assisted living residents stay in their "home" on an average of only two years, and fewer than one-third actually do die while they live there. Of the remaining number, over one-half must enter a nursing home to live out what remains of their lives.

The corporations that own assisted living facilities would, I'm certain, be horrified to learn that I believe that a number of them (or at least many of the people who work for them) are as dishonest as the day is long. Furthermore, while the hue and cry is loud and irate about scams that are deliberately directed against seniors, why is the problem that I've addressed any less awful? As far as I'm concerned, *any* method that seeks to misrepresent information to those who need the most honest of facts is nothing shy of fraud. We don't have to stand still for any smoke and mirrors, either. As I always advocate, writing a well-documented letter to the correct people and agencies works wonders. (Remember my part in the dismissal of incompetent and deceptive staff at the first facility that housed my mother?) Each state, for example, has ombudsmen in its state long-term care division. These advocates look out for the health and well-being of the elderly who are in a caretaker situation. Check the **Area Agency on the Aging** closest to the city where the facility in question is located (usually several organizations to a state). A national contact is the Consumer Consortium on Assisted Living; contact these folks at 703-533-8121. The **Assisted Living Foundation of America (ALFA)** is another. This organization is the overseer of nation-wide facilities and many times will interject on behalf of residents. If there's a problem or if you simply wish to find out information about assisted living, contact ALFA by calling (703) 691-8100. Visit its site at www.alfa.org.

The federal agencies wish to hear, too, so don't forget to contact the US Department of Health and Human Services, among others. Above all, don't become (or remain) a victim. You have the power to effect change. Go for it!

Weatherization and Energy Bills:
    If you're too hot or too cold because you're having problems paying your heating and cooling bills, then help is on the way.

Over two million seniors now receive assistance and you can, too, even if you own or rent your home or apartment. The first contacts to make are your local utility offices to see if there are special programs for seniors, including discounts or reduced fees. If, God forbid, an office threatens to cut off the gas, power, or phone, then immediately call (and *write*) your state's Public Utilities Commission to act as your advocate. There are national offices to help in your search for financial assistance as well. One is the **State Weatherization Office** for your area and the other is a federal program, the **Low Income Home Energy Assistance Program**.

The U. S. Department of Energy heads up the State Weatherization Offices and their support regions. By implementing energy-saving measures in low-income homes, this program works to correct the lopsided energy burden faced by low-income Americans. Depending on the state in which you live, you may write, phone, fax, or e-mail the program manager for your region.

Atlanta Department of Energy Region: If you live in Alabama, Arkansas, Florida, Georgia, Kentucky, Mississippi, North Carolina, South Carolina, Tennessee, Puerto Rico or the Virgin Islands, then your program manager is Bernadette Cross. Write Ms. Cross at 730 Peachtree Street, NE, Suite 876, Atlanta, GA 30308 or call her office at (404) 347-2838. E-mail or fax your inquires to bernie.cross@hq.doe.gov or (404) 347-3098.

Denver Department of Energy Support: States that fall within this region are Colorado, Kansas, Louisiana, Montana, Nebraska, New Mexico, North Dakota, Oklahoma, South Dakota, Texas, Utah, and Wyoming. Your program manager is Marian Downs, 1617 Cole Boulevard, Golden, CO 80401. Her phone number (303) 275-4812; the fax is (303) 275-4830, or contact Ms. Downs by e-mail (marian.downs@hq.doe.gov).

Boston Department of Energy Support: Your states of residence are Connecticut, Maine, Massachusetts, New Hampshire, New York, Rhode Island, and Vermont. Your contact is program manager Christine Reinfelds at One Congress Street, Suite 1101, Boston, MA (02114). Other means of contact are by telephoning (617) 565-9708, faxing (617) 565-9723, or e-mailing (christine.reinfelds@hq.doe.gov).

Chicago Department of Energy Support: Your contact person is Celeste Moerle, (206) 553-2200. Write Ms. Moerle at 800 Fifth Avenue, Suite 3950, Seattle, WA 98104.

Another great source for aid is the **Low Income Home Energy Assistance Program** (**LIHEAP**). Even though eligibility varies from state to state, the total household's income must not surpass $150% of the poverty level or 60% of the state's average income. (This is an important aspect as one state's median might be $50,000 while another may be $150,000.) Payments from LIHEAP may be cash, vouchers, or payments to third parties, such as your power company. Because the LIHEAP Coordinators are by state rather than by region, I'll simply include the national address, which is **Administrator for Children and Families**, 370 L'Enfant Promenade, Fifth Floor West, Suite 509, Washington, DC 20444.

Dental Care:
Okay, so your gums are bleeding and that left molar makes you moan and groan day and night. Are you going to allow your teeth to fall out because you either can't afford dental care or simply aren't able to travel to the dentist? Let's hear a resounding "NO" since there are programs for this health-related service, too, and often regardless of your income. You may be able to receive such aid as free or low-cost dentures and repairs, senior discounts anywhere from 15% to 80%, free at-home care, and free dental implants.

Most states have programs such as this for the elderly, and often dentists contribute their time and expertise just for this cause. Low-cost care is also available through dental schools, many of which will even set up a payment plan if the services aren't free (and many are). Contact your state **Dental Society** or dental schools to find out the requirements.

Some states actually have "Dentists-on-Wheels" programs. This service brings a dentist straight to your doorstep if you're physically unable to make the trip yourself. Again, the service may be either free or on a sliding scale payment plan. Contact your state's Dental Society or your nearest **Community Health Center** for more information.

VITA/TCE Programs and IRS e-file:
Is there any one of us who likes taxes? Excuse me, but I didn't hear anyone reply in the affirmative. Unfortunately, though, just like clockwork, every year Uncle Sam comes a'marching with his greedy hands outstretched, and you must deliver whether you're a senior citizen or not. While you may not be able to avoid this dreaded time, there are ways to make the process a little easier, compliments of dear 'ole Uncle Sam himself.

The **Volunteer Income Tax Assistance/Tax Counseling for the Elderly** is a free service for the elderly that joined several years ago with the IRS's free service, **e-file**. The upshot of the combination is a great help to senior taxpayers. There are no fees for tax preparation or for electronic filing, and refunds are received in half the time. Because your tax returns are correct, there's less chance of Mr. Taxman knocking on your door, especially as you receive a proof of receipt from the IRS. This service is also very convenient and may be found at libraries, local community centers, and so forth.

So how does it work? The IRS trains volunteers to prepare basic returns free of charge for individuals of low to moderate income, those with disabilities, non-English speaking taxpayers and, of course, the elderly. This procedure is performed at VITA locations. Volunteers also prepare free basic returns at local TCE sites for those who are sixty years or older. For the nearest location, contact the IRS Taxpayer Education Coordinator at your local IRS office or call AARP at (1-888) 227-7669.

Legal Services
In addition to tax assistance, older Americans who belong to AARP may partake of the organization's **Legal Services Network**. Tested and proven, this service should be nationwide by the time you're reading this chapter. Check your yellow pages under "Attorneys" or the associations section under the

subheading, **AARP**-Legal Services Network or check **AARP**'s Web page. You can also write for a list at **LSN Fulfillment**, P.O. Box 100084, Pittsburgh, PA 15290. Here's what you get:

- A free half-hour consultation by phone or in person, whichever you choose.
- Preparation of a simple will. Individuals pay $50 and couples pay $75.
- Preparation of a Durable Power of Attorney and a health-care Power of Attorney/Living Will. This is the best of the deal as far as I'm concerned. For $35 you may choose a person who is capable of handling your finances and medical decisions if you're unable to do so physically or mentally.
- Billing in matters of probate by the hour at twenty percent off the lawyer's usual hourly rates.
- In Social Security cases, the attorney charges a twenty-percent reduction and his or her fees can't exceed twenty-five percent of a lump-sum award.
- A lower percentage rate is charged for personal injury or damage suits if settled before court action and, to make the pie tastier, the lawyer can't deduct his or her expenses from the client's share of the settlement.

Even though death knows no age limitations, it does seem that it faces us more the older we become. The death of a loved one is difficult enough without having to worry about expensive lies that take advantage of the grieving family. While the majority of funeral homes are reputable and honest, just as with every other business there are unscrupulous individuals out to make a buck (and a lot of bucks, in this instance). Respond to deceptive claims in the following ways:

1. Buying a casket or even an urn for cremation is *not* a necessity. Quite literally, the funeral home can cremate in a box and the ashes may be placed in a baggie. This may sound rather irreverent, but it just goes to show that you don't have to pay the price that the director says you do.

2. Refusal to discuss prices over the phone is *against* the law. The Federal Trade Commission's (FTC) requires funeral homes to provide consumers with any price when requested.
3. Law does *not* require a burial liner or a vault. Moreover, neither will preserve the body forever. Don't be pressured into this purchase, either.
4. A grave marker *doesn't* have to be purchased from the funeral home. In fact, buying from a third-party (usually a company that specializes in such) will save a substantial amount of money.

A funeral may be as simple or as elaborate as the family wishes. Just try to make sure that your sorrow doesn't get in the way of your good sense so that it's your wishes that count (or that of the deceased) and not that of the funeral home.

Before I close this chapter, I want to leave you with a few last agencies that exist solely to serve the aging. Please contact each of them *before* the need arises. The **American Association of Homes and Services for the Aging** provides brochures on housing options and information on community services for those who live at home. Contact these folks at 901 E Street, NW, Suite 500, Washington, DC 20004; (202) 783-2242; http://www.aahsa.org. The **National Academy of Elder Law Attorneys** is an organization that provides you with information on what to seek in this type of specialized lawyer, including living trusts, guardianships and conservatorships, and medical decision-making. Write them at 1604 North Country Club Road, Tucson, AR 85716 or call at (520) 881-4005. The **National Association of Professional Geriatric Care Managers** refers you to care managers in your area. It also publishes a fee-based directory of care managers listed by state and by qualification. Contact the Association by writing the same Tucson address as above or by calling (520) 881-8008. The **Older Woman's League** (666 Eleventh Street, NW, Suite 700, Washington, DC 20001) provides information on caregivers' concerns and referrals to local caregivers. Give the League a call at (202) 783-6686. The **Well Spouse**

Ellen Phillips

Foundation sponsors programs and local support groups for spousal caregivers. Call this organization at (1-800) 838-0879/ (212) 644-1241 or write to 610 Lexington Avenue, Suite 814, New York, NY 10022. Finally, the **National Meals on Wheels Foundation** makes grants to local programs that provide free and nutritious meals to homebound seniors. To contact the group in your area, call (1-800) 999-6262. A sourcebook site that offers an overwhelming amount of helpful information about all aspects that affect older Americans is the **Eldercare Web** (www.eldercare.com). It offers over 4,000 reviewed links regarding health, finance, housing, and any other topic you can think of.

Seniors, I salute you!

Agencies and Services

A Consumer's Guide to Postal Crime Prevention, a booklet that helps prevent mail fraud and theft, may be ordered from your local post office or by calling (202) 268-4293.

The **American Association of Homes and Services for the Aging** provides brochures for services of those who live at home. Contact the Association at 901 E Street, NW, Suite 500, Washington, DC 20004; (202) 783-2242.

For information about assisted living, contact the **Assisted Living Foundation of America**. Visit its site at www.alfa.org or call (703) 691-8100.

The **American Association of Retired Persons** is a watchdog agency that provides a wealth of services to its members. Contact the AARP at 601 E Street, NW, Washington, DC 20049 or call at (202) 434-6030.

The **Carrier Alert Program** is one in which your mail carrier watches your mailbox for accumulated mail, possibly signifying assistance. Call your local post office. Also ask for a copy of *A Consumer's Guide to Crime Prevention* or obtain a copy by calling (202) 268-4293.

Contact your state's **Dental Society** for its services offering free or reduced fees for low-income and/or disabled senior citizens.

The **Eldercare Locator**, a national directory that helps to locate local support resources, may be reached at (1-800) 677-1116. The online site is www.elderweb.com.

Order the book *Free Stuff for Seniors* by writing FC&A Publishing, 103 Clover Green, Peachtree City, GA 30269.

The **Low Income Home Energy Assistance Program** provides special energy services to low-income seniors. Write Administrator for Children and Families, 370 L'Enfant Promenade, Fifth Floor West, Suite 509, Washington, DC 20444 for information.

One of the best organizations that help with a variety of problems is the **National Association of Area Agencies on the Aging**. Write to 112 Sixteenth Street, NW, Suite 100, Washington, DC 20036 or call (202) 296-8130.

The **National Academy of Elder Law Attorneys** provides information on legal services. Call at (520) 881-4005 or write to 1604 North Country Club Road, Tucson, AR 85716.

A referral service to area care managers, the **National Association of Professional Geriatric Care Managers** also publishes a directory for such. It may be ordered from 1604 North Country Club Road, Tucson, AR 85716 or by calling (520) 881-8008.

The **National Caregivers Association** can help to provide some relief for exhausted caregivers. Write the organization at 10605 Concord Street, Suite 501, Kensington, MD 20895. They can also be reached at (800) 896-3650 or at www.nfcacares.org.

If you suspect you've been victimized, contact the **National Fraud Information Center**, P.O. Box 65868, Washington, DC 20035 or call the **U.S. Justice Department** at (202) 514-2001. Contact Justice, too, at (202) 514-0301 if you believe you're the victim of discrimination relating to a disability.

National Meals on Wheels Foundation provides localities with grants for homebound seniors' meals. To find out the group in your area, call (1-800) 999-6262.

The **Office of Fair Housing and Equal Opportunity** at the U.S. Department of Housing and Urban Development assists with complaints about discrimination because of age or disability. Call (1-800) 669-9777.

The **Older Woman's League** helps with caregivers' concerns and referrals to local caregivers and may be called at (202) 783-6686 or write to 666 Eleventh Street, NW, Suite 700, Washington, DC 20001.

Operation Match helps to pair people looking for affordable housing with someone who wishes help with housing expenses. Contact the Eldercare Locator at (1-800) 677-1116.

Patient Assistance Programs help provide free or low-cost prescription drugs. Call your drug manufacturer for more information.

"Protecting Older Americans Against Overpayment of Income Taxes" may be ordered from (202) 224-5364 or by sending a postcard to the Senate Special Committee on Aging, G31 Dirksen Senate Building, Washington, DC 20510.

The **U.S. Department of Health and Human Services** (1-800) 447-8477 assists if you feel you're the victim of Medicare fraud or abuse. **The Civil Rights Division** at the U.S. Justice Department assists with disability discrimination, and HUD's **Office of Fair Housing and Equal Opportunity** helps with housing discriminatory practices. Contact both of the latter two departments at (202) 514-0301 and (800) 669-9777, respectively.

VITA/TCE is a tax service for the elderly. Contact your local IRS office or call AARP at (1-888) 227-7669.

Weatherization Offices, a service of the U.S. Department of Energy, assists the low-income elderly with financial needs. Contact your region's program manager.

Call the **Well Spouse Foundation** at (1-800) 838-0879 for information on local support groups for spousal caregivers. Write to 610 Lexington Avenue, Suite 814, New York, NY 10022.

www.seniors.gov is a fantastic site with collaboration between the AARP and the federal government.

Chapter 12
Corporate Etiquette

"I'm rarely wrong, but when I am it's inconsequential."
– **Marvin Packer**

It's too bad that Mr. Packer's quote seems to be the attitude of many in the corporate world. Often we see an excessive air of superiority to the customer, an attitude of almost "I'm OK, you suck!" Whether it be poor Customer "Service" or the lack of response we get when we air our problems to many in management positions, me thinks these higher-ups need a *big* lesson in corporate etiquette. In large part, the Consumer Revolution will dose out the medicine, but it's up to the executives to swallow it and then try to get-well-quick. Then and only then can consumers rest easy in the assurance that shoddy products and unfair or negligent services have been placed on the back burner – forever. Just as important, however, is that companies also will relax in the knowledge that their products and services are the best around, thereby leading to fewer and fewer complaints. Finally, don't forget that customers surely will return to shop at companies and businesses that make them feel appreciated and take care of service needs.

Let's take customer service departments first. Who among us hasn't experienced the frustrations of dialing a company's number (and sometimes we even have to pay for the call) and having to punch in thirty-three menus in the hopes of reaching a real live person on the other end? Or maybe after punching the thirty-third, we get a human, only to be placed on hold for anywhere between ten and forty-five minutes. Then, to add insult to injury, we may be disconnected and have to begin the entire process over. Boy, are we really hot by this point! Or maybe we do eventually speak with a customer service representative and he or she is rude, defensive, uncooperative, or just downright ignorant. Whose fault is this? I maintain that the problem lies not necessarily with the individual but with the company itself. Studies show that customer access and a satisfactory response makes all the difference in the world to their decisions to continue doing business with a particular company. After all, statistically, when one average dissatisfied customer tells eleven other people and those eleven tell five more, we're already up to sixty-seven bad word-of-mouthers. This doesn't count the number of folks that the sixty-seven approached. The worse kind of publicity? You betcha.

Even though I'm notorious for blaming many of our woes on the customer service representatives, I maintain that their employers place most people within the industry in an uncompromising position. Whether it's a lack of training in product knowledge, overloaded with calls, or no authority to truly solve problems, these worker bees become the culprit for our anger. Add to this equation a "never admit fault" philosophy and throw in a general need for more civility (a little kiss-up never hurts) and it's no wonder we are quick to rant and rave at these poor individuals.

As a consumer, you know what *you* should do when faced with a crummy item, service, or person, but what should business owners or corporate officials do to ensure that consumers obtain the help they need and deserve? Heads up, Honchos, this one's for you.

- **Make sure that all your employees understand the customer is *Number One*.** Everyone is to be treated with equal respect. And while I don't advocate unhappy customers cursing and screaming, still they don't deserve to feel devalued. Consumers with a legitimate gripe should expect a prompt resolution or at least the satisfaction of someone listening to their tales of woe. The outburst can actually be abated or even stopped if your employee listens (or at least pretends to). Sometimes, that's all we want – to be heard and to know that our views are important. This then leads me to the second point.
- **Never argue with a customer, even if he or she is in the wrong.** Imagine yourself in the customer's

shoes. Wouldn't *you* be upset, too? If he or she wants to vent, then let the venting begin, but <u>don't</u> take it personally – it's not about you! Don't interrupt or try to defend the company. "Do unto others" is the perfect treatise, especially under these circumstances.

- **Always promptly return phone calls**. This is simple, common courtesy, and we need more mannerly traits in today's rampaging society. Even better, after the problem is resolved, write a short note of apology and stress that the customer should feel free to make future contacts.

- **Make your product or service easy to purchase – and to complain about**. Is the customer hassled with loads of paperwork and other dribble, such as ferocious or harassing or simply untrained sales clerks? What if they can't get any results from online customer service? Or, on the other hand, when a shopper enters your place of business (whether online or your bricks-and-mortar stores), is there any person available to help him or her? I've often needed some assistance and have literally walked the entire length of a store to find someone who doesn't tell me to "go to the next department." Indeed, I've also been treated the same way by companies who have set up a Web site that isn't prepared to handle traffic, specifically with regards to a lack of response to customers. Excuse me, but remember Rule Number One!

- **Don't blame the defects on anything other than the company's errors**. For example, if that high-priced car or even the cheap model rolls off the assembly line full of poor quality parts, then it's your responsibility to accept and acknowledge the fact that the company screwed up. If there's a problem with the plane's computers, don't blame the delay on the poor baggage handlers. Consumers are not dumb; don't treat us as if we are.

- **Use customer satisfaction surveys.** You might be surprised when you read these. The real kicker, however, is to learn from these surveys so that your business doesn't continue to make the same mistakes over and over again. According to a recent study by Perdue University, fewer than ten percent of customers regularly let companies know how they (the companies) are doing. Even worse (or should be) to the eyes of the companies themselves, research shows that consumers simply stop buying the product or service from that particular business or manufacturer.
- **Don't use a voice mail system unless absolutely necessary**. The "thirty-three" options get mighty tiresome and aggravating. *Absolutely necessary* does not mean continuous use on a daily basis. And while we're on the subject,

- **Have a good call center**. As absolutely infuriating as it is for all those options and all that wasted time, consumers' blood pressure goes even more ballistic when they are the ones paying for the call. Be sure your company has a toll-free number and that it stays open, preferably twenty-four hours a day.
- **Empower employees**. If businesses would just open their eyes and understand that this empowerment would stop a multitude of problems pretty darn quick, we'd see a whole new world of customer satisfaction. When employees are trained to work successfully with problems and issues and to resolve the complaints,

there would be far fewer needs for irate purchasers or complaint ("A rose by any other name...") departments. Experiment yourself and you'll see just how easily most of us are made more than happy with a simple apology, the defective item replaced or repaired, or maybe a slight adjustment to the bill.

- **Provide a money-back guarantee**. The company's profits soar when satisfied customers continue to buy from it (and they tell everyone else to do so). Also, you need to clearly state the return policies. Ditch the fine print and the gobbledygook.

- **Make it easy to contact you directly**. An available e-mail address is a nice option as is a cooperative executive secretary.

- **Promptly respond to customer complaint letters**. Usually, these letters are written as a final resort. If you don't respond in a speedy fashion or, worse, not at all, your competitor will thank you.

- **Executives should experiment with calling their own customer "service" numbers**. Once you see for yourself just what we peons go through on a daily basis, you'll understand why consumers stay irate.

- **Treat customers like members of your own family**. Consumers are the reason for your huge salaries, stock options, and other perks. If they (finally) feel that their opinions are valid and important, your profits will wildly increase.

Okay, Big Bosses, so you like what I've said so far (or you'll at least accept it as good business practices). What can you do to ensure happy workers for your company? This is important, too, since a cheerful work force means better service, which in turn leads to more satisfied customers. If the employees who man your corporation, business, or mom-and-pop store aren't exactly turning cartwheels in glee when Monday morning rolls around, then you need to address this area as well.

Our economy went from great into the grave. Because of the scarcity of good people in a very tight labor market, many companies have had to resort to the "warm body" hiring approach. If one can use a telephone or move from one in-store counter to another, he or she often rapidly finds a job. (Why do you think that McDonalds and others are paying their staff twice the minimum wage to flip burgers beneath the Golden Arches?) Unfortunately, Mr. and Ms. Warm Body – especially if they're good at what they do - either aren't made to feel appreciated or a better offer comes along and they hit the road. Moreover, because so many people do move along to other jobs so quickly, companies don't wish to invest a lot of time and money. And guess what? If no time or money is invested, if these employees don't feel valued, then they do move on. The vicious cycle continues, and the consumer once more is the loser.

As we go to press, Kmart, the granddaddy of all discount stores, just filed Chapter 11. Beset on each side by Wal-Mart and Target stores, analysts suggested that Kmart should have booted out its unproductive stores and turned others into superstores that carry groceries and so forth. When I read this news, it reminded me of a sketch I read about a year ago on Charles Conaway, the former Chairman, and the measures he initially took to guarantee pulling the company back up by its bootstraps, one of which was to provide employee incentives. For example, he's credited with introducing a twenty-four hour customer service center that rewarded those employees who provide superior service. Mr. Conaway even took matters a step further by ensuring that store managers' bonuses were tied to how well they responded to complaints. (Frankly, since the great Sam Walton died, Wal-Mart's customer service hasn't been up to the stupendous par it once was. Its corporate heads are smart enough, however, to maintain a loyal customer base by supersizing all over America.) Perhaps if Kmart can keep Conaway's strategies while restructuring the corporation, we'll hopefully see some future positive difference. In fact, if more corporate heads would follow his earlier lead regarding employee morale when he first came onboard last year, plus go by the following tips, then employees and, thus, consumers would be a great deal happier.

- **Pay the best wages possible**. By doing so, you'll show respect for the employee's talents and what he or she can do for your company. To be sure that the salary is fair, check around with other companies in your field.
- **Remember the perks**. Paid holidays and vacation time are basic benefits, but don't stop there. Employees feel valued and more respected when they work for a business that offers other packages. These may include benefits, such as a company medical plan, dental plan, paid sick leave, paid personal leave, paid maternity leave, life insurance, short and long-term disability, educational help, and so forth. (These days, folks are looking for companies that really go a half-dozen steps further and offer in-house daycare, gyms, cafeterias and other "luxuries."
- **Cosset Miss/Mr. Doesn't Know-It-All**. If you're confident enough about your own abilities to lead the pack, then some subtle flattery won't hurt you a lick. Statements that begin with, for example, "As I'm sure you already know" (whether he or she really knows at all) make the employee feel important. Persons who feel this way will usually push themselves to the limit, which ultimately leads to a more successful company (and more bucks lining your and your investors' pockets).
- **Be detail-oriented**. When we screw up, we panic. It may not be as obvious as an overt fit of hysteria, but we are forced into the old fight-or-flight mode. When FOF occurs, we can make mistakes and the company ultimately suffers. Executives and managers can help to prevent this, however, by taking a positive approach. For instance, one way to calm your employee is to be calm yourself in order to reduce the frantic one's anxiety. Ask questions, like "First, tell me what you did or said?" Then lead this person through his or her explanation or problem, until the point where it may be corrected. By the way, this approach is exactly what a good complaint letter does when it's addressed to you.

- **Don't fight anger with anger**. Not only do people panic when they've done something wrong, they often get angry when they're placed on the defensive. Even if they misperceive what you're saying, they're still ticked. Not the most ideal situation for employer-employee relationships, huh? Just as I advocate to my readers that anger promotes anger and to avoid the appearance of this emotion like the plague, it's vital that bosses do the same. Rather than risking the loss of an employee, who actually may be quite good at his or her position, revisit the sore spot at a later time. Even ten or fifteen minutes later can be a cooling-off period — for both of you.

- **Compromise when necessary**. Yes, I know you're the head honcho. Yes, we all realize you make a trillion dollars a year by running your company. These do not detract from the issue at hand, though. You *are* only human, after all, and your viewpoint isn't the be-all-to-end-all. Compromises can many times be the most effective way to deal with differing views. In addition, respect your employees' opinions. After all, these people are the ones in the trenches and know what's going on – many times a lot better than you do. Forget mission statements. They do not motivate. Employees are motivated by success, which then should become better job security and pay for all.

- **Make advancement possible within the company**. Regardless of how little, there always should be room for advancement. This could be at a minimum of more job responsibility on up to a new job title and/or more salary. Give staffers the opportunity to advance and they'll excel even more.

- **Celebrate achievements with every person in the company**. When something terrific happens – maybe landing a big account – then include your staff in the "celebration." From the lowest rung of the ladder on up to your corporate vice presidents, express your personal gratitude for a job well done. Believe me, a little effort and pats-on-the-back on your part will always result in employees' greater effort.

- **Above all, don't forget that there would be no profitable company without loyal employees**. While from an economics viewpoint it may be good business to hire those young hotshots (who earn less than the old-timers), remember that loyalty must reciprocate loyalty. Don't expect your employees to be ethical and productive while you hand out pink slips to some who have worked hard for the company, especially for those who have been faithful employees for twenty years or more. Offer incentives to retire if you must; this is a better way to purge than the old heave-ho that everyone knows about - and fears.

One of the most dreaded *goodbye-don't-let-the-door-slam-you-in-the behind-on-your-way-out* apprehensions is when the staff begins to hear the term/threat "merger" tossed around the office. After speaking with a number of people who have found themselves either remaining on the inside after the fact or those who see themselves looking in but remaining out, I firmly believe that few occurrences strike more terror into the hearts of personnel than the prospect of a merger. Yes, some folks will be shown a severance package, but for countless others, the success of such a step may create very big opportunities. In fact, even these soon-to-be former employees can view this step as a chance to move on to another and more profitable venture.

So I advise readers who fall within either of these categories to stay in touch with one another. Even you (lucky) people who are asked to remain may find that your departing co-workers may become the best of connections for future endeavors. As a matter of fact, think seriously if you really want to stay with Company X. Are the slots being opened by departing workers ones in which you would be interested? Perhaps a promotion? On the other hand, if you're not the happiest with the proposed action, then maybe this is the time to pull up stakes yourself and move on.

And remember, Bosses, if you don't have loyal employees who do their jobs well without constantly having to look over their shoulders, there won't be loyal customers. And without loyal customers, there won't be you!

Chapter 13
Follow the Leader

"With the proper direction and perseverance, one can obtain almost any goal."
- Ellen Phillips

So many folks have thanked me for including templates for them to follow in the final chapter of *Shocked, Appalled, and Dismayed!* Because of these comments, I feel it necessary that I offer a smattering in this book, too. I've also discovered over the years that many would-be complainers or just the average person is more prone to write if a specific guide is placed before them.

While I know that a whole pile of consumers follow the step-by-step process and the sample letters, it's simpler for others to "borrow freely" from a form letter. Of course, their own documentation and information are placed within the blanks, but a fill-in-the-blank-camera-ready-copy is almost as easily accomplished as closing one's eyes. So one day if you prefer to be a bit lazy or don't have the time to go back to the relevant chapters to search out the steps in order to write your letter, then make sure your recipients are up-to-date, sit back, and follow the (*Ellen's Poison Pen*) leader. Note that some templates contain a longer list of carbon copies, depending upon the complexity of the situation.

Airlines

[Your street address]
[Your city, state, zip code]
[Today's date]

[Name of recipient, title]
[Name of airline]

[Street address or post office box]
Atlanta, GA 30600 (As an example, I'm using the state of Georgia for the purpose of copying the Georgia Office of Consumer Affairs.)

Dear Mr./Ms. _____:

I am a faithful and long-standing customer of _____ Airlines, and I am certain that you wish to be made aware of my outrage because of an appalling situation that recently occurred.

On _____[date], I traveled from _____ [city and airport] on flight #_____ to my destination, _____ [city and airport] (copies of tickets/boarding passes enclosed). Imagine my shock when [here, state the problem: flight canceled; luggage didn't arrive with you; unhelpful personnel; stale peanuts; etc.].

When I attempted to first solve the problem myself, I [state what you did, to whom you spoke and when, and so forth]. However, no one seemed the least bit sympathetic to my very real plight. [If there are applicable federal regulations, such as the ones I wrote of in *Shocked, Appalled, and Dismayed! How to Write Letters of Complaint That Get Results* and in this book, state them here.]

I cannot believe that you are aware of or condone this manner of what I believe to be unprofessional [rudeness/unfeeling/unhelpful/sucks raw eggs] attitudes on the part of your airline and its employees. I am certain you wish to investigate this matter immediately and thoroughly.

I look forward to hearing from you within thirty days with the resolution which is fairly owed to me: _____ [two first-class tickets/new luggage/fresh peanuts].

Thank you.

Sincerely,

[Your name]

Enclosure

cc: The Honorable Norman Mineta, Secretary
United States Department of Transportation
400 Seventh Street, SW
Washington, DC 20590

Office of Intergovernmental and Consumer Affairs
United States Department of Transportation
400 Seventh Street, SW
Washington, DC 20590

Jane F. Garvey, Chief
Federal Aviation Administration
800 Independence Avenue, SW
Washington, DC 20591

Office of Consumer Affairs
United States Department of Commerce
Room 5718
Fourteenth Street and Constitution Avenue, NW
Washington, DC 20230

Helen McMurray, Chief
Consumer Protection Division
Office of the Attorney General
State Office Tower, 25th Floor
Columbus, OH 43215

The Honorable Thurbert E. Baker
Attorney General of Georgia

Office of the Attorney General
40 Capitol Square, SW
Atlanta, GA 30334

Jeff L. Milsteen, Deputy Attorney General
Office of Consumer Affairs
2 Martin Luther King Drive, Suite 356
Atlanta, GA 30334

I am using the contact name for Ohio as an example for a consumer in that state to copy.

*****

Automobiles

[Your street address]
[Your city, state, zip code]
[Today's date]

[Name of recipient, title]
[Name of automobile manufacturer]
[Street address or post office box]
Lansing, MI 69823 (As an example, I am using the state of Michigan for the purpose of copying Michigan's attorney general.)

Dear Mr./Ms. _____:

The trust and loyalty I have placed in _____ Motors for many years has shockingly not been merited with regard to my current model, _____ [name of car and ID number]. I am certain that you will agree that I have been subjected to [harassment/ill mannered employees/ a kick in the hiney], all of which besmirches the fine name of _____ [name of corporation].

377

I purchased my vehicle on _____ [date] from [dealership] in
_____, _____ [city and state]. Imagine my dismay when the
following problems began to occur: [document the date,
problem, what you did, to whom you spoke, etc.]

1.

2.

3.

4.

5.

This horrendous problem has caused me a great deal of
emotional, physical, and financial hardship [one, two, or all
three, if applicable]. I might add that all of my family, friends,
and colleagues who have observed what I have suffered are
equally appalled at what has transpired with your company's
practices. [implied threat of profit loss]

All I ask is what I am fairly owed: [state what this is]. I am
sure you will wish to investigate this matter promptly and
thoroughly, and I look forward to hearing from you by [date].

Thank you.

Sincerely,

(Your name)

Enclosure

cc: The Honorable Donald Evans, Secretary

United States Department of Commerce
Fifteenth Street and Constitution Avenue, NW
Washington, DC 20230

Howard Beales, Director
Office of Consumer Protection
Federal Trade Commission
Pennsylvania Avenue and Sixth Street, NW
Washington, DC 20580

The Honorable Roy Cooper
Attorney General of North Carolina
P.O. Box 629
Raleigh, NC 27602-0629

Alan Hirsch, Special Deputy Attorney General
Consumer Protection Section
Office of the Attorney General
P.O. Box 629
Raleigh, NC 27602-0629

The Honorable Jennifer Granholm
Attorney General of Michigan
Office of the Attorney General
P.O. Box 30212
Lansing, MI 48909-0212

Robert Shelton, Executive Director
National Highway Traffic Safety Administration
400 Seventh Street, SW
Washington, DC 20590

Ms. Marion Blakely, Acting Secretary
National Transportation Safety Board
490 L'Enfant Plaza, East, SW
6th Floor
Washington, DC 20594

Clarence Ditlow, Executive Director
Center for Auto Safety
2001 S Street, NW, Suite 410
Washington, DC 20009

Automotive Consumer Action Program
8400 Westpark Drive
McLean, VA 22102

Cleo Manuel, Executive Vice President
Consumer Federation of America
1424 Sixteenth Street, NW, Suite 604
Washington, DC 20036

I'm using the contact name for the state of North Carolina as an example for a consumer in that state to copy.

*****

Contracting Services

[Your street address]
[Your city, state, zip code]
[Today's date]

[Hoke MacMillan, Attorney General]
[Office of the Attorney General]
[123 State Capitol Building]
Cheyenne, WY (As an example, I am using the state of Wyoming for the purpose of writing *to* the Wyoming Attorney General.)

Dear General MacMillan:

I am outraged that I continue to be harassed by [name and address of company], especially following the dreadful mess the employees made of my bedrooms and the carpets (see enclosed copy of letter). To add insult to injury, I received today a late notice from [name of contracting company]. Colorado's Insurance Commissioner Kirven suggests that I request that you use the full force of your office to take care of this problem once and for all.

- I thought I surely had corrected the matter when I last spoke with [name of person] on [date]. I [spat at/ cursed/informed] him in no uncertain terms that I was tired of being hassled, that I owed nothing, that my homeowners insurance company had informed me that neither the company nor I owed a penny more to [name of contracting company], and that I had maintained copious notes about this entire inexcusable and appalling matter.

- After explaining that the charge [name of contracting company] continued to bill was based upon <u>its errors and correcting its mistakes</u>, [employee name] promised to red flag my account; I was to receive no more bills. The statement received today (attached) credits me with the wallpaper ($352.80) but still maintains that I owe $247. I **owe for neither**.

After I have been forced to expend an enormous amount of time and aggravation with regards to the numerous problems forced upon me by [contracting company] since [date], enough is enough. I truly do not understand if some of its employees are ignorant of procedure, ignorant of dealing with insurance companies as a whole and with informed customers, or the company itself is simply a fraudulent one. It is definitely my opinion that one or more of the contentions listed is the reason why I have been treated in this manner for [length of time].

Thank you so much and I look forward to hearing from you by [date].

Ellen Phillips

Sincerely,

[Your name]

Enclosure

cc: Christopher Petrie, Assistant Attorney General
   Office of the Attorney General
   Consumer Protection Unit
   123 State Capitol Building
   Cheyenne, WY 82002

   William J. Kirven, III, Commissioner
   Department of Insurance
   1560 Broadway, Suite 850
   Denver, CO 80202

   Ken Salazar, Attorney General
   Office of the Attorney General
   1525 Sherman Street
   Denver, CO 80202

I'm using the contact names and addresses for the state of Colorado as examples for a consumer in that state to copy.

*****

Frauds and Scams

[Your street address]
[Your city, state, zip code]
[Today's date]

[The Honorable Bill Lockyer, Attorney General]
[Office of the Attorney General]
[1300 I Street, Suite 1740]
Sacramento, CA 95814 (As an example, I'm using the state of California for the purpose of writing to the Attorney General of California.)

Dear General _____:

My [father/grandma/black sheep of the family/pet pig] has recently fallen prey to what I believe to be an illegal sweepstakes activity. In my opinion, [name of organization] has defrauded me by mail of [sum], and [I/he/we]turn to you for your personal intervention.

- When my relative, [name of relative] received the sweepstakes notice, it emphatically stated that he would receive [sum] simply by sending in his entry blank (copy of notice and entry blank enclosed). The inference, however, was that by purchasing the [magazines, collectibles/porcelain potty], my chances of a larger amount would be even better. On [date], I mailed a check to [company] (copy enclosed).
- The following week [or whatever date] I received a second notice that assured me of additional prize money if I ordered more of [company's] products (copy enclosed). I did so in the amount of [sum].
- The president of [company] ostensibly wrote the third letter I received (copy enclosed). [name of person] promised that my prize checks were immediately forthcoming from the first two orders, and I would claim another check if I placed a third order.
- By this time, I realized that I had been victimized. I wrote to [company] (copy enclosed) and demanded a refund of the [sum] I had previously paid. I also explained to [name] that I believed his/her company was an illegitimate one and that I would write to the consumer protection agency in my state if

my letter were ignored. I received no response. Since I believe this matter to be one of mail fraud, I then contacted the postmaster at my branch office, [name], who is investigating himself; however, [name] recommended that I write directly to you, as the offending company's Attorney General's office is directly in charge of fraudulent activities.

Even though this amount may be never recovered, if I could be assured that this organization does not defraud other citizens, my fears would be somewhat alleviated.

Any assistance that your office can provide is greatly appreciated, and I look forward to hearing from you by [date].

Thank you.

Sincerely,

[Your name]

Enclosures

cc: Robert S. Mueller, Director
Federal Bureau of Investigation
935 Pennsylvania Avenue, NW
Washington, DC 20535

The Honorable John E. Potter
Postmaster General
475 L'Enfant Plaza,West., SW
Washington, DC 20260

Mark R. Shurtleff, Attorney General
Office of the Attorney General
State Capitol

Room 236
Salt Lake City, UT 84114

I'm using the contact name for the state of Utah as a Utah consumer.

*****

<u>Health Maintenance Organizations</u>

[Your street address]
[Your city, state, zip code]
[Today's date]

[Name of recipient, title]
[Street address or post office box]
Phoenix, AZ 85007 [As an example, I am using the state of Arizona for the purpose of copying the Arizona Department of Insurance]

RE: Policy [#]

Dear Mr./Ms._____:

I am absolutely **appalled** at the manner in which certain members of your staff have treated me. Furthermore, it is my belief that your company has [defrauded? mistreated? annihilated?] me of insurance benefits for which I signed a contract and always pay said premium in full. I am certain that you have no knowledge of such activities and will, therefore, launch an immediate and personal investigation into the situation. While I am including copies of all charges and communications for your perusal, the following brief history should provide an overall status of this egregious issue.

- Because of [cite the specific reason] my [relative] was admitted on [date] to [the park/football game/General Hospital] in [city, state]. Because she had some problems, her hospital stay extended until [date] for a total of [sum], after insurance payment.
- As you can see by the enclosed documentation, [include all chronology]
- Even after repeated requests, I have never received the appeals information; thus, here is my own attempt. I have also checked similar hospitals around the Washington, DC area, and my hospital's charges **are** "usual and customary. [List the hospitals here.]

I cannot believe that you [love/push/dupe/condone] these types of behaviors on the part of your company. When I searched for reputable insurance companies back in 1999 that would best meet the needs of my family, I decided upon [name of company] for a variety of reasons. Moreover, I should not be held accountable for your company's irresponsible **in**action. However, I am to blame for my naïveté in continuing to have some faith that your organization would fulfill its obligations. I hope that my loyalty was not totally displaced, and that you grant me *immediate* assistance with this horrific problem.

Thank you, and I look forward to hearing from you by [date].

Sincerely,

[Your name]

Enclosures

cc: The Honorable Michael Mangano, Inspector General
United States Department of Health and Human Services

200 Independence Avenue, SW
Washington, DC 20201

The Honorable Elaine Chao, Secretary
United States Department of Labor [covers all health plans]
200 Constitution Avenue, NW
Washington, DC 20210

David B. Irvin, Senior Assistant
Attorney General and Chief
Office of the Attorney General
Consumer Litigation Section
900 East Main Street
Richmond, VA 23219

Theodore V. Morrison, Chairman
Bureau of Insurance
State Corporation Commission
P.O. Box 1197
Richmond, VA 23219

Sally J. Duren
Virginia Department of Health
Managed Health Care Insurance Plans
2542 North Vermont Street
Arlington, VA 22207

Charles R. Cohen, Director
Arizona Department of Insurance
2910 North Forty-fourth Street
Suite 210
Phoenix, AZ 85018-7256

Nancy Davenport-Ennis, Executive Director
Patient Advocate Foundation
753 Thimble Shoals Boulevard, Suite B
Newport News, VA 23606

Ellen Phillips

I'm using the contact names and addresses for the Commonwealth of Virginia as examples for a consumer in that state to copy.

*****

Nursing Homes and Assisted Living

[Your street address]
[Your city, state, zip code]
[Today's date]

[Name of recipient, title]
[Name of airline]
[Street address or post office box]
Austin, TX 78711 (As an example, I am using the state of Texas for the purpose of copying the Texas Agency on the Aging.)

Dear Mr./Ms. _____:

I am appalled and disgusted at the conditions under which my [name of relative] resides at [name of facility]. Without going into all of the unpardonable details, I will simply document the one or two issues of most concern. I trust you will personally investigate the situation without delay.

- I originally met with [name of staff member] on [date]. [Staff member] assured me that [relative] would be provided with quality care under the best of circumstances. Her direct quote regarding staff was "We are your employees. We do whatever you ask." Just to make sure, however, we decided to pay the extra $280 monthly to ensure that Mother's more specific needs would be addressed and, additionally, cared for. [Staff

388

member] also promised conditions, such as weekly church services, plenty of staff, delicious and nutritious meals (with special dietary issues cared for), seating and activities by cognitive levels, a hospitality committee and a staff guardian angel to make Mother feel welcome and more "at home." Because the facility is so beautiful and [staff member] so convincing, Mother agreed that [facility] could be the best place for her to live, as she was unable to live at home any longer.

- Staffing is the primary and most serious alarm. [Document conditions].
- I find it also deplorable to observe **horrifically unsanitary conditions.** On each visits, I unobtrusively watch employees stand over the fruit basket(s) and [handle everything in the basket(s)/take bites from the fruit and put it back/eat from a resident's plate, or so forth]. How do you think matters like this affect gentle ladies and gentlemen who are assured that [facility] is their "home"? Do you believe that these same types of upsetting activities and accidents occur at *real* homes? [Document examples.]
- A specific instance occurred recently with my mother. [Relate details.] It is evident to me that [facility] is leaving itself wide open for a lawsuit, and this is an event that both corporate and the [local] facility would wish to avoid at all costs. Additional staff would be far less expensive than a mega-million dollar endangerment or even a negligent death suit.

It is incomprehensible to me that you would have knowledge of or condone gross neglect such as what I have described (and which does not begin to tell the full story). Therefore, I demand a personal investigation as well as a personal explanation.

Thank you, and I look forward to hearing from you by [date].

Sincerely,

[Your name]

cc: The Honorable Tommy Thompson, Secretary
US Department of Health and Human Services
200 Independence Avenue, SW
Washington, DC 20201

The Honorable Michael Mangano, Inspector General
US Department of Health and Human Services
200 Independence Avenue, SW
Washington, DC 20201

Judy Conover, Director
Assisted Living Foundation of America
10300 Eaton Place, Suite 400
Fairfax, VA 22030

Melissa M. Gordon, Ph.D, Executive Director
Department of Senior Services
770 Washington Avenue
RSA Plaza, Suite 470
Montgomery, AL 36130

Robert B. Culver, Executive Director
Area Agency on Aging
115 A Washington Street, SE
Huntsville, AL 35801

Mary Sapp, Executive Director
Texas Department on Aging
P.O. Box 12786
Austin, TX 78711

I'm using the names and addresses for the contact persons for the state of Alabama for consumers in that state to copy.

*****

Products

[Your street address]
[Your city, state, zip code]
[Today's date]

[Name of recipient, title]
[Street address or post office box]
Newark, NJ 07103 [As an example, I am using the state of New Jersey for the purpose of copying the New Jersey Consumer Affairs Division]

Dear Mr./Ms _____:

On [date], I purchased the *Zippadee Dooda* vacuum cleaner [or whatever the item] for _____ [price] (copy of receipt enclosed), and I was appalled the very first time I attempted to use it.

The vacuum made such horrendous noises when plugged in that I feared it might explode and [destroy my home, burn my face, take my life and all those lives within a thirty-mile radius]. Unfortunately, when I attempted to return the vacuum to [name of store], your manager, [name], refused to exchange this item, as he refused to believe that it was defective.

I am immediately shipping this shoddy product back to you and I expect [a new one/your money back/a credit to your account/the recipient's investment accounts] within the next three weeks.

Thank you.

Sincerely,

[Your name]

Enclosure

cc: Howard Beales, Director
    Office of Consumer Protection
    Federal Trade Commission
    Pennsylvania Avenue and 6th Street, NW
    Washington, DC 20580

    Kenneth Weaver, Chief Postal Inspector
    United State Postal Service
    475 L'Enfant Plaza West, SW
    Washington, DC 20260

    Ann Brown, Director
    Consumer Product Safety Commission
    4330 East West Highway
    Bethesda, MD 20207

    Debra Martinez, Chairwoman and Executive Director
    New York State Consumer Protection Board
    5 Empire State Plaza, Suite 2101
    Albany, NY 12223

    Thomas Conway, Bureau Chief
    Consumer Frauds and Protection Division
    Office of Attorney General
    120 Broadway

New York, NY 10271

The Honorable John J. Farmer, Jr.
Attorney General of New Jersey
Office of the Attorney General
Richard J. Hughes Justice Complex
25 Market Street, CN 080
Trenton, NJ 08625

I am using the contact names and addresses for the state of New York as an example for a consumer in that state to copy.

*****

Retail Service Companies

[Your Street Address]
[City, State, Zip]
[Date]

[Name, Title]
[Name of Company]
[Street Address]
Columbia, SC 29250 (As an example, I'm using the state of South Carolina for the purpose of copying the state's Commission of Consumer Affairs.)

Dear Mr./Ms. _____:

I have attempted to solve this intolerable problem with your company to no avail; therefore, I trust you will personally intervene so that the situation may be immediately corrected.

- [Document point by point. Each bullet corresponds with what has chronologically occurred. Depending upon the type of home service, specify the particular problem(s). For instance, a cleaning service may continue to leave the lights on when departing; the personnel may continue to place bedspread on the wrong way or leave pictures askew after dusting, etc. Did the client find anything broken? If so, then state the replacement cost. Have notes been left to the person in charge designating these areas of concern?
- A tree or lawn service may top or thin trees incorrectly – if so, then the client will wish full payment reimbursement plus the cost to replace the trees. A lawn service may skip a week and still wish to be paid. Perhaps the workers mow the grass too closely when in the middle of a drought. The client should expect reimbursement for sod, etc.
- Specify by date, names of persons with whom the client has spoken and the response/lack thereof, prior correspondence, and other pertinent information.]

I have been a loyal customer for [number of months or years] and have always promptly paid the bills [if this is the case]. Because I anticipate that loyalty to be reciprocated, in addition to what I believe your company owes me, I also expect [a free month's worth of work/groveling at my feet/the hand of your eldest son]. My neighbors to whom I have recommended your service are also looking forward to my hearing from you by [Date].

Thank you.

Sincerely,

[Client name]

Enclosure(s)

cc: Dr. Lonnie Randolph, Jr., Chief
Commission on Consumer Affairs
P.O. Box 11549
Columbia, SC 29211

Phil Leventis
Chairman of Banking (in case you had to borrow the funds to pay for the job)
1015 Sumter Street
Columbia, SC 29201

Trudie Bushy, Executive Director
Call for Action, Inc. (helps settle disputes between consumers and small businesses)
5272 River Road, Suite 300
Bethesda, MD 20816

Between the templates found in this chapter and all the sample letters found throughout, almost every problematic situation is covered. Even if you don't see your own particular issue highlighted, you still should be able to follow what's written or cut-and-paste, and so forth. Above all, you've discovered that **you** can do anything possible to resolve the conflicts in your life the "write" way.

Ellen Phillips

Epilogue

"If you would be remembered, do one thing superbly well."
- Saunders Norvell

Final food for thought comes from an old Chinese tale, entitled *Holding Up the Sky* (or, in purchasing language, "I'll Do My Part to Fight Back and Win").

One day an elephant saw a hummingbird lying flat on its back on the ground. The bird's tiny feet were raised up into the air.
"What on earth are you doing, Hummingbird?" asked the elephant.
The hummingbird replied, "I have heard that the sky might fall today. If that should happen, I am ready to do my bit in holding it up."
The elephant laughed and mocked the little bird. "Do you think those itty, bitty feet could hold up the sky?"
"Not alone," admitted the hummingbird. "But each must do what he can and this is what I can do myself."

With respect to Hummingbird's philosophy, ***Fight Back and Win! How to Work <u>With</u> Business and Get What You Want*** demonstrates how each of us can make a difference, not just for our own individual purposes but also for society as a whole. As worthy soldiers, we'll join the fight for a variety of complaints and other issues. And combined with the information discovered in *Shocked, Appalled, and Dismayed! How to Write Letters of Complaint That Get Results*, I charge both consumers and companies to respect and to respond to each other. Each reader is urged to become a savvy consumer, empowered to become a major force in that Consumer Revolution. You have the knowledge and the ability to write <u>all</u> types of letters to achieve your own satisfactory results, thereby winning the battle for consumer — and personal – rights. And the best part of all is when you find yourself as a comrade of

397

sorts with the company that, in your opinion, used to do you wrong, and when we work together, both groups can realize great accomplishments to make winners of us all.

ABOUT THE AUTHOR

Ellen Phillips is a retired English and speech arts teacher. Also, as a professional storyteller, Phillips credits her "tale-telling," as well as her natural theatrical flair, for the creative and humorous touches found within her books. She attributes her consumer zeal, assertiveness, and tenacity to her early battles to overcome crippling polio and nephritis. However, Phillips maintains that she owes her tenderness, compassion, and concern for the underdog to her family and, most especially, to her grandchildren. She credits her husband, Bruce, for his patience and stamina in putting up with her complaining nature.

Printed in the United States
754800003B